Data Cartels

DATA
CARTELS

*The Companies That Control
and Monopolize Our Information*

Sarah Lamdan

STANFORD UNIVERSITY PRESS
Stanford, California

Stanford University Press
Stanford, California

©2023 by the Board of Trustees of the Leland Stanford Junior University. All rights reserved.

Printed in the United States of America on acid-free, archival-quality paper

Library of Congress Cataloging-in-Publication Data

Names: Lamdan, Sarah, author.
Title: Data cartels : the companies that control and monopolize our information / Sarah Lamdan.
Description: Stanford, California : Stanford University Press, 2022. | Includes index.
Identifiers: LCCN 2022010953 (print) | LCCN 2022010954 (ebook) | ISBN 9781503615076 (cloth) | ISBN 9781503633711 (paperback) | ISBN 9781503633728 (ebook)
Subjects: LCSH: Information services industry—Law and legislation—United States. | Information services industry—Social aspects—United States. | Cartels—United States. | Antitrust law—United States. | Data protection—Law and legislation—United States. | Freedom of information—United States.
Classification: LCC KF2848 .L35 2022 (print) | LCC KF2848 (ebook) | DDC 343.7309/99—dc23/eng/20220520

LC record available at https://lccn.loc.gov/2022010953
LC ebook record available at https://lccn.loc.gov/2022010954

Cover design: David Drummond
Cover image: Optimarc/Shutterstock
Typeset by Elliott Beard in Adobe Garamond Pro 11/15

For library workers everywhere

CONTENTS

Preface — ix

Acknowledgments — xv

1   The Data Cartels: An Overview — 1

2   Data Brokering — 27

3   Academic Research — 50

4   Legal Information — 72

5   Financial Information — 94

6   News — 112

CONCLUSION: Envisioning Public Information as a Public Good — 127

Notes — 145

Index — 197

PREFACE

I GOT INTO STUDYING DATA ANALYTICS companies by accident. I'm a law professor, and for over a decade, I was also a law librarian who worked at law schools and law firms. That means I've spent a lot of time using Lexis (RELX's legal information platform) and Thomson Reuters's Westlaw, the "gold standard" research products for the legal profession. In my role as a librarian, I spent so much time training students, and my colleagues, about how to use these products that some days I felt like little more than a glorified product rep for their parent companies, RELX and Thomson Reuters.

In 2017, someone sent me a news article reporting that another division within RELX called LexisNexis, and Thomson Reuters were vying to help the U.S. Immigration and Customs Enforcement (ICE) build its "extreme vetting" surveillance program.[1] By 2017, ICE had solidified its reputation as the cruel immigration police ruthlessly separating families and deporting people who'd lived in the United States for their whole lives. This news story about LexisNexis and Thomson Reuters came out amidst other reports of ICE agents raiding workplaces and holding children in cages. So I was stunned to see the signatures of LexisNexis and Thomson Reuters employees who attended ICE events meant for companies trying to do surveillance work for the nation's cruelest cops. Suddenly, the stacks of Lexis and Thomson Reuters books, records, and the Westlaw and Lexis printouts cluttering my office seemed unsavory.

Not only was the possible Westlaw-Lexis-ICE connection unsavory, using legal research products linked to ICE surveillance could run counter to ethical convictions held by both librarians and lawyers. Both professions prize confidentiality, and they protect people from unwarranted government intrusion. If Lexis and Thomson Reuters were working for ICE, it would raise uncomfortable questions: Was I training immigration lawyers to use products that help ICE arrest their clients? Were people who used my library giving their data to ICE?[2]

My concerns intensified when I tried to discuss the issue with the companies. I wondered how, as a profession, we'd failed to notice that Westlaw and Lexis's companies were also building surveillance products for police and ICE agents, so I asked my school's Lexis and Westlaw representatives about what their companies were doing with ICE. The companies' product reps were usually helpful and eager to assist, so I expected prompt, reassuring responses. I was accustomed to the companies lavishing us with gifts and attention. When I was in law school, I got points for using Westlaw, which I eventually turned in for a designer handbag and silver watch. The companies even hired attorneys who were available 24/7 to answer our research questions by phone or online chat. I knew them as benevolent, generous entities that wanted to please their customers.

"Surely this is a misunderstanding," I thought, hoping the people who worked at Westlaw and Lexis could clear up the issue with an easy explanation. I wanted to find peace of mind with companies that I'd trusted, and that I relied on for so much of my job. But when I brought my concerns up directly with vendors, they didn't do anything to assure me that our data was safe from being sold to ICE or law enforcement. They weren't even willing to issue a promise to my law school that our personal data wouldn't end up in ICE's data systems.

RELX, especially, exerted its power. A Lexis representative started camping out at my law school, calling my work phone, and my boss, demanding that I speak to her manager. She also started monitoring me through my students, asking them to report back to her if I talked about

LexisNexis's ICE contracts.[3] A blog post that a librarian and I wrote about the issue for the American Association of Law Libraries was erased moments after it was posted, and the organization replaced it with a single sentence: "*This post has been removed on the advice of General Counsel.*"[4] The takedown was an aberration: librarians are not the type to censor. They're usually the ones fighting censorship. Spurred by this baffling takedown, I started digging for answers to my questions about the companies' data businesses in earnest.

Ever since, I've been trying to connect the hidden informational world of data analytics companies like RELX and Thomson Reuters. I wasn't trying to find proof that these companies were harming the public—I was actually trying to do the opposite. Learning that Westlaw and Lexis's corporate overlords were helping ICE track people and feeding problematic predictive policing systems with flows of personal data shattered my career. I couldn't, in good conscience, train hundreds of new lawyers to rely on companies that were selling their future clients' data to police and ICE officers. Law enforcement data brokering conflicted with the confidentiality obligations and zealous advocacy responsibilities inherent in the immigration law and criminal defense work that most of my students go on to do. I kept hoping that I'd find something that would prove the ICE story wrong.

But the more desperately I searched for information that would prove that I was mistaken, the more my research surpassed my worst suspicions. I uncovered a web of information and data analytics products that hurt people in multiple information markets. These companies were building policing products. They were also making "risk" products that help our landlords, bosses, insurers, and healthcare systems decide whether to give us care and services that we need. They were selling "academic metrics," data analytics products that determine whether scholars will get tenure or grant funding using outdated, elitist, and discriminatory ratings systems. They were paywalling critical information, including law and science, so people who aren't wealthy, or affiliated with wealthy institutions, can't get access.

With every information market I investigated, I found a different group of people uniquely oppressed by data analytics companies. Immigrants' rights groups are fighting to get data analytics companies' invasive personal data dossiers removed from ICE's digital surveillance programs. People of color are disproportionately made targets by predictive policing algorithms. Academic scholars' research is trapped behind the companies' paywalls, and their funding and tenure depend on the companies' metrics. Pro se litigants, including prisoners, can't see the legal information that's relevant to their cases because it's only available on the companies' platforms. The best financial data is only accessible to people who can afford pricey data analytics products. Data analytics companies have even paywalled news resources from the public, making it so that people can't get critical updates on local and national emergencies.

The companies hadn't always been quite as ethically fraught as they've become in recent years. When I was introduced to these companies as a new librarian in the early 2000s, they called themselves academic, legal, news, and financial "publishers." Their various publishing brands seemed like separate, standalone platforms: Elsevier, LexisNexis, Thomson Financial, Reuters news, and Westlaw had different purposes and unique customers. But over the past decade, the companies switched their business models from publishing to data analytics, winding down their publishing businesses while spending billions of dollars to hire thousands of technologists and build data analytics development labs.

Today, the companies are no longer publishers that sell journals or casebooks, they're data analytics firms that sell "risk solutions" and "business insights." They sell informational content, a slurry of structured information and unstructured data points. They sell published content, and they also sell predictions and prescriptions they make with their algorithms, machine learning, "AI," and other data-crunching technologies. They make "academic insights," "legal insights," "financial insights," "law enforcement insights," and any other "insights" their technologists can formulate.

As data analytics companies, these gigantic corporations dominate multiple information markets with some of the biggest troves of personal data and academic, legal, financial, news, and other information on the planet. They can use these raw informational ingredients to cook up even more information products in their technology labs. They can sell raw data, structured information, and analytics-driven "answers" to a broad range of consumers across major industries and institutions.

It might be fine to have information markets run by a few data analytics companies if the companies were operating with good ethics and public interest goals in mind, working towards providing better access to essential information and protecting intellectual freedom.[5] But my research has led me to believe that the dominant data analytics firms are not operating with the public interest in mind. Instead, they're impeding information access and privacy, privatizing and paywalling information that should be public, and exploiting people's personal data. Just before this book went to press, two different public interest organizations filed separate reports to the Federal Trade Commission (FTC) complaining about how the companies' strongholds in the legal information market and the academic information market were harming consumers.[6] One complained that Westlaw and Lexis were blocking consumers' access to "the laws of the land" even though access to the law is guaranteed by law. The other warned that Elsevier's stronghold on the academic journal market puts government-funded scientific research on platforms that subject their visitors to personal data collection without an opt-out.

Perhaps the most shocking aspect of the FTC reports is that most people, and possibly even people working at the FTC, don't know that Lexis and Elsevier are parts of the same company. The companies have hidden the full spectrum of their business models. They keep their products in the various information markets relatively siloed so consumers can't see the full span of their data analytics business. Few people know how much information these companies control. They don't know that Lexis is also ICE's biggest data broker, or that Elsevier's academic journals and BePress's journal preprint sharing system are under the same corporate umbrella, giving RELX primary control of both published and unpublished scholarship systems.

Data technologies are simultaneously miraculous tools for sharing knowledge and dangerous tools for controlling information flows. Like most people, I was in awe of the first data technologies that companies, including data analytics firms, provided. Databases were life-changing inventions. It was thrilling to be able to pull up news articles by the dozens instead of rummaging around in dusty old stacks or squinting through the viewfinder of a microfilm machine. When Westlaw's KeyCite replaced paper Shepard's legal citator volumes, it felt fantastical that a tiny icon could indicate whether the law was still good, like some magic informational thermometer popping out of a judicial turkey.

But as information technologies and platforms have proliferated, I've grown more wary of the seemingly miraculous computers and data systems, and the private companies that are building our new information infrastructure. A lot of the "bells and whistles" on our digital products take power away from the humans making choices, replacing our wishes with automated selections that benefit the data companies by forcing certain content in front of readers and making other content prohibitively expensive or harder to find. Our informational services also seem to be collecting more and more personal information about us, forcing us to trade our privacy in order to access information. In addition, they're taking over markets by squashing competitors with lawsuits and hostile takeovers, pushing out startups that have more public interest-oriented offerings. A few companies are cutthroat, dominating information markets by crushing innovative new information enterprises.

The chapters of this book share what I've discovered as I've peeled back the lid on this can of worms I opened by accident back in 2017. Along the way, I've met activists and workers in every informational market I discuss. Their stories show that data analytics companies don't just hurt libraries or financial markets, they have an impact on real people who rely on information, which is all of us.

ACKNOWLEDGMENTS

FIRST AND FOREMOST, TO EYAL, thank you for supporting me and believing in me no matter what, and for always making me laugh. Thanks B and E for being fantastic and so, so fun. You, Kansas (and I guess, also, Barkley) are the best buddies a girl could ask for. Thanks also to all of the Shiks, Lamdans, and Flams who have supported me and patiently listened to me talk about libraries and data companies for years on end. Special thanks to Nina and David for giving me life and to Yonathan Partouche for giving me an awesome office.

Thanks to everyone at Stanford University Press who made this book possible, and especially Marcela Maxfield, Susan Karani, David Horne, and Sunna Juhn. Your patience, feedback, and attention to detail transformed my unruly drafts into an actual book. I also want to thank my research assistants Simone Harstead, Alex Matak, Gregory Minnig, and Rachel Goldman for participating in the research that formed this book. To Max Behrman, Meghan McDermott, Daniel Peña, Bryce Renninger, B Taylor, and all of my other FOIA seminar and data privacy seminar students—thanks for contributing to our class discussions and research adventures. The semesters we shared provided joy and new insights about data issues.

The highlight of writing this book was the friends I made along the way. So many people shaped and informed the stories and ideas in the book. In the data brokering world, thank you to Mizue Aizeki and Em Puhl at Immigrant Defense Project, Jacinta González at Mijente, and Julie Mao at Just Futures Law. Your advocacy and research are inspiring. I am grateful for the tireless dedication to tech justice of William Fitzgerald and everyone at The Worker Agency. I'm also so grateful for Emma Pullman, Albert Fox Cahn, and Alvaro Bedoya's work. Your efforts have shaped my understanding of the companies at the center of law enforcement data brokering.

In the open access world, I am indebted to everyone at SPARC, Public. Resource.Org, Library Futures, and IOI, and especially to my heroes Heather Joseph, Carl Malamud, Nick Shockey, Kaitlin Thaney, Jennie Rose Halperin, Claudio Aspesi, Nicole Allen, and Kyle Courtney. Getting to know you has made these pandemic years so much better. Observing the conscientious, thoughtful ways you approach challenges makes me a better advocate, and your work moves us closer to an equitable information infrastructure.

I am also indebted to my library privacy heroes Dorothea Salo, Alison Macrina, and Shea Swauger. You've lit up my library world and taught me so much about data privacy. Thank you also to Eira Tansey for demonstrating the ways librarians can create socially responsible professional communities that are brimming with both insight and kindness. Thanks, also to Patrice McDermott, Michael Morisy, Ian Head, and all of the other freedom of information advocates building community around government transparency. I also have to thank Library Twitter. You deliver joy and librarian wisdom every single day, even during tough times.

This book could not have been written without my dear law library friends, and especially everyone involved with the Boulder Conference on Legal Information. I owe so much to my mentors and role models Susan Nevelow Mart and Barbara Bintliff. I did this research as part of the community they've created over the years, which has generated so much of our in-depth legal information scholarship. I also relied on the research and support of critical legal information literacy scholars Julie Krishnaswami, Nicholas Mignanelli, and Nicholas Stump, and the research and feedback of legal information scholars including Paul Callister, Shawn Nevers, Anne Klinefelter, Rebecca Fordon, Nicole Dyszlewski, and Olivia Schlinck. Thank you, also, to Library Freedom Project members Deborah Yun Caldwell, Qiana Johnson, Frans Albarillo, and Marisol Moreno Ortiz, who are patiently and expertly approaching legal information privacy issues one source at a time.

A million thanks to my CUNY colleagues and friends, and especially to Meg Wacha, Roxanne Shirazi, Maura Smale, Mariana Regalado, and Polly Thistlethwaite, who work hard on privacy and access issues across the CUNY library system. Thank you also to Matthew Gold at the Graduate Center for supporting this work. In the law school library, thank you to Julie Lim for bringing me in, to Yasmin Sokkar Harker for being my librarian partner-in-crime for almost a decade, and to the research magic and support of Doug Cox and Kathy Williams. And thank you to all of my CUNY law colleagues beyond the library, and especially to Ruthann Robson, Rebecca Bratspies, and Sarah Valentine for being fantastic mentors as I drafted this book, to Julie Goldscheid, Allie Robbins, Andrea McArdle, and Sofia Yakren for listening and supporting me throughout the project, and to Susan Bryant and Charisa Kiyô Smith for organizing such thoughtful spaces to share our scholarship.

Plenty of scholars beyond my own institution were part of making this book. At the Engelberg Center at NYU School of Law, I am so grateful to Michael Weinberg and Rochelle Dreyfuss for their thoughtful and formative feedback on my drafts, and I can't thank Michael and Katrina Southerland enough for organizing opportunities for the Engelverse to convene and share ideas. Thanks to Anil Kalhan and Kit Johnson and everyone else who supported my initial research on this topic and shared in the concerns the research raised. I appreciate everyone who held conversations around my work: Shalini Ray and the 2019 Emerging Immigration Law Scholars Conference; Emily Drabinski and the Mina Rees Library speaker series; Matthew Garklavs at Pratt Institute Libraries; Melissa Villa-Nicholas and the University of Rhode Island's GSLIS Voices for Information Equity Series; Karen Levy, Eliza Bettinger, Kim Nayyer, and the Cornell University's Tech/Law Colloquium; Stephanie Warden and Julie Bracket of University of Wisconsin Superior's Data Deluge speaker series; Joachim

Neubert and Semantic Web in Libraries SWIB21 Conference; Karen Stoll Farrell and Ethan Fridmanski at the University of Indiana; Jordan Hale and Ian Goldberg University of Waterloo's CrySP Speaker Series on Privacy; and every institution and person who engaged conversations around topics in this book. Thank you so much for convening students and scholars to discuss data analytics companies. Each conversation taught me something new and provided ideas that shaped this book.

This book wasn't just inspired by conversations, it was also inspired by formative, groundbreaking scholarship. Thanks to Julie Cohen, Jathan Sadowski, and James Grimmelman, whose writing expanded my understanding of informational capitalism. Thanks to Rashida Richardson, Andrew Guthrie Ferguson, and Hannah Bloch-Wehba, whose research on data analytics and policing illuminated the practical and legal problems inherent in datafied law enforcement. I couldn't have written this book without the scholarship of copyright experts including Jason Schultz, Aaron Perzanowski, Michelle Wu, and Amanda Levendowski. Meg Leta Jones's writing on technological exceptionalism was also inspiring, as was Safiya Umoja Noble's work on algorithmic bias.

Thank you to Sam Biddle, Shoshana Wodinsky, and McKenzie Funk for writing the brilliant pieces that shaped my understanding of how data brokering plays out in practice. Nantina Vgontzas and Meredith Whittaker's perspectives on the bigness of big tech also gave me so much hope and inspiration. Thanks also to organizations including the Brennan Center for Justice, the Center for Democracy & Technology, Jack Poulson's Tech Inquiry, Wolfie Cristl at Cracked Labs, and Justin Sherman at Duke's Sanford School of Public Policy for fantastic in-depth reports on data brokering and data privacy.

Last but not least, thanks to everyone doing the daily work of advocating for government transparency, open access, and data privacy. Your work makes our informational futures brighter.

Data Cartels

1

THE DATA CARTELS
An Overview

> *Information, knowledge, is power. If you can control*
> *information, you can control people.*
>
> Sarah Schafer, "Vonnegut and Clancy on Technology,"
> December 15, 1995

THE INTERNET IS A VAST circulatory system of fiber-optic cables connecting data servers; a web of cords, tubes, and wireless radio waves laced over cities and under oceans. Information is the lifeblood of the internet, the substance that flows through those cables, cords, and tubes—the arteries of our digital world. Without informational content flowing through it, the internet would be an empty, hollow network, a virtual ghost town. People expect to find a wealth of information online. We depend on the internet's information flows to get what we need, from the mundane, such as finding the best local pizza place, to the more weighty, such as finding the best health care options for a chronic illness. An information-free internet would have little worth.

For the internet to work, we need information to flow continuously and consistently, routed in the right directions. Like human circulation, the internet's circulation can be finicky: digital apps, search-bars, and platforms work best when they have optimal amounts, and types, of information. If information isn't flowing well, critical public information won't reach those who need it. Conversely, bad information flows can also put private information in places it wasn't intended to go.

This book is about how a few companies are messing with the internet's circulatory system. They're jamming up the arteries, stopping some information from getting where it needs to go and diverting other information to places it shouldn't be. When you need to know whether plumes of smoke from a nearby fire are toxic, you don't want the answer to be trapped behind a paywall. When you post something on social media or fill out a dating profile, you'd probably prefer those records not be routed to employers, landlords, and police without your consent.

Data analytics companies like RELX and Thomson Reuters are erecting those information-blocking paywalls and selling our personal data. They privatize critical news and legal, medical, and financial information that should be public. They also restrict access to the resources we use to make informed decisions about our health, our finances, and our legal rights. They even route our private information to law enforcement, insurance companies, employers, and other entities that make big decisions about our lives. These entities use data analytics companies' informational products to assess our personal "risk" levels and decide whether to track us, arrest us, or deny us services we need. Data analytics companies aren't just selling raw data and information, they're also selling predictive and prescriptive products they make with their information and data stockpiles.

The data analytics companies are acting like cartels, taking over markets for different categories of information and exploiting their stronghold on multiple information sectors to amass more power and profit. Their behaviors have vast and pervasive consequences for everyone—and the behaviors are perfectly legal. How can something legal so fundamentally disrupt values, like government transparency and personal privacy, that are supposedly integral to our democracy? To answer this question, we need to first understand who these companies are.

All about Data Dealers

RELX and Thomson Reuters call themselves many things—publishers, business services solutions, research platform providers—but at the end of the day they're information dealers. They've amassed abundant informational troves: thousands of academic publications and business profiles, millions of data dossiers containing our personal information, and the entire corpus of U.S. law. The companies are the culmination of information market consolidation that's happening across media industries, from music and newspapers to book publishing. Reed Elsevier LexisNexis (RELX) is a Frankenstein-ian amalgamation of publishers and data brokers, stitched together into one big informational giant. Thomson Reuters is also an amalgamation of hundreds of smaller publishers and data services. Dozens of companies that started as specialized publishers of news,[1] scientific reports,[2] case law,[3] or stock prices[4] have melded into mountains of informational content under just a few corporate umbrellas.

RELX and Thomson Reuters aren't the only information companies around, but they are uniquely large and sprawling. There are plenty of data brokers out there, and there are other academic journal companies. There are also a plethora of financial data companies. But there aren't any other information providers who are all of these things at once. RELX and Thomson Reuters dominate many informational markets simultaneously. Most information companies specialize in a particular type of information. Oracle and Equifax are major data brokers, but they don't also run legal information platforms. Bloomberg L.P. is a powerful financial information provider, but it doesn't also control access to thousands of academic journals. CNN is a major news source, but it doesn't sell personal data dossiers on the side. In contrast to these specialized information providers, RELX and Thomson Reuters don't focus on one information sector. Rather, they lead legal information, financial information, academic research, and personal data markets all at once. Thomson Reuters even runs one of the world's main news services and RELX has a leading news archive. Each market the companies dominate is massive on its own.[5] Combined, the markets comprise much of the information that people need to make critical legal, financial, and science-based decisions.

RELX and Thomson Reuters are conglomerates, multi-industry behemoths that control broad swaths of resources. They're the informational equivalent of Nestlé, the giant food company that owns everything from Cheerios to Hot Pockets and Perrier. Nestlé's products are so varied and ubiquitous that they're practically unavoidable. People continue to buy

Nestlé's food, beverages, and baby formula even though the company is "one of the most hated companies in the world" for convincing parents to starve their children with watered-down formula and draining towns' reservoirs to make bottled water.[6] Consumers buy Nestlé products not because they prefer Nestlé, but because they have little choice.

Similarly, RELX and Thomson Reuters sell so much informational content that it's hard to avoid them even though we hate them. Librarians and researchers revile the data analytics companies for charging outrageous prices and stealing academics' labor. Yet they have little choice but to comply with the companies' terms because there aren't alternative sources for the information they need. As one writer explains, "If a candymaker decided to charge $5,000 for an organic chocolate bar, consumers wouldn't respond by stealing the pricey bar; they'd simply buy another brand of chocolate, and the initial company would either adjust its price or go bankrupt," but "When a publisher of academic journals decides to charge $5,000 for a yearly subscription . . . subscribers might grumble about the price but they will often still pay it" because they have no other option.[7] Like Nestlé, Thomson Reuters and RELX are too big to fail, even when they do things consumers don't like. In the digital ecosystems where we spend more and more of our lives, we can't opt out of information. It is as critical a part of our digital internet infrastructure as roadways and water systems are to our physical infrastructure. While few of us adore our cable companies or electricity providers, we have little choice but to pay their bills each month, even when they leave us in the dark or raise their prices.

Companies like RELX that sell things millions of people rely on choose whether to run their businesses in ways that benefit consumers or in ways that decrease our quality of life. We've seen this play out with other digital market monopolists such as Amazon, the internet's major shopping platform. At the start of the Covid-19 pandemic, the cost of hand sanitizer and protective masks doubled on Amazon as the platform's vendors gouged prices. The platform is such a pervasive retailer that people had little choice but to buy the ridiculously overpriced products or go without the important pandemic protections.[8] Luckily for consumers, Amazon decided to be a benevolent shopping dictator, opting to remove price-gouged items from its website.[9] If Amazon hadn't made that choice, people would have been left either paying hundreds of dollars for a box of face masks or waiting to see whether the government would intervene to ensure reasonable prices.[10]

RELX made a similar choice to play the role of benevolent informational dictator during Covid. Its academic content product, Elsevier, temporarily expanded access to Covid-19 research, taking down some of its pricey paywalls.[11] But the company's benevolence is for a limited time only: Elsevier only promises free access "for as long as the COVID-19 resource center remains active."[12] RELX will eventually snap the paywalls shut, closing its Covid resources from the public once again.

When the paywalls return, librarians and scholars, who bear the brunt of data analytics companies' unfriendly consumer practices, won't be surprised. Libraries, as the main gatekeepers of informational content (and the only institutions with sufficient budgets to afford RELX's and Thomson Reuters's platform and product fees), are used to the companies' anticonsumer practices. Among librarians and scholars, RELX and Thomson Reuters aren't known as benevolent—they're known as bullies. The companies exploit scholars' free labor and then steal the fruits of their research, paywalling their work so that only subscribers can see it. The companies also crush competition, including cool new library vendors. Librarians have watched the companies acquire innovative startup competitors or sue them out of business. Longtime librarians know better than to get too excited about or grow too attached to fledgling information companies, because they'll eventually either be swallowed or strangled by a company like Thomson Reuters or RELX. The companies also force libraries, and their institutions, to accept tyrannical contract provisions. The companies make libraries agree to product-tying "big deals" and compel them to sign nondisclosure agreements that prohibit them from discussing their contract terms with others.[13] RELX's Covid generosity was a deviation from the company's normal consumer practices. Just as Amazon usually is known as a corporate miscreant that destroys small businesses and implements abusive labor practices, RELX and Thomson Reuters are generally seen as villains, not saviors.

Consumer protection laws and antitrust regulations were meant to prevent companies like Amazon and RELX from using their market power in ways that hurt consumers. Government officials recognize the immense power market-dominating companies have over consumers' lives. They know that when companies dominate markets, consumers have little choice but to buy from them, even if their services are subpar and even when their practices are exploitative.

Exploitation is more likely the more enmeshed a company is in our social fabric. It's easy to take advantage of people when you control resources that play central roles in their lives. Some resources are so intimately bound to humanity that they aren't just things we buy, they are essential to who we are. Information companies sell those kinds of essential resources. The goods and services data analytics companies provide aren't merely products we buy and sell, they are products derived from us. Data analytics companies capitalize on the invisible, ethereal products of our minds. Industrialists profited from mining, logging, and other trades that strip value from our land, but unlike historical extractive ventures, data isn't cut from trees or extracted from earth, it's harvested from humans. Companies like RELX and Thomson Reuters appropriate our informational labor.[14] They siphon intellectual and social output, co-opting our artistic and scholarly work and vacuuming up the digital exhaust we release through our wearable devices and online activities.[15] They take things that we make, turning our output into something they can own and store like wheat in silos.

They also privatize public informational resources that we, collectively, pay for. Information is a communal creation, a by-product of social connection. We fund most of the world's legal and scientific information, paying taxes that support public schools and national grant programs in order to promote progress in science and the humanities. Our taxes also pay legislators, regulators, and judges to make public law. Besides being something we fund and create, information is also a social necessity—we must see and share information to participate in human life.

The companies ramp up prices for things that should be free, charging more than fair market value because they know that information is unique and nonfungible—each journal article and court opinion contains findings that can't be duplicated by another source. If they need particular information, consumers will have to pay whatever the companies charge. In the last decade, companies have been especially ruthless in raising prices on critical information. In the academic information market, publishers like RELX's Elsevier increased journal prices by 300 percent from 1986 through 2006,[16] even as the transition from paper to digital format has decreased the costs of producing journals by eliminating printing, handling, and shipping expenses.[17]

The companies also exploit the people who produce information. They've figured out how to get new content for free from academics who must publish to get hired and tenured, and by scooping up public records and putting them behind paywalls. It's easy to make tons of money when you are reselling the free labor of law school's student-run law review editorial boards, and when you aren't paying the scientists and researchers that make your informational content. Both RELX and Thomson Reuters also capitalize on the troves of materials that they get through taking over competitors. By buying out publishers, the data analytics companies have accumulated centuries' worth of science, financial, news, and U.S. law records. RELX and Thomson Reuters own among the most complete digital sets of those resources in the world.

What Makes These Companies Data Cartels?

Market leaders and exerting market power aren't necessarily bad—market leaders can exert their power for good, making life more convenient, efficient, and affordable for consumers. It's certainly not illegal to compete for a larger market share by building better products, and successful competitors shouldn't be punished for winning over consumers.[18] Problems only arise when enterprises use their market control to exclude competition and exploit consumers. The line between fair market power and unfair monopoly power is hard to draw. When does a company cross the boundary that separates competitive market participants who happen to have the best, most popular products from anticompetitive monopolists who maintain their power with unfair practices? According to the law, monopoly power is problematic when companies dominate markets and use their power to bar competitors from entering the market, and when they use their power to exploit consumers.[19] Market share alone doesn't make a company harmful, it's how the company wields that power that matters.

One potentially harmful way that companies wield their power is by partnering with other dominant companies, working together to corner and keep market control. Those partnerships are called cartels, "alliances of rivals" that collude to increase their profits and dominate markets.[20] The word "cartel" is often used to describe illicit markets like drugs or organized crime, but in fact, there are cartels in all sorts of markets. Canada's maple syrup cartel controls syrup prices all over the world.[21] In the early 1900s, cartels controlled markets for goods including lightbulbs and cheese.[22] In the late 1990s the U.S. Department of Justice labeled a cluster of pharmaceutical companies as cartels when they collectively inflated prices for the vitamins that food companies use to fortify their cereals and beverages.[23]

As with monopolies, what counts as a cartel is malleable—an illegal cartel in one jurisdiction could be a permissible market collaboration in another. Just as not all market leaders are monopolists, not all cartel-like behavior is prohibited. For example, OPEC (the Organization of Petroleum Exporting Countries) acts like a cartel, setting the world's oil prices and oil production quotas to prevent oil prices from fluctuating in ways that would harm both oil producers and purchasers. OPEC's collaborative control of the oil market is distinctly anticompetitive, but it's accepted as legal.[24] Similarly, in the United States we let public utilities operate like monopolies and cartels, collectively controlling electricity, water, and other infrastructure, so long as they provide equal, affordable services to consumers.

One common characteristic among most illegal cartels is collusion. But collusion is hard to prove. By definition, collusion is a secret agreement. Plans to fix prices or intimidate consumers aren't usually broadcast to the public, nor are they recorded in board meeting agendas. Collusion is usually tacit. As 1700s-era economist Adam Smith put it, "People of the same trade seldom meet together, even for merriment and diversion, but the conversation ends in a conspiracy against the public, or in some contrivance to raise prices."[25] Although it's rumored that RELX and Thomson Reuters cooperatively decide which competitors to wipe out and which to let stay, and gossipers say they work together to distribute various content affiliates, none of these suspected agreements are substantiated on any record.

Evidence of collusion or not, it's clear that RELX and Thomson Reuters share a vision for the future of informational markets. Together, they are twisting traditional content publishing into data analytics businesses. In comparing news information cartels to traditional oil cartels, journalist and media professor Ben Bagdikian explained that even though OPEC members sometimes disagree and compete, making such enemies of each other that they have brutal shooting wars between themselves, "when it comes to the purpose of their cartel—oil—they speak with one voice."[26] RELX and Thomson Reuters also speak with one voice when it comes to information markets, advancing unified agendas and goals. Together, the companies are moving lockstep away from publishing and towards data analytics. They're dragging their customers with them, even as their research products turn into data products, and they're crushing competitors along the way. Their lockstep moves thwart competition and consumer choice: consumers can expect similar services, products, and treatment from their brands. Sharing information markets between themselves has solidified their market power and kept antitrust regulators at bay.[27]

Even if data analytics companies are acting like cartels, it's up to regulators and courts to decide whether they're violating U.S. antitrust laws. RELX and Thomson Reuters dwell in the liminal space between fair market power and unfair monopoly. They are market superpowers that seem to leverage their power in various markets to take over others. They also seem to work in tandem, deciding when to take down competitors or whether to allow a lesser competitive threat to coexist in their shared marketplace. They've been subject to antitrust investigations on more than one occasion, but the government has largely allowed them to dominate major information flows in our digital ecosystem.

Companies like RELX and Thomson Reuters have been depicted as octopus-like monopolies with tentacles wrapped around multiple industries. The tentacles also wrap around government regulators that they've captured with their lobbying influence, revolving doors, and government clientele.[28] They restrict competition by using their tremendous size to take over markets, and by leveraging their power across multiple markets. In the past, octopus monopolists like the Standard Oil Company, an industrial-era oil enterprise, and telecom giant AT&T were broken up by the government for violating antitrust laws.[29] But today the companies that constitute our digital infrastructure engage in Standard Oil–style behavior, and antitrust law has not reined them in.[30]

Without antitrust safeguards, a few digital companies have been able to take over a largely unsettled digital frontier. Big-tech companies treat our relatively new digital infrastructure like children with fresh, pristine snow, building their forts across the entire expanse. A few companies have colonized broad stretches of the internet ecosystem, becoming digital company towns that run everything online.[31] For instance, Amazon runs almost our entire digital mercantile, acting as a shopping mall with storefronts for every vendor, transporting goods across the world, giving customer reviews, and even selling more cloud storage space than any other company. Facebook is our main public square, serving as our central meeting center, news aggregator, and classified ad system. Microsoft and Google are our primary personal assistants, helping us map and organize the internet's content, providing our mailing system, and helping us plan our online lives with calendars, meeting spaces, and other virtual tools. Data analytics companies like RELX and Thomson Reuters run the libraries and reams of knowledge that the infrastructure depends on, from grand digital archives to the mundane filing systems at the foundations of our businesses and bureaucracy.

Even though these companies are far-reaching corporate octopuses, the government hasn't intervened to stop their expansion. The main reason we aren't breaking up digital octopus enterprises has little to do with companies' market power and a lot to do with government choices about how to enforce antitrust laws. Over the years, antitrust enforcement has slid from its original, robust *Standard Oil* strength to become a weaker legal tool. In the 1970s, "Chicago School" economists including Milton Friedman and their legal disciples such as Robert Bork convinced lawmakers that too much government intervention in market affairs would crush our economy. Lawmakers and antitrust regulators absorbed those warnings, and today they only enforce antitrust laws in limited cases, when they're convinced that a firm's activities are economically harming consumers. While European antitrust enforcement focuses broadly on fairness, shepherding companies with too much market dominance away from monopolistic behaviors, today's U.S. antitrust enforcement declines to intervene absent economic consumer harm, even if companies are harming competitors, or even democracy.[32]

The government's failure to intervene is seeming, more and more, like a tactical mistake. After decades of letting tech companies enjoy unfettered growth, companies such as Google, Amazon, and Facebook have taken over hundreds of competitors to become unstoppable internet giants.[33] With their market power, the companies have implemented a slew of troubling practices. They pilfer people's personal data and offer people unsafe products and bad financial advice that consumer protection laws are supposed to prevent. Their products and platforms sow misinformation that fosters fascist movements and even genocide. Now, regulators, lawmakers, and even the White House agree that we need to rein in big tech.[34] But experts fear that it's too late to curb the tech companies' power.[35] Google, Amazon, and other companies that make up our internet's infrastructure have developed into powerful "net states" that act like governments. Their tentacles are so deeply entrenched in our online ecosystems that they've become impossible to pull back without destroying our digital world.

The big-tech companies are a cautionary tale about how powerful tech enterprises can become in our digital ecosystem. The U.S. government is trying to untangle the big-tech mess, hiring antitrust lawyers to investigate companies such as Facebook and Amazon and bringing the companies' CEOs to testify before Congress. But acting post hoc, after the damage is done, is far more complex than preventing the companies from multimarket domination. It's not too late to loosen data analytics companies' tentacles before they dig in too deep. If big tech shows us anything, it's that it's unwise to ignore ever-sprawling tech enterprises.

But the government isn't paying enough attention to the data companies. Even though data analytics firms are sowing digital harms similar to those of the other big-tech companies, their CEOs aren't sitting in front of Congress, explaining their anticompetitive practices. RELX and Thomson Reuters are billion-dollar enterprises with larger profit margins than big-tech companies, but they don't receive the same attention that big-tech companies get from reporters or regulators. Despite their immense sizes and profits, they are generally ignored in tech investigations and studies.

The data industry "operates in the shadows."[36] Most consumers don't even know that these information companies exist, let alone what their names are. One *New York Times* exposé about GPS-tracking tech companies brushed aside companies like RELX and Thomson Reuters, dismissing them as nameless entities *you've probably never heard of.*[37]

Without attention, the information companies are becoming larger and more embedded in our digital infrastructure. Today, RELX is so large that it's considered Europe's biggest media company by market capitalization.[38] Thomson Reuters similarly strives to be the primary platform monopolist for professionals—Google but "without the garbage."[39] The data analytics companies may not catch the eye of antitrust enforcement, but their "bigness" causes problems for consumers.

The Problem of Bigness

The main way that data analytics companies are exploiting their cross-market bigness is by using their massive information collections to make even more products. The companies build on their informational domination by multiplying their existing information troves through data analytics software to make more information, creating "entirely new data asset[s]."[40] The companies can "double-dip" with their data assets, selling raw data, and also selling structured information made from that raw data. Not many information companies are equipped to build the type of billion-dollar data analytics business RELX and Thomson Reuters built because a company needs stockpiles of information to run through its data analytics systems. RELX and Thomson Reuters are among the few companies that have enough informational and analytical power to mix and match their collections to make new information to sell.

RELX and Thomson Reuters were well positioned to become data analytics giants because they have been stockpiling raw data and information for decades. When data analytics became a thing, RELX and Thomson Reuters were in the best position to capitalize on it. Commercial data analytics services are fairly new, made possible by mass digitization and mass data collection. Information was clunky and varied in its physical form—papers, books, cassette tapes, records, photographs, paintings, newspapers, blueprints, and pamphlets had different modes of transmission and storage. Now, information can flow in one form: binary code beaming through fiber-optic cables. Digital information is far easier to transport, store, and share. A TikTok dance video can sit on the same USB drive as an image of a Monet painting and the *Lord of the Rings* trilogy, and all three types of media can be sold in a single informational bundle. Digital information is also easier to transport. Publishers used to send crates of books and CDs to libraries and stores, but digital information can be disseminated without postage or brick-and-mortar warehouses.

Not only is information easier to transport than ever, there is also far more of it. The world produces more data than ever because we've infused our world with data collectors. The internet of things embeds data collection into the items we use every day: traversing the streets, using home appliances, and even wearing clothes creates billions of data points for data analytics companies to use. RELX and Thomson Reuters are collecting it all, from corporate and government pamphlets to your license-plate-tracking data.

People use the words "data" and "information" interchangeably, but they are two different things. Data is the binary, raw material of information, and information is structured, processed data. Datasets contain unorganized facts, quantities, characters, and symbols that have not been processed. Data's disorderly particles of information can seem arbitrary. Consider the randomness of the following dataset: "UT, 1234, Joe, Circle, SLC, 8015553211, 84084, Smith." When this string of data is interpreted, organized, and formatted, it becomes information: Joe Smith, 1234 Circle, Salt Lake City, UT 84084, (801) 555-3211.[41] Information is designed to be informative, to *tell* you something, while data is merely a collection of recorded, but unsorted, values. Data analytics companies control warehouses of data *and* they build analytics software that transforms data into information, selling that data analytics output as well. Instead of "big data," data analytics companies deal in "big information," structured informational products extrapolated from data.

RELX and Thomson Reuters are capitalizing on the glut of information they've amassed by hiring thousands of technologists to build AI and machine-learning software to churn the information from their troves into new informational by-products.[42] Their analytics software works like those Play-Doh fun-factory extruders that blend disparate chunks of colored clay into singular products—spaghetti-noodle hair or thick tubes, depending on the filter. Instead of clay, data companies extrude raw data into new information. The companies' analytical tools add value to datasets by quickly answering questions that once took intensive research to solve. For instance, data analytics software can chart the major themes in a musician's songs.[43] Historically, researching the themes in Taylor Swift's records would have taken hundreds of hours of careful listening, writing, and mathematical work. An algorithm does all of that work in seconds.

Analytical products transform companies like RELX and Thomson Reuters from mere content providers into oracles that guide decision making in governments and corporations. The companies have so much data and information that they can use their informational power to forecast future outcomes. Data analytics companies don't just sell information, they sell predictions (Who will commit a crime? What is the most profitable choice?) and prescriptions (Deny insurance due to likelihood of fraud. Fund that science project.) for governments and companies to follow.[44]

The more data firms collect, the more power they have. Larger datasets can generate more useful, high-value information.[45] From a data analytics perspective, data becomes more valuable as its volume increases. Consider the name of your favorite type of candy. Alone, that tidbit of information isn't very valuable. But when you combine that data with other data points, like your age, income, and other shopping preferences, your candy preference becomes more useful. On an even larger scale, if you can link your candy preferences with the preferences of your friends, with financial data about the candy industry, with legal information about recent candy patent filings, or with news archives about the candy business, you've created actionable market data.

Data analytics companies blend academic research with financial reports to help grant funders game academic funding by predicting what projects will make the biggest profits. They blend collections of court opinions with lawyers' and judges' personal data to help lawyers game the legal system by suggesting which judges are most likely to agree with their arguments.[46] Some data analytics projects benefit the public, but the companies' projects benefit their biggest customers: insurance companies; big law firms that represent major banks and corporations; and government agencies that decide things like who gets surveilled, who gets social security benefits, and who gets custody of their children. Their products meld critical public information with our personal data to judge us and sort us by how "risky" we are. By infusing personal data with other types of information, RELX and Thomson Reuters products can be used to sort people, and their assets, into risk categories and to make predictions about future events. The companies can sell traditional informational content, personal data dossiers, *and* software-driven guesses at whether banks, landlords, insurers, employers, public institutions, and police can trust us.

Until the last decade or so, both companies considered themselves publishers, not data services. They printed out stacks of scholarly journals and volumes of case law reporters, chronological compilations of U.S. court opinions. But, as it did with other physical media, from Blockbuster videos to Empire records, digitization has toppled traditional publishing. Thomson Reuters may call itself a news company, but Reuters news has been reduced to around 10 percent of the company's revenue as it makes the transition to data analytics software services.[47] Similarly, RELX is "winding down" its publishing services to focus on data analytics.[48]

By collecting both structured information products (legal codes, published articles, financial reports, and so on) and also raw data from tens of thousands of sources, RELX and Thomson Reuters aggregate ever more grist for their informational mills. With their stores of information and data-analytics products, companies like RELX and Thomson Reuters aren't taking over the information commons, they're creating new, private, walled-garden information ecosystems in multiple informational markets. Just as Facebook and Amazon make password-protected, closely controlled online platforms, RELX and Thomson Reuters make virtual, subscription-access and pay-per-view libraries and files.[49] Historically, information was envisioned as a common resource.[50] The centuries-old concept of a "marketplace of ideas" was not meant to be a for-profit business. But RELX and Thomson Reuters run closed information universes where they curate informational resources and decide who can access them. Like Facebook and Amazon, RELX and Thomson Reuters have privatized, and now control, social spaces that used to be public. They are the informational landlords that decide who can *swim in the ocean of knowledge*.[51]

Who Gets Hurt?

The inability to access critical knowledge is more than a mere inconvenience—in some cases, it can lead to more serious, life-and-death problems. In Tanzania, scientists and doctors can't see up-to-date malaria research even though Tanzania is teeming with malaria-carrying mosquitoes. Tanzanians are at risk of a deadly but preventable disease because malaria research is too expensive for researchers to access.[52] Paywalls can also keep people from being able to represent themselves in legal matters. Incarcerated people with limited access to legal information can't properly prepare to appear before parole boards and court judges because RELX and Thomson Reuters law products for correctional facilities often offer the bare minimum legal resources, which are insufficient to help inmates make their case.[53]

Data analytics companies' walled gardens also increase misinformation, propaganda, and fake news. In a walled-garden informational ecosystem, "[t]he truth is paywalled but the lies are free."[54] Well-curated digital archives and content streams ensure that people are well informed. The major data analytics companies are among the main providers of accurate financial, legal, and scientific information that shapes our understanding of the world.[55] When paywalls keep people from accessing and sharing accurate resources, low-quality content fills the informational voids beyond the garden walls. Information access prevents the public from falling prey to political high jinks. When the public can't see information, officials can alter facts. In the last few years, India's government lied about the dangers of Covid-19 and the U.S. president used a Sharpie marker to rewrite the path of a hurricane.[56] These falsehoods can dominate news feeds when factual stories are paywalled.

Even inside the companies' walled gardens, information quality is declining. In striving for bigness, the companies are sacrificing quality for quantity. The data analytics companies have become so focused on building the biggest information warehouses that their own content stockpiles are becoming diluted with information of varying quality. In the past,

Thomson Reuters and RELX companies were specialized information providers, deliberate about quality control, carefully editing out bad information from their products. They didn't just provide content, they also vetted it. But as data analytics companies, RELX and Thomson Reuters aren't as careful about curating information or selecting the best, most useful information for consumers. Instead, the companies provide tons of mediocre information. They behave less like information specialists and more like digital wholesale clubs, selling informational content in bulk. RELX even depicts its company as a giant funnel that ingests thousands of datasets from numerous sources and "cranks through" its databases with "Big Data technology."[57] The system that "cranks through" the data is a black box system, which means we can only see data going in and data products coming out—the actual data analytics process is a mystery. Even the companies' data analytics specialists aren't sure how, exactly, its products are made because there is so much data and so many data-sorting moves happen so fast. The companies are informational Costcos or Sam's Clubs, selling economy-sized information by the bucket.[58] But unlike Costco, which carefully selects high-quality products for its Kirkland label, the data analytics companies aren't so careful about quality control.

RELX alone boasts about having over sixty-five billion "science records," 3 petabytes of legal data, and more than sixty-five billion pieces of personal data collected from more than ten thousand sources.[59] But it doesn't promise that all of this content is accurate. Companies like RELX have high profit margins but they don't allocate their profits towards vetting the data and information they sell. Instead, they use their profits to buy and create more and more data and informational products, growing the size of their offerings rather than improving the quality of the products they offer.

The lack of quality control hurts consumers. The companies' citators (reports that tell lawyers whether cases and statutes are still good law) are inaccurate, leading lawyers, and even judges, astray.[60] RELX's Elsevier puts out reports that are later retracted.[61] Thomson Reuters's and RELX's personal data dossiers come with disclaimers warning consumers that their data suppliers may provide erroneous information. Instead of vetting the billions of personal data points they sell, the data analytics companies urge consumers to seek redress from their downstream data providers.[62] These mistakes can have serious consequences, especially for Black, brown, and overly surveilled people, who are likely to have more erroneous data in their RELX and Thomson Reuters dossiers. People, especially Black men, have been mistakenly arrested by police on the basis of data dossiers provided by private corporations. When erroneous data dossiers are algorithmically paired with photos, police get facial recognition products that are wrong 96 percent of the time, and more likely to be wrong when they are identifying people with Black or brown skin.[63] Incorrect information is especially problematic when RELX and Thomson Reuters sell their data dossiers and data analytics products to law enforcement agencies and other institutions that make big decisions about our lives.

And these companies can sell more data than the tech companies we hear about in the news. Both RELX and Thomson Reuters collect billions of personal data points from thousands of sources. RELX's files are more revealing than our Social Security numbers. There are few, if any, personal data collections more robust than the companies' dossiers. In some respects, RELX and Thomson Reuters know more about us than we even know about ourselves. News reports focus on how invasive Facebook and Google's data is, but those companies' personal data caches are merely a sliver of RELX's and Thomson Reuters's dossiers. Thomson Reuters personal data products include information from social media, blogs, chat rooms, and other platforms *plus* data from thousands of public records sources including DMVs and courthouses, as well as news, academic, and financial databases.[64] RELX sells data from big-tech platforms such as Twitter and YouTube *and* Accurint's deep-dive credit and background check reports.[65]

RELX and Thomson Reuters sell this personal data to the government,[66] insurance companies, health care providers,[67] landlords, and police. The data companies call their personal data products *risk solutions* because they assess how "risky" we are on the basis of hundreds of personal data points, including data reflecting our criminal and financial histories, as well as data identifying whom we associate with. Basing decisions about whether to insure people, whether to hire people, and whether to incarcerate people on bad data is as dystopian as a Ray Bradbury book. People can't get basic housing when RELX-data-fueled tenant screening software falsely labels potential tenants as high risk.[68] Immigration and Customs Enforcement (ICE) used predictive policing systems stocked with Thomson Reuters data to track down immigrant parents and separate them from their families.[69] ICE also pays LexisNexis almost $17 million for its personal data dossiers.[70] Both Thomson Reuters and RELX are Palantir data partners, supplying the data that fuels Palantir's predictive policing software. The government's invasive surveillance tech relies on RELX's and Thomson Reuters's data.

In addition to fueling predictive policing software, data analytics companies partner with "designer data" firms that specialize in specific data types of biometric and geospatial data. We worry about biometric data products like Clearview AI's facial recognition databases, but like information about our favorite candy, biometric data must be paired with other data to be useful. Biometric and geolocation surveillance products need supplemental data supplies to work. Like the name of your favorite candy, the location of someone's phone or car isn't very useful unless you know who the person is, who they associate with, and what they're up to. RELX and Thomson Reuters provide the data dossiers that match faces and cell phones to names, addresses, and associates. The companies give law enforcement agencies the informational links that connect someone's DNA to their address, their address to their workplace, their workplace to their work associates, et cetera.

The companies' personal data brokering businesses make their expansion across multiple information markets especially fraught—when companies like RELX and Thomson Reuters take over too many disparate information markets, they can combine information services that should be separate. Lawyers' research data shouldn't be in the same product suite as government surveillance data, and lawyers shouldn't have to rely on research services run by the same company that the police use to track their clients.[71] The findings of researchers doing nonprofit, public interest research shouldn't belong to the same companies whose products determine what research gets funded and which researchers get tenure.

Inadequate Legal Solutions

Even though data analytics companies are exploiting our informational needs and outputs, lawmakers and regulators are not intervening to clip the companies' far-reaching tentacles. There are no simple explanations for why the United States has failed to pass comprehensive data privacy laws or build public access systems for our digital infrastructure. The federal government is only beginning to scrutinize big tech, but it's leaving data companies out of its inquiries. Without attention, data analytics companies flourish while their big-tech counterparts face increasing regulatory and social scrutiny. Big-tech CEOs run a gauntlet of congressional questioning and antitrust litigation, but big information companies don't, even though they're the result of aggressive informational takeovers and anticompetitive practices worthy of the kind of antitrust scrutiny that Facebook and Amazon receive.[72]

A big reason data companies get away with turning our public information into their private property is plain old American capitalism. In the United States, private, for-profit ownership is more than a financial model, it's a core belief. Both public information access and private, unsellable personal data are anathema to the free market because they don't leave companies with anything to buy or sell. In the U.S. iteration of free market capitalism, virtually anything can be commercialized, even our personal information, laws, and public research.

Since the 1970s, we've stripped down business laws, antitrust protections, commercial codes, and securities regulations to threadbare, minimal protections to help U.S. businesses to make as much money as possible.[73] Legal safeguards protecting our information infrastructure have only grown weaker as our digital ecosystem has grown. The same antitrust laws that successfully prevented Microsoft from dominating the web browser market in the 1990s failed to rein in Facebook's social media domination less than twenty years later.

This lack of regulation is especially pronounced in digital markets. Around the time of Microsoft's rise, President Clinton removed regulatory safety rails that guaranteed public access to informational services to make way for digital media companies like satellite radio and national news corporations.[74] Clinton-era policies replaced the promise of information services such as guaranteed phone lines and local news with "access," the promise that there would be free market choices for those who sought them.[75] Clinton hailed digital deregulation, saying it would "promote competition as the key to opening new markets and new opportunities." Instead of competition, without regulation, telecommunications mega-giants like AT&T and Clear Channel digital radio took over telecommunications markets, eliminating competition. We similarly saw our information commons privatized by publishers that are now the legacy companies of our data analytics giants.

Despite the overwhelming evidence that digital monopolists are destroying competition, politicians are living in the past, imagining informational capitalism as the startup boom they saw in the 1990s, when a bevy of innovative new enterprises disrupted markets every day. This vision of "big tech" is mistaken and outdated. The dot.com boom burst long ago, and today's data markets aren't brimming with healthy competition. In the real world, several huge data companies dominate, and new companies can't compete, leaving consumers stuck, relying on unregulated informational dynasties that have no competitive incentive to treat them well.

Without new laws, regulators and courts are left retrofitting old, outdated legal concepts to today's data problems. Many of the laws used to regulate today's data practices were passed in the 1990s or before. The pre-internet, paper-era laws are ill-equipped to regulate today's informational infrastructure. The government shoehorns new data problems into old laws like a wayward crab trying to fashion its shell from washed-up litter. Courts use intellectual property rules meant to protect individuals' "creations of the mind" to protect corporations' data portfolios. Financial regulators apply the same laissez-faire approach to data ventures as they did to industrial-era ventures even as modern data practices threaten civil rights and liberties in unprecedented ways.[76] In our current legal schemes, data companies can squeeze as many advantages as possible from the markets in which they participate, without government safeguards and oversight.

Even antitrust law, which is especially designed to protect consumers from too-big companies, isn't in the right shape to protect people from data analytics companies' harm. Regulators cannot enforce Chicago

School–era antitrust doctrine to break up data monopolies, so the news, trade publishing, and academic publishing markets are each dominated by five companies. Music has its own the "big three" oligopoly of companies.[77] Legal professionals only have two legal information products to choose from. Different types of media fold into one another—TV companies buy publishers, news companies buy music labels, and data analytics firms buy journal platforms as the government watches from the sidelines.

Another reason the government doesn't intervene to regulate the data analytics industry is that federal, state, and local agencies themselves rely on the data companies' products. Without Thomson Reuters and RELX databases, the legal information that lawmakers, courts, and agencies rely on would stop flowing. Government surveillance programs wouldn't work. Child welfare agencies and other social services wouldn't be able to predict future interventions or generate lists telling them which benefit recipients might commit fraud or default on paying their debts. State DMVs would lose valuable revenue they get from selling our data.

Data analytics companies have become ingrained in government systems, and the two are codependent. Thomson Reuters has at least 512 federal government contracts, and RELX has at least 527 contracts with various government agencies. The companies supply everything from identity verification data for the Department of Treasury, to legal information platforms for Department of Justice lawyers, to financial data services for the Securities and Exchange Commission, to Elsevier's e-learning system for nurses in VA hospitals.[78] This codependence is also demonstrated by the revolving doors between the government and the data companies. Government agencies are hungry for tech talent in their ranks,[79] and data companies want an insiders' scoop on which products their government clients want. It's no surprise that James Dinkins, the general manager of Thomson Reuters's surveillance products, was the executive associate director of Homeland Security Investigations under President Obama, and that LexisNexis's current head of federal strategy led the Office of Personnel Management before coming to the data company.[80] Former police commissioners sit on data companies' boards of directors.[81] The government is a data company partner, not a data company regulator. On top of the human connections between the government and data companies, there's also the financial one: data companies spend millions of dollars supporting tech-friendly candidates and legislation. RELX alone spent $2.38 million on lobbying and $903,563 on political campaign contributions in 2020.[82]

Without government intervention, people have tried to solve data problems on their own. Activists have tried to curb data companies' bad practices. Several libraries walked away from RELX's exorbitant Elsevier contracts.[83] Groups have marched in front of Thomson Reuters's and RELX's headquarters to protest the companies' ICE contracts. These types of individual actions raise public awareness, but they don't stop data exploitation: only government intervention can stop it. Anything short of government action merely puts the government's responsibility to ensure safe, equitable infrastructure onto individuals, and it lets the data companies make the rules.

Like social media and other media industries, the data industry won't effectively govern itself. When left to their own devices, industries push consumer protection duties onto consumers with ad campaigns, community advisory boards, and other public relations glosses. Like plastics companies convincing us that it is our job to recycle and keep the earth clean, data companies convince us that digital "hygiene" is our cleanliness problem instead of their exploitation problem. When data companies tell us to clear our cookies if we don't want them to get our data, or when they tell us to affiliate with a university if we want to see science, they are shifting their social obligations on to consumers instead of fixing their harmful practices.

A New Outlook on Data Regulation

Instead of leaving data analytics companies to their own devices, we could intervene to make sure they stop harming consumers. History gives us a roadmap for how to regulate data companies and infrastructure. The United States regulates critical, communal resources, including industries that provide public goods and services such as water companies and power plants. The companies enjoy some monopoly power in exchange for government oversight. The U.S. also regulates critical environmental resources like air and water to prevent industries from destroying them.

But the government tends to avoid intervening in market affairs until catastrophe forces its hand. Lawmaking is often a post hoc affair. We aren't willing to interrupt the free market unless the dangers of continuing are too great to bear. Environmental law only coalesced when deadly toxic smog threatened entire towns and Ohio's Cuyahoga River literally caught fire. The Consumer Finance Protection Bureau was created only after the economy collapsed under the weight of abusive investment banking practices. We like to let the free market hum along until something so bad happens that it grinds the market to a halt, making it impossible to move forward without addressing the problem.

In the case of data infrastructure, we have the opportunity to act sooner, before the data problems get out of control. Right now, we are courting digital catastrophe. Unbreachable paywalls, big-data policing, and the data-fueled spread of misinformation are destroying lives. We are seeing information run astray, giving way to conspiracy theories and even government insurrection. These informational problems are warning signs that we need government intervention. Today's information crises are a digital river on fire.

To fix the information problems that data companies cause, we'd need some new laws. The legal schemes that scholars and judges have applied to digital problems don't fit. We don't have sufficient data privacy or information access laws to govern nongovernmental, third-party data companies like RELX and Thomson Reuters. Property, contract, constitutional, and other legal doctrines are blunt, imprecise tools for dealing with data analytics companies. The data laws we do have only address specific data types (health data, financial data, and so on) instead of the broad data analytics schemes we have today. Old information laws are ill-equipped to fix new data problems. The people who wrote the laws did not envision an internet-based society, nor did they predict the ways we use and share data and information today.

The ideal information laws would treat information policies as a spectrum. On one side of the spectrum, laws would guarantee open access to critical, public information, and on the other side of the spectrum, laws would safeguard personal, private information. But until the federal government creates comprehensive information access and data privacy laws, lawyers will have to keep pulling all the arrows from the quiver of American law, hoping that they will strike down various data problems as they rise. The chapters of this book demonstrate how our current laws (or lack thereof) have been used to try to solve data problems, and how they have fallen short. Each chapter explores a different market that the data analytics companies control, either by monopoly, duopoly, or oligopoly. While not every market is divided between RELX and Thomson Reuters, you'll see how they play power roles in all of them. Each market raises unique information access and privacy issues, so they are worth examining one by one. The chapters examine both the data companies' roles, and the laws that govern them, as they serve as the government's major data brokers, as they dominate the academic research market,[84] as they disseminate legal information and services to the entire legal profession,[85] as they sell the corporate financial information needed to make sound investment decisions, and, finally, as they report and archive the news.

The final chapter offers advice on how to improve our information and data infrastructure. The solutions in this book undoubtedly omit some legal experts' pet prescriptions for regulating data and information flows. The sprawling, inconclusive field of tech and data law is ever-changing and too vast to summarize in this book. Information capitalism, like industrial capitalism of the past, can't be easily reduced to a single cause, effect, or solution. Like other systemic injustices, systemic informational inequality is the result of a convergence of many policies and laws, a perfect storm that promotes and sustains data cartels. We must revive the idea that information is a public good.

One thing to keep in mind as we pick through the various laws: laws are decisions made by people. They're human constructs, not godly decrees. Interpreting legal rights and doctrines is an art form similar to translating tarot cards or tea leaves. Legal interpretations are part alchemy, part political will, and part emotional reaction. Justice Souter describes law as an "ipse dixit" (Latin for dogmatic and unproven statement) effort to balance "liberty" and "security" interests.[86] Others compare law to Calvinball, the game that cartoon character Calvin played with his stuffed animal tiger, in which rules were made up on the spot. We pretend that lawyers and Supreme Court justices know something we don't, when really, interpreting the Constitution is not so different from interpreting a literary passage or poem. I tell you this not to turn you into a legal nihilist, but to empower you to participate in law and policy making. The experts sitting in law firms' corner offices or in justices' chambers are well versed in the law as we know it, but you can help design legal solutions they haven't even thought of.

Participate in information law and policy not just because you can, but also because it's important. Information is power. Information can make people wiser, and it can be a tool of oppression. Communities of color, and poor communities, are more likely to endure overpolicing and oversurveillance. Data will be used to track and arrest nonwhite, nonwealthy people, to deny people services and privileges. Protecting people's informational rights will improve digital equality. The UN's Universal Declaration of Human Rights includes "receiving and imparting information" as a right. But merely saying that something is a right doesn't do anything to protect it. If receiving and imparting information is a human right, then it requires legal protection. We have to create laws and policies to protect and enforce rights, or else rights are no more than platitudes.

This book is meant to introduce a broad informational problem and invite creative, new legal solutions instead of recycling old legal ideas. Most of all, I hope this book sparks ideas for information science and information law scholars and activists by stringing together a bunch of previously disparate problems (academic paywalls! access to law! surveillance!) under one umbrella, where they belong. Because so many of our informational problems, especially in libraries and academic institutions, are caused by the same few companies.

2

DATA BROKERING

DATA BROKERS—entities aggregating and selling personal data—have become a hot topic among privacy activists.[1] Tech journalists are calling out companies such as Facebook for bartering user data, and condemning Clearview AI for selling facial recognition information to the government. But RELX and Thomson Reuters are vintage, original data brokers. They've been selling personal data since the 1990s, almost a decade before Facebook even existed.[2]

Of all of the informational markets RELX and Thomson Reuters participate in, data brokering markets are the creepiest—companies are turning your data into a product. Data analytics businesses like RELX and Thomson Reuters sell personal data and information to government agencies, including law enforcement, and to private firms including insurance companies and health care providers. While RELX and Thomson Reuters are far from the only data brokers out there, they're among the few that specialize in government and "risk" data products that predict whether we'll repay our loans or commit crimes. The companies also use their personal data dossiers to create data products in the other informational markets they occupy. The companies' "academic metrics," "legal insights," and financial data products are created by running a slurry of our personal data through data analytics software with other datasets the companies own.[3]

There are two types of data brokering: commercial data brokering, in which companies crunch our data to sell us things, and institutional data brokering, in which companies sell our data to the government and other institutions that determine our rights and privileges.[4] RELX and Thomson Reuters specialize in the latter type of personal data services, selling your data to the people who decide whom to criminalize and whom to deprive of services and benefits. RELX and Thomson Reuters are among the companies that sell the data products that power government surveillance programs and other operations assessing how likely we are to be criminals, "fraudsters,"[5] or bad employees. Child welfare agencies, landlords, banks, and even hospitals depend on the companies' "encyclopedic dossiers" with their billions of data points from thousands of sources.[6] Public institutions and private firms make decisions based on streams of our medical, religious, and political information, and other intimate data.[7]

Commercial data brokering is bad for privacy, but government data brokering is worse. It's not merely meddlesome and invasive—the government's data programs can strip you of your liberty. Your data dossier can get you arrested or deported, altering the course of your life.[8] Companies like RELX and Thomson Reuters participate in peoples' surveillance, arrest, and deportation. It's no coincidence that they've earned the Orwellian nickname *big brother's little helper*.[9] They help the government, your employer, your landlords, your insurance companies, and all sorts of other big decision makers spy on you. In her book *Weapons of Math Destruction*, mathematician Cathy O'Neil calls these types of data products "translators of moral choices," reducing our rights to algorithms.[10]

Companies like LexisNexis and Thomson Reuters dove into data brokering long before it turned into a multibillion-dollar industry.[11] They built their data brokering businesses on policing software made by people like Hank Asher. Asher is known as "the father of data fusion."[12] A reformed drug smuggler, he dedicated the latter half of his life to fighting crimes with data. He developed some of the first government data broker products, including Accurint and ChoicePoint. Today, Asher's products constitute the core of RELX's and Thomson Reuters's risk products. Asher started building data analytics products in the 1990s, when he figured out that he could buy government and company databases stocked with personal information.[13] Government agencies were game to capitalize on their personal data collections. In the pre-internet days, government data was like "underappreciated real estate": cheap and largely overlooked bundles of information.[14] As a Washington State employee put it, the DMV isn't just a public-safety agency, it's "very much a data-sharing agency."[15] Asher collected all sorts of public records, including arrest records, land sale recordings, and data rolls from DMVs.[16]

Asher also figured out how to link personal computers and build algorithms to organize and sort his data troves. By the early 2000s, nobody could match Asher's data collections and mining software. Even the government couldn't compete—its own data systems were siloed and slow compared to Asher's nimble data tools. Hundreds of police departments started using Asher's AutoTrack, a product that could instantaneously find peoples' driver's license records with no more than a name. In the wake of 9/11, Asher formulated a "high terrorist risk factor" algorithm and sold it to the White House for $8 million. A few years later, RELX bought Asher's entire company.[17]

By the time RELX bought Asher's business, RELX and Thomson Reuters were already well-positioned to offer new data products to their already-established government customers. The companies were selling legal products to prosecutors—it wasn't a stretch to also sell data products to the law enforcement officers. Companies like RELX and Thomson Reuters were already embedded in government offices and contract procurement systems, so expanding into data analytics was more like selling a new product to existing users than starting out in an entirely new marketplace.

In 1997, RELX rolled out its first "risk management" tool: a product that helped child support officers find and punish parents who fell behind on payments.[18] Soon the company was building all sorts of personal data fusion and analytics tools for the government, going to agency investor days to help the government build more data-analytics-based programs.[19] By 2009, RELX was on the verge of monopolizing the electronic public records market for law enforcement.[20] The Federal Trade Commission

(FTC) intervened, forcing RELX to divest some of its personal data analytics products to Thomson Reuters. RELX gave its competitor Choice-Point's Consolidated Lead Evaluation and Reporting (CLEAR) research platform, which is now Thomson Reuters's main "risk" product.[21]

"Risk product" is a vague term. The companies describe their science and legal information products with specificity, listing all of the database features and search functions, but they don't say much about what is in their risk products or what they do. They just vaguely claim that the products will make communities *safer*.[22] Like other tech companies building creepy tech, they describe their data brokering businesses with fuzzy terms. There are plenty of "business solutions" and "data integration" firms, but there are few tech companies that out themselves as spyware and surveillance businesses. Similarly, nobody calls themselves a government data broker. It's bad PR to say you're selling people's data to the police.

Instead of explaining what its products do, the LexisNexis "Special Services"[23] landing page shows rows of American flags waving in the breeze alongside the quote "Integrity. Honor. Trust." Thomson Reuters Special Services (TRSS) promises to "help professionals achieve mission objectives," but the company doesn't clarify that the "professionals" are law enforcement agents and the "mission" is filling arrest, detention, and deportation quotas.[24] It's not unusual for policing programs to be advertised with vague, fluffy rhetoric. In the 1980s the government used a cartoon canine to convince kids to report people to the police. While McGruff the Crime Dog seemed earnest about safety, the underlying campaign was less about safe neighborhoods and more about convincing kids to pass information to cops.[25] TRSS and LexisNexis Special Services, Inc. (LNSSI) are fighting the same "War on Crime" McGruff was taking a bite out of back in the 1980s, but they've replaced human intelligence with more powerful data dossiers.

Just as a cartoon dog probably won't stop crime, even policing with the most powerful data analytics is unlikely to make the world any safer. Using data to police people has become common practice, but it hasn't decreased crime. Instead, the government's partnerships with third-party data providers have embedded the discriminatory policing problems of the McGruff era into digital policing infrastructure. While data surveillance long predates the internet,[26] in the United States, digital surveillance and policing programs ramped up after 9/11. The attacks happened in the same span of time that people started shedding more digital exhaust as the internet, cell phones, and other digital tools became more prevalent. The USA PATRIOT Act eased the way for government agencies to procure records from data companies,[27] and the NSA started sifting through tons of phone, email, and other personal data records to track Muslim people and their communities.[28]

Despite backlash over its invasive post-9/11 data-based surveillance programs, the government hasn't rethought its use of data dossiers. Instead, it's gone hard in the other direction, supporting datafied decision making in child welfare decisions, financial crimes enforcement, and decisions about whose taxes get audited.[29] The U.S. Postal Service even tracks our social media posts to "assess threats to Postal Service employees and its infrastructure."[30]

Today, the government is one of the biggest consumers of personal information dossiers. RELX sells data brokering products to more than 7,500 federal, state, and local government agencies. Seventy percent of local governments and 80 percent of federal agencies use RELX data products, including 2,100 police departments and 955 sheriff departments.[31] TRSS supplies data brokering services to federal and local law enforcement agencies, the Department of Defense, the Department of Justice, and intelligence agencies. TRSS also had over $39 million in data brokering contracts with Immigrations and Customs Enforcement (ICE) in 2020.[32] In the private sector, RELX provides data analytics products to 95 percent of the top one hundred personal insurance companies, 76 percent of Fortune 500 businesses, and seven of the world's top ten banks.[33]

Data analytics companies play a big role in many agencies' decision-making processes, but it's hard to figure out exactly how the government uses data analytics products. It's nearly impossible to parse the thousands of local, state, and federal government data contracts and memoranda to figure out who is accessing the data services and what they're using them for. This obscurity seems intentional. The contracts and descriptions are "purposefully dense and dull." The companies and institutions involved make "the most interesting stuff . . . the most impenetrable" to prevent the public from discovering just how our personal information is being used by powerful decision-making entities.[34]

We may not know exactly how the data products are being used, but we do know they digitize historically prejudiced policies and programs. Spying on citizens with help from private companies isn't new. AT&T fed people's information to the government during the Prohibition era, the NYPD had wiretapping agreements with phone companies in the early 1900s,[35] and the FBI intercepted activists' cables during the civil rights movement.[36] Historical surveillance programs were often racially motivated and racially focused, from informants who spied on Black people in the 1800s to the FBI's COINTELPRO surveillance program that tracked civil rights activists including Rev. Dr. Martin Luther King Jr., Malcolm X, and the Black Panther Party.[37] Data analytics partnerships merely datafy these types of surveillance programs, including their tendency to disproportionately target Black people and marginalized groups.[38]

Ruha Benjamin correctly calls data-based government programs "the datafication of injustice." Data analytics companies' services amplify that injustice. Data-based programs could be built anew, to erase or correct injustice. But instead, they are built upon the foundations of historically racist criminal and social services programs.[39] Adding data analytics to historically discriminatory criminal justice, child welfare, insurance, and healthcare systems doesn't decrease injustice. Instead, it infuses discriminatory systems with biased data and information.[40]

Like other digital innovations, data analytics embeds the inequities, marginalization, and biases of our analog world into technological systems.[41] Data profiling, like all profiling, is based on assumptions, and those assumptions aren't neutral. Just as algorithms are biased by the assumptions of their architects,[42] data collections themselves are also biased. Overpoliced people, especially Black people, are overrepresented in police records. Because Black people are more likely to be subject to police interactions, they have disproportionately more legal writeups than the others. They're also more likely to have rap sheets and be named in gang databases. Over a century of systemic racism also makes it more likely that Black people will have more interactions with social services and child welfare agencies than white people. All of these government records end up in data dossiers. If you're looking at the data dossier of a Black man living in the United States who's been at the receiving end of generations of racism and criminal injustice, it's statistically likely that their profile will contain more information than a white person's data dossier, and that a Black person's profile will be associated with more friends and family members ensnared in the same overpolicing system.

Redlining, workplace discrimination, and racist financial treatment may also inaccurately make people appear more financially risky. White and wealthy families are less likely to have records in government welfare systems, and they're less likely to utilize government services such as food stamps or public medical assistance. The disproportionately large data dossiers end up harming Black people. For instance, the disparate data dossiers make Black children the focus of child welfare algorithms, which makes Black children more likely to be tracked and their families disparately subjected to state intervention.[43]

When data is removed from its context, it is easier to draw discriminatory conclusions from it. For instance, if you lack a credit history because redlining prevented you from getting a mortgage, the racist origins of the related data won't be explained in a data dossier. A story from data specialist Steven Rich demonstrates how technically accurate data can, without context, paint an inaccurate picture. [44] One day, Rich was driving his truck, when he suddenly slammed on the brakes. His GPS map flashed a warning: "Hard Braking: Sudden hard braking increases the odds of losing control of your car." If braking data is relayed to his car insurance company to determine whether Rich should get discounts for good driving, this warning would likely hurt his chances. But on the day Rich hit the brakes, the GPS didn't tell the full story: the reason Rich pumped the brakes is because a car suddenly swerved into his lane, right in front of him. If he hadn't hit the brakes, he would have been in a wreck. Without context, data can be not just incorrect, but harmful.

Data products don't just perpetuate systemic racism, sometimes they amplify it. In certain situations, data companies and the government purposely gather more data about some marginalized groups than about others. Data brokers and the U.S. military have been known to buy Muslim dating app data without users' consent.[45] The government also demands more data from people who seek its services. People who are poor, sick, or disabled are also forced to trade personal data in exchange for basic resources. When services are provided through online platforms, data becomes a cost of entry. Filling out online Supplemental Nutrition Assistance Program (SNAP) registration forms, going to a health clinic, scheduling paratransit program rides, participating in stores' rewards programs and opting into store credit cards, and completing online surveys for coupons are all activities that involve swapping data for necessary benefits.[46] All of this data can become fodder for risk analysis and surveillance.

Discriminatory data collection is cyclical—people with more robust data dossiers are more likely to be listed on data-driven hot lists and found in search results, which makes them more likely to be subject to police trackers and agency interventions. Those additional run-ins with the government result in more records being added to their data dossiers. For example, the Chicago Police Department's failed "Strategic Subjects List" program, which used a computerized algorithm to rank people's likelihood of committing a crime, didn't reduce gun violence, but it did result in disproportionate police contact with people who appeared more on the lists. People with more data in the system showed up more prominently in the system, and they subsequently had more police interactions that created even more data in their files.[47]

Similarly, undocumented immigrants are more likely to be tracked by immigration enforcement the more they comply with U.S. laws. They generate digital "paper trails" by getting licenses and insurance, paying bills, sending kids to school, filing taxes, working, and participating in society. Social participation makes people more "findable." The U.S. government encourages immigrants to assimilate, applauding people who perform "model citizenship," but it builds systems in which people who follow government rules and live model "American lives" are most likely to be snared by ICE.[48]

Data analytics also makes already unjust programs worse by replacing smaller data collections with huge data dossiers. Human intelligence is limited—people can only collect so much information on their fellow humans. But personal data dossiers like the ones RELX and Thomson Reuters sell contain more information than humans could ever gather on their own. RELX and Thomson Reuters are at the top of the personal data food chain. Big-tech companies like Amazon and Google are first-party data collectors—they gather data directly from you. You consensually trade information with those companies in exchange for the products and services they offer, whether it's one-click shopping or free email. Beyond those "first-party" data brokers, there are also smaller "second-party" data brokers that collect specific types of data (like financial or criminal data) or share data in smaller consortia. But data brokers like RELX and Thomson Reuters acquire billions of data points from a vast array of data sources, including the first- and second-party data collectors. They've been called "shopping malls for information," offering an array of data types for a broad spectrum of customers.[49]

There are only a few of these giant, third-party data brokers.[50] Their massive personal data collections are stuffed with billions of public and proprietary records from thousands of different places, updated in real time.[51] They have dossiers on millions of people, including over two-thirds of U.S. residents, which probably includes you.[52] Data brokers like RELX and Thomson Reuters have so much data that they know more about you than your family and friends do.[53] With that much data, their customers can capitalize on the "dossier effect"—a single query can compile "huge dossiers containing extensive information about you from many diverse sources."[54]

RELX calls its millions of unique personal datasets LexIDs. The company uses the LexIDs in their "risk" analytics products.[55] Our LexIDs, and our Thomson Reuters CLEAR profiles, are like social security numbers, identifiers associated with our identities. RELX and Thomson Reuters associate these identifiers with everything from our consumer data, social media activity, warranty registrations, magazine subscriptions, religious and political affiliations, and other details about our daily lives.[56] When database technologies started taking off in the 1970s, people worried that universal identifiers such as social security numbers would be used to create invasive "master files" detailing our personal lives. Computer science experts urged Congress to limit the use of universal identifiers, including social security numbers, to prevent the government from building systems of digital personal dossiers.[57] Fifty years later, the government buys those invasive dossiers through companies like RELX and Thomson Reuters, and uses them in the types of invasive ways that 1970s-era data experts feared.

Unlike the government, private data companies don't have to limit their data use to certain purposes, nor do they expunge their data as part of their records management practices. Thomson Reuters and RELX save our data indefinitely without deleting it, layering new data on top of old. They combine different datasets to create mosaics of our lives: where we go, who we know, and what we do each day.[58] Even if you try to opt out of data collection by avoiding social media, the companies create "shadow profiles" about you based on the data your friends, family, and associates trail behind them when they go online.[59] If you try to remove your online data, companies like Thomson Reuters can make you reappear, from "invisible to stark visibility."[60]

Institutions from insurers to law enforcement use data brokers because dossiers of data are far more useful than singular sources of data. GPS data alone doesn't do much more than tell someone where you've been, but when you combine GPS data with someone's social media posts, home address, and marriage and criminal records, it's far more revealing.[61] That's why DNA companies,[62] license-plate-reader companies,[63] and predictive policing software companies like Palantir and CopLink[64] partner with data brokers like RELX and Thomson Reuters. Without more data, their DNA and license-plate recordings and their predictive policing algorithms aren't as useful.

Government institutions also use data brokers to get around the Fourth Amendment's warrant requirements. The Fourth Amendment protects people from warrantless searches of their persons, houses, papers, and effects.[65] But over the years, the Supreme Court has made so many exceptions to the warrant requirement that the Fourth Amendment has been compared to Swiss cheese—full of holes.[66] The Court decided that law enforcement doesn't need a warrant to search open fields[67] or things in "plain view."[68] Law enforcement also doesn't need warrants to search information gathered by nongovernmental third parties. In the 1970s, the Court said that people don't have legitimate expectations of privacy in information they voluntarily give away to banks and other entities.[69] This "third-party doctrine" was conceived before data brokers existed, in an era when people handed over information knowingly and consensually, like a businessperson giving their records to an accountant or someone describing a crime to an informant.

The third-party doctrine makes less sense in the 2000s, when we give information to third parties all the time, unintentionally and involuntarily. Voluntarily telling someone something is much different than digital information sharing, which is often involuntary and totally beyond our control. But even though our data constantly flows to third parties without our knowledge and consent, courts have, so far, maintained the third-party doctrine for data companies' dossiers. The Supreme Court may eventually curtail the third-party exception to the Fourth Amendment. In 2012, Supreme Court Justice Sonia Sotomayor suggested that the third-party doctrine is outmoded, calling the warrant exception "ill suited to the digital age."[70] In 2018, the Court exempted cell phone location data from the third-party doctrine.[71] But the Court is still a long way off from getting rid of the third-party doctrine for our data.[72]

Because the government doesn't need warrants to use data brokers' products, RELX and Thomson Reuters can help police "buy their way around" warrant requirements.[73] Without constitutional safeguards, the data analytics companies don't merely help police conduct warrantless searches in individual criminal cases. They also replicate portions of the government's surveillance infrastructure beyond the scope of government oversight. For instance, after 9/11, federal and state officials joined forces to create a network of government-run fusion centers to share information. Civil rights experts decried the massive data-sharing networks, saying that they posed serious risks to our civil liberties.[74] Today, RELX runs its own private, third-party data center where thousands of law enforcement agencies consolidate and share their data. The company's Public Safety Data Exchange compiles federal, state, and local law enforcement data, links it to our LexIDs, and makes it available to RELX customers in products with names like "Accurint Virtual Crime Center."[75] This private fusion-center-like product is advised by former FBI, secret service, and metropolitan police department employees. LexisNexis's Data Exchange may not be a government surveillance program, but it sure feels like one with its government customers and ex-law enforcement leadership. Unlike government's fusion centers, which are subject to government oversight and public scrutiny, RELX's private data center operates without transparency or government supervision. Safeguards that protect people's civil liberties against government surveillance don't apply to RELX's private data centers.

Civil rights concerns about data brokers are compounded by the fact that, unlike government data collections, people can't correct erroneous data in the private companies' dossiers.[76] The data brokers are selling imperfect data to law enforcement, employers, health care providers, and other institutions making our life-altering decisions, and the subjects of that data have no way to fix it. Even when consumers' insurance rates double because of faulty LexisNexis data, or when people's credit scores sink because LexisNexis switches their names with someone else's, there is no easy way to correct a data profile.[77]

The inability to correct erroneous personal data is especially problematic because third-party data brokers' data is the lowest-quality data. It's hard to effectively vet data when it's constantly pouring in from thousands of sources. So instead of fact-checking its data troves, the companies send its customers disclaimers about the veracity of their data collections. When librarian Shea Swauger requested his personal data file from Thomson Reuters, the file arrived with a cover letter saying that the company doesn't "warrant the comprehensiveness, completeness, accuracy, or adequacy" of Shea's information.[78] So when Shea saw errors in his forty-one-page Thomson Reuters dossier, including the wrong marital status, age, and addresses, he had little power to correct the information, even though it's being sold to institutions that make decisions that effect his life. The disclaimer attached to its data dossiers makes it clear that the company isn't interested in fact-checking its personal data products. Thomson Reuters brushes aside its responsibility to sell accurate information with a note saying, "The nature of the information and the collections processes self-limit the ability of any aggregator to independently verify and/or validate any of the database contents."[79]

With this warning, the companies put the onus on consumers to contact the original data providers and ask them to correct their files. It would take a huge amount of time to figure out where the bad data came from.

The companies don't list any of their ten-thousand-plus data sources, and each source has its own unique system to navigate and people to talk to. That's why repairing your data dossier's errors has been described as a task that "few people would have the time or patience to embark upon."[80]

Using erroneous data to make decisions can violate people's civil rights. LexisNexis had to disable one of their data analytics products in Aurora, Colorado, over fears that people would be falsely arrested on the basis of bad or outdated information. Lumen is a facial recognition tool that instantly matches photos from dating profiles, security cameras, and even phones to jail-booking photos.[81] It turns out that the jail-booking photo database included people who were wrongly arrested, were acquitted of crimes, or had already served their sentences.

Despite their biases and errors, companies are building more and more data products to make decisions for agencies. If all you have is a hammer, everything looks like a nail, and if all you have is data, every problem looks like one that can be solved with data analytics, even when the problems are very human, sensitive ones involving life, liberty, and property. In *Automating Inequality*, Virginia Eubanks says that the government is using digital decision making to create efficiencies and ease administrative burdens.[82] Data-powered tools like Lumen make policing less burdensome by giving cops plenty of leads and fast answers. That's why, even knowing about the potential for mistaken identification, police in Aurora, Colorado, want their Lumen access back. As one officer explained, they're "just biding . . . time until LexisNexis allows us to have access again."[83]

Datafied decision making may be fast and convenient, but it contravenes government's obligations to solve social problems and improve municipal life. By dehumanizing choices that have an impact on human life, the government avoids difficult political conversations about social justice and about who deserves rights and privileges in our communities.[84] In many cases, datafied decisions make social problems worse for people already facing the brunt of social injustices. Dehumanizing innovations are often tried on oppressed people.[85] Landlords test facial recognition surveillance systems in primarily Black apartment complexes.[86] The government deploys large-scale data surveillance programs against immigrants. The Department of Homeland Security (DHS), including ICE and Customs and Border Patrol (CBP), is casting a thick web of data-powered surveillance systems across the U.S. border and in the nation's interior, and it's using RELX's and Thomson Reuters's data services.[87] DHS is testing out data-powered technology on immigrants, including predictive policing software, automated license-plate-recognition surveillance, automated facial and DNA identification, and phone-hacking technology.[88] They're also testing out digital tools of incarceration including ankle monitors and other devices that create "digital jails" and "virtual borders" that track immigrants and limit their freedom to move.[89] These experimental surveillance technologies are fueled by data analytics' companies' dossiers.

DHS's surveillance tools are deployed cruelly. They help ICE catch people off guard, finding and detaining targets by surprise as they are going about their daily lives. They catch people in moments of weakness, without warning. ICE agents tracked down and detained a ten-year-old girl as she was being transported in an ambulance right after she had surgery. Agents detained a high schooler hours before his senior prom. They also arrested parents visiting their U.S. Army sergeant son-in-law at his base on the Fourth of July. ICE's raids and arrests are swift and surprising. As one teacher whose students' parents were taken by ICE agents described it: "One moment they're living life . . . and then they're gone, their car just sitting on the side of the road. It feels like a death."[90]

While data analytics companies don't make all of the surveillance technology that leads to these arrests, their data helps agents piece together mosaics of immigrants' lives. The most common questions among immigrants at the receiving end of ICE arrests and raids are "How did they pick me as a target?" and "How did they find me?"[91] The answers to these questions can often be found in subjects' data dossiers. Data analytics companies' products "form an ever-evolving, 360-degree view" of people's lives by supplying up-to-the-minute information about workplaces, locations, associates, affiliations, and so on.[92] The companies also use their dossier power to help ICE agents sort through billions of data points in a single keyword search, making instantaneous hot lists and maps listing targets and showing where to find them.

Newfangled surveillance technologies aren't just used on immigrants. Police use data-fueled surveillance tools to track protesters and activists.

This type of activist surveillance has been compared to civil-rights-era spying: "COINTELPRO for the tech age."[93] Thomson Reuters and RELX sell data for these types of surveillance programs as well. Thomson Reuters sold its CLEAR services to Minneapolis police to track protesters after police killed George Floyd in 2020.[94] In Aurora, Colorado, the police who used LexisNexis's Lumen (the problematic facial recognition product) deployed the tool to identify protesters as well.

Other government agencies and private companies beyond law enforcement also use data to determine whether we can access health care, education, housing, and employment.[95] These data analytics programs don't involve police, but they still disparately harm oppressed people—in this case, poor people and people of color who are more likely to interact with social services or be denied insurance, housing, health care, employment, and other services often provided by private institutions.

Child welfare agencies replace human decisions with data products that decide when a child is at risk of abuse or neglect.[96] Child welfare data is as biased and erroneous as policing data. The Illinois Department of Children and Family Services stopped using child welfare data analytics products after the product they were using mistakenly flagged thousands of kids as being at imminent risk of death.[97] Los Angeles County ended a similar deal after the data led to thousands of false positives for child abuse there, as well.[98] The federal government has run into comparable problems when it datafied decision making in its social service programs. When the Social Security Administration started using LexisNexis's Accurint to determine whether people getting government assistance had unreported assets that could disqualify them, bad data falsely listed people as owning real property. Across the nation, extremely low-income elderly people and people with disabilities had their benefits suspended on the basis of the erroneous information Accurint provided.[99]

Private lenders, landlords, banks, and employers also use data analytics products. These decision makers hope that data analytics products will make their work more efficient, but they ultimately embed errors into their decision-making processes. A bank using LexisNexis data locked a customer out of her bank account when Lexis mixed up her data with a sibling's data.[100] A Michigan man was denied a job after his LexisNexis-data-powered background check matched him with a criminal record belonging to a different man with the same name.[101] In Texas, tenant screening services using LexisNexis Risk Solutions data ended up making erroneous housing "blacklists" because data mistakenly marked people as having been evicted. Tenants had little recourse to clear their rental histories, leaving them unable to secure housing.[102]

Data companies' products don't just contain data they're not supposed to contain, they're also used in ways they aren't supposed to be used. Improper use and mission creep are especially likely when it comes to personal data collections. In 1976, U.S. senators warned that a glut of government information "creates a temptation to use it for improper purposes."[103] This warning has proven true in cities like San Diego, where data from smart streetlight cameras installed to solve violent attacks is instead used to arrest people for minor crimes such as illegal dumping and vandalism.[104] It has also proven true in New York City, where video recorded by digital kiosks was purposely kept separate from the NYPD's camera system until someone started smashing the kiosks.[105] Then, civil liberties concerns fell by the wayside and the kiosk footage was sent to police for use in law enforcement.[106]

Our current data privacy laws don't prevent police and other people from using data products beyond the purposes of their contract. We put safeguards on other tools used by law enforcement and government agencies. While we give police high-powered tools to do their jobs, such as guns and warrants to search peoples' homes, we also give strict rules limiting when the tools can be used. When police are in the field, they wear cameras so we can review the film and hold them accountable. There are repercussions when police misuse their weapons, including disciplinary action, dismissal, and lawsuits.[107] There are no similar consequences when police abuse their data broker subscriptions, and in most cases, nobody monitors or audits how data companies' products are used once they're purchased.[108] Police must show probable cause before a judge will give them a warrant, but they can search our data whenever they want with the data companies' products.[109] And they do. The FBI's National Crime and Information Center database gets used around fourteen million times every day.[110] Even in the 1990s, agencies such as the U.S. Marshals ran around twenty thousand data broker dossier searches a month. And we don't know how employees are using these products.

Nobody monitors how data brokers' products are used to ensure they're being used for their assigned purpose. When the FBI subscribed to ChoicePoint in the 1990s, the agency's general counsel encouraged employees to "use ChoicePoint to your heart's content."[111] Without safeguards, people with access to data analytics products *will* use them to their heart's content, far beyond their intended function. When LexisNexis provided limited Accurint to law schools, my law students called the product their personal stalking service, and they used it to spy on exes and high school enemies. Without oversight, it's no surprise that today police are also using their departments' data analytics services to stalk exes and satisfy voyeuristic curiosity.[112] In 2013, the Minnesota Police Department discovered that over half of its eleven-thousand-person police force made "questionable" searches on their databases.

Regulators and legislators have pushed for more oversight on data brokers, but their efforts have not succeeded. In 2014, the FTC urged Congress to pursue privacy legislation to curb data brokers' collection tactics,[113] but when Senators John Rockefeller IV and Ed Markey introduced the Data Broker Accountability and Transparency Act, it didn't go anywhere.[114]

In fact, Congress hasn't passed much data legislation lately. The federal government has essentially stalled out on comprehensive data privacy plans. Even as other countries move forward and pass laws and regulations limiting data brokering and making data programs more transparent, we haven't followed suit.[115] Other countries make data companies conduct privacy audits, allow people to erase and amend their personal data dossiers, and bake privacy measures into data-processing technology. But in the United States, we haven't done anything to reign in data brokers.

Our existing data laws are outdated and piecemeal. We have a patchwork of data privacy provisions sprinkled across different statutes. The Family Educational Rights and Privacy Act of 1974 (FERPA) protects students' educational records; the Health Insurance Portability and Accountability Act of 1996 (HIPAA) protects electronic medical records; and the Children's Online Privacy Protection Act of 1998 (COPPA) protects children's data online. A constellation of laws protect our financial information, including the 1978 Right to Financial Privacy Act (RFPA), the Gramm-Leach-Bliley Act of 1999, and the Fair Credit Reporting Act of 1970 (FCRA).[116] The Freedom of Information Act (FOIA) blocks the release of personal information from government files.[117] In some situations, data brokers actually help skirt these laws. For instance, the companies' data products bypass FCRA requirements, even though their products are used just like credit reports. FCRA is supposed to ensure that the records that lenders, employers, housing providers, and government agencies use to make decisions are accurate and fair. The law gives consumers the right to access their credit reports and limits the sale of reports to a list of "permissible purposes." FCRA also requires companies to correct inaccurate information. But LexisNexis and Thomson Reuters put disclaimers on their products saying they aren't consumer reports, even though companies use their reports the same way they use credit reports from Equifax, Experian, and TransUnion—the big three credit bureaus that are subject to FCRA.[118]

A few other federal laws are supposed to prevent the government from collecting and using our data without getting a warrant first. The Privacy Act of 1974 requires agencies to notify the public when they plan to create new systems of records, and it gives the public rights to access and correct those records.[119] But the Privacy Act was written before data brokers existed, so it assumes that the government is making and maintaining its own records systems, not that it's streaming third-party data collections. The law doesn't apply when data brokers create their own datasets, even if those datasets will eventually be used by the government. For instance, if the U.S. Marshals Service (USMS) creates its own database containing fugitive's data, it must follow the Privacy Act's requirements.[120] But if the USMS uses a data broker instead, the Privacy Act doesn't apply.[121]

Another law, the Electronic Communications Privacy Act (ECPA), prevents the government from getting computer transmissions and other electronic communications without a warrant.[122] But ECPA doesn't cover data brokers' dossiers. It was passed in 1986 to update the federal Wiretap Act of 1968, so it's based on wiretapping logic—it focuses on situations in which the government is spying on conversations, not on neutral information repositories. Like the Privacy Act, ECPA predates cloud computing and other nonconsensual data storage. Its scope is limited to communications stored on a third-party server for fewer than a hundred-and-eighty days. ECPA doesn't account for the ways data brokers collect and supply data, so data brokers provide warrantless-search-accommodating loopholes to the law. While it prohibits the government from getting your text messages from Verizon without a warrant, if Verizon sells your data to Thomson Reuters, ECPA's warrant requirements don't apply. Companies subject to ECPA's warrant requirements can simply sell their data to data brokers who roll that data into their dossier products and sell them to the government.[123]

Without up-to-date federal laws, states and localities are dealing with data brokers on their own. States including California, Vermont, and Illinois have passed laws that create data broker registries and force data companies to give people access to their dossiers.[124] On the other end of the spectrum, some states, such as Florida, sell and share people's data—marriage records, beverage licenses, concealed weapons permits, worker compensation data, and more.[125] Inconsistent legislation means that people's protection from data brokers varies according to where they live. Californians have more control over their data dossiers than Floridians do.

People have also looked to the Fourth Amendment, trying to find legal grounds for reining in data brokers. Not surprisingly, the U.S. Constitution doesn't talk about data brokers. In fact, it doesn't directly address privacy at all. Around the time that Kodak introduced its first box camera, opening the gates for amateur photographers to snap candid pictures of people, legal scholars Louis Brandeis and Samuel Warren tried to fashion a privacy law. In their law review article (the most famous law review article of all time!), the lawyers described a "right to be let alone" and suggested a common law cause of action against public disclosures of private facts.[126] Their conception of privacy law was provocative, but hard to implement in practice.[127]

The Supreme Court is still struggling to articulate workable legal privacy norms without positive law prescriptions.[128] The Court has extrapolated privacy protections from the First Amendment's freedom of association; the Fourth Amendment's prohibition against unwarranted searches and seizures; the Third Amendment's prohibition against quartering soldiers in people's homes without consent; and the Fifth Amendment's protection against self-incrimination.[129] As we've seen, the Fourth Amendment seems especially applicable to data analytics companies that supply information to the government. When the government uses data analytics products that sort through millions' of peoples' personal data without a warrant, it could be considered a violation of the Fourth Amendment. But, in addition to the third-party exception, there is another loophole that helps the government skirt constitutional provisions when they use data brokers: the state action requirement.

Hoping to prevent excessive government intervention in our private lives, the Supreme Court limited constitutional requirements to "state actors," but there's no clear rule for who is, and who isn't, a state actor.[130] In cases when people and companies work closely with the government, it's hard to draw the line between who is a state actor subject to Fourth Amendment requirements and who is a private actor whose products can be used without a warrant.

Courts have used various tests to try to differentiate between state and private actors, with relational names like the entwinement test,[131] the sufficient nexus test,[132] and the symbiotic relationship test.[133] All of these tests have been used to decide whether overlapping relationships confer constitutional requirements on companies working with the government, and, like relationships themselves, all of them are mushy and variable. In 2014, a law student wrote an entire article mulling over whether Batman is a state actor when he helps police fight crimes.[134] It's just as complicated to figure out whether a data company is a state actor when it helps police fight crimes. So far, the Supreme Court has declined to say one way or another. But the Court has refused to call other companies that run online services state actors even when they perform government roles, such as running financial markets and serving as people's primary information conduits and forums.[135] Twitter wasn't even given state actor status when the president himself used it as his main megaphone, so it's unlikely that data analytics companies would get state actor treatment.[136]

Some legislators have tried to close the constitutional law loopholes for data brokers, but so far they haven't succeeded. Ron Wyden, an Oregon senator especially concerned with data surveillance, has tried to pass laws with names like The Fourth Amendment Is Not For Sale Act that would restrict the government's use of data brokers, but none of the proposed legislation has been adopted.[137]

Even as Senator Wyden tries to pass bills to make data brokers more accountable to consumers, data analytics companies are using other parts of the Constitution to limit their own accountability. In some situations, they're invoking the First Amendment to escape liability when they share incorrect information or use our data in harmful ways, asserting that our data dossiers are their constitutionally protected speech. When states sued Standard & Poor's for sharing the bad data that spurred the 2008 financial meltdown, the company's legal counsel compared Standard & Poor's' data to newspaper op-eds, arguing that the company's data deserves the same constitutional protections as people's opinions.[138] Lawyers have also invoked the First Amendment to convince courts that forcing platforms like Google, Yahoo!, and YouTube to take down personal online content would violate the companies' free speech.[139] Claiming free speech protections for data collections has been called "the most convenient defense" for data companies trying to sidestep privacy regulations or tangled in litigation because their bad information has harmed people.[140]

As an antidote to data companies' claiming information about us as their speech, some legislators have suggested that we pass laws designating our personal data as our personal property. They figure that, if we own our intellectual property, perhaps we should have the same rights to our data output. Although imbuing our data exhaust with personal property rights may sound like a simple fix in theory, assigning personal property rights to our data would raise a slew of practical problems. There are good reasons that judges don't confer property rights to the information collected in phone books, databases, or our DNA.[141] Granting people property rights over the products of our human intellect—poems, plans, and ideas—is different from giving people the right to own plain facts.

Propertizing personal facts would make reporting them much more time-consuming and less efficient.[142] Reporting and receiving news and other nonfiction would involve a volley of permissions and purchasing. Imagine having to pay Viola Davis each time you use her name in a movie review or having to get permission to reprint Michael Phelps' arm measurements in a book about Olympic swimmers. When the 9th Circuit Court of Appeals considered whether people's personal video performances in films were their copyrighted materials, it opined that treating each person's video performance as their property would "be a logistical and financial nightmare," turning a "cast of thousands into a . . . copyright of thousands."[143]

Restricting personal data flows would also stifle productive data projects. Data can be used for social good: we can trace pandemics, smooth out traffic, and plan better cities with open data collections. Big-data collections are uniquely able to quickly identify correlations and patterns, allowing us to do fast analyses that are otherwise impossible, like matching illnesses to genetic traits or predicting health outcomes on the basis of geography.[144]

Propertizing personal data would also make our lives less convenient. Our weather apps and traffic maps rely on our personal data to tell us how to get places and whether to take an umbrella when we go. If you owned your data, companies would have to bargain with you for your information, interrupting the smooth flow of personal information that greases the wheels of our online platforms.

Making our data into personal property could also perpetuate inequality. Poorer people may be pushed to sell their data even when it's not in their best interest. Data could become the new plasma—a billion-dollar industry that "depends on the blood of the very poor."[145] Just as plasma centers underpay people, giving them $30 for $300 worth of plasma, an exploitative data industry could induce cash-strapped people to sell their data for less than it's worth. Despite the practical issues, data ownership is a popular idea—according to one survey, 79 percent of consumers believe they should be compensated when their data is shared.[146] Members of Congress sponsor legislation like the Own Your Own Data Act, promising to give people exclusive rights to their online information.[147]

If the government doesn't intervene to regulate data brokers and personal data analytics' risk products, these companies will keep building more and more data analytics inventions for a data-hungry risk sector. Data analytics is a fast-growing industry, and companies like RELX and

Thomson Reuters are ready to rake in profits in the data marketplace. Back in 2004, Chris Hoofnagle foreshadowed a datafied future powered by companies like ChoicePoint. He warned, "If we are ever unfortunate enough to have George Orwell's Big Brother in the United States, it will be made possible by the private sector."[148]

Data brokering is a sprawling business, but it's just one slice of the data analytics companies' products. In their data brokering business, companies like RELX and Thomson Reuters mine and use our personal data without consent, but in other sectors, like academic and legal information, the companies hoard information and wall it off, restricting public access. This leads to a range of different consequences and inequities that will be explored in the next few chapters.

3

ACADEMIC RESEARCH

ACADEMIC RESEARCHERS SOLVE some of the world's toughest problems. When a social or scientific dilemma looms large, we gather experts and dispatch them to address it. We collectively fund the experts with government grants, giving them the financial support they need to do the work, whether it's curing cancer or curbing climate change.[1] Academic researchers take on humanity's biggest economic, political, and social questions for the greater good. When researchers solve the world's mysteries, they publish their findings in academic journals.

As taxpayers, we fund researchers so their expertise can improve our lives.[2] Research drives technical innovation, contributes to economic growth, and improves our health and environment.[3] Access to scientific information is so important for humanity that the United Nations calls it a human right.[4] Academic research plays such an integral part in protecting us from diseases and disasters, and helping us invent new technologies, that it seems like something people should be able to access if they need it. But, like most digital informational content, a few companies turn academic research into their products to sell. A small oligopoly of publishers own most of our academic journals, even though we paid for much of the work printed on the journals' pages.[5]

RELX's Elsevier dominates the cadre of companies that control the academic research market. Elsevier used to be an academic publisher, but today the company calls itself an "information analytics business."[6] The company has shifted its focus from providing access to journals to providing data analytics products ("academic metrics"). Elsevier is reducing publicly funded science into fodder for RELX's data analytics software. Instead of focusing on selling critical scientific information at an affordable price, the company is concentrating on developing software that sifts through the company's "vast corpus" of academic data to draw "insights" from—and monetize—the entire research process.[7]

Elsevier treats academic research not like a publicly funded resource, but like its own private portfolio of copyright assets. Even though it doesn't curate, author, or edit any of the research, Elsevier profits off of every step of the research process. Elsevier sells both raw academic content *and* data analyses about the people and institutions that create and use that content.

Companies like Thomson Reuters and RELX can dominate informational markets because they have huge collections of raw materials that have been gathered over centuries. In information markets, the companies with the biggest information troves win. Scrappy upstarts can't reproduce the deep wells of information that these other companies have collected. This is especially true for Elsevier in the academic information market. Elsevier has been publishing scientific research for over five hundred years. During the Renaissance, Elsevier's namesake, Louis Elzevier, published foundational scholarly works by Desiderius Erasmus and Galileo.[8] When academia became a "publish or perish" profession in which people who want professorial jobs churn out dozens of articles and monographs, Elsevier was best positioned to publish those works.

Elsevier was also the first major academic publisher to occupy the digital research marketplace. In 1971, Elsevier acquired the only company that was using a database to produce scholarly journals, becoming the first to digitize its collection. When the internet became a new venue for sharing knowledge, Elsevier was the first company to provide copyrighted journal materials online. These early entries into digital academic publishing set Elsevier up to be a leading academic content provider. Now Elsevier is part of RELX, and it publishes more than five hundred thousand scholarly articles annually in twenty-five hundred journals. Its extensive scholarly archives contain over seventeen million documents and forty thousand ebooks.[9]

Elsevier's gigantic stockpile of academic content didn't just make it an unbeatable academic research provider, it also primed the company to become a leading academic data analytics firm.[10] The companies' millions of academic research materials are ideal data vectors—data analytics companies can put their research databases online and collect tons of personal data about both the people who write the materials and the people who access them.

Elsevier and Thomson Reuters both jumped on the data analytics bandwagon in the early 2000s, just as the world was figuring out ways to collect and use people's digital data. The companies launched competing "academic metrics" products called Scopus and Thomson Science (now known as Clarivate).[11] The companies don't call Scopus and Clarivate data analytics products. They are referred to instead as an "abstract and citation database" and an "index of journal articles"; however, both products collect and sell author and user data, not access to academic research. The companies harvest data from their abstracts and indexes and make the data into products that could predict which researchers, and which research projects, will be the most lucrative investments for funders. Academic metrics don't help researchers do their work, they help grant funders divvy out money and institutions decide which hires will make them appear the most prestigious according to the predictions generated by the slurry of academic data run through RELX and Clarivate analytics systems.[12]

Even though Elsevier is the largest publisher of academic research, it's not obligated to focus on publishing the best science for the public good. So it doesn't. Instead, Elsevier focuses on crunching academic researchers' data in new ways to make money off the research process. It slices and dices its academic databases to make article-level "impact" metrics,[13] journal-level metrics that rank journals' prestige and predict citation trends,[14] and author metrics that assess the people who do the research.[15] This barrage of analytics turns universities and grant funders into rich data sources for the analytics companies, and it also turns them into academic bean counters that depend on metrics to make choices about who to fund and support.

Clarivate and Elsevier's data analytics products don't just analyze the impact of academic research articles and their authors, they also analyze data collected before and after journals are published. The companies have expanded their analytics to encompass both the prepublication research cycle and the postpublication research evaluation process.[16] They have figured out how to extract profits from every part of the research process. Their analytics products monetize the entire "knowledge production cycle."[17] Elsevier has acquired and extracted data from platforms where researchers share their preprint drafts, such as BePress, Mendeley, and SSRN.[18] Elsevier also sells analytics products that evaluate research impact, connect researchers for networking and job hunting, and facilitate research collaboration after papers are published.

Even though Elsevier rakes in profits from data analytics, it doesn't use that financial fortune to discount its journal collection or make it more accessible to the public. Instead of easing access to academic information, Elsevier shuts off its informational assets to anyone who can't pay the company's high prices. Online access was supposed to erase barriers to knowledge by routing the "information highway" through our home computers, phones, and watches. Online information access could revolutionize access to knowledge by sending academic research to anyone who needs it, anywhere in the world. But when you're a for-profit analytics company that sees academic content as a stockpile of raw materials instead of as individual human insights, you'll try to squeeze as much profit as possible from your digital collections. Instead of making information access better, Elsevier sets up artificial barriers to entry around its materials, fencing them behind digital "walled gardens."

Elsevier should be paid market value for its services, but it shouldn't be allowed to wall off critical public knowledge by charging exorbitant access fees. Yet Elsevier's prices are so high that many institutions cannot afford to access scientific research. Seventy-five percent of academic research is paywalled, and it usually costs around $30 to look at a single journal article. The paywalls and high prices make it so that many people can't access crucially important information when they need it. Doctors battling malaria outbreaks in Africa can't read reports about life-saving medications and measures. They can't afford to read past the articles' abstracts.[19] Researchers are limited to using whatever materials they can access.[20]

Prohibitively expensive academic research prices can hamper public health and innovation. A researcher asked scientists all over the world to try to access state-of-the-art research on eye diseases and found that almost half of the world's researchers could only access around half of the articles.[21] While the U.S. institutions could access most of the paywalled articles, researchers in Ecuador and Pakistan couldn't access any paywalled articles at their institutions. The access disparities stratify wealthy countries' libraries from developing companies' libraries, deepening the chasm of inequality. In 2008, Harvard researchers could peruse almost 99,000 academic journals but the best-funded research library in India subscribed to 10,600. Some sub-Saharan African university libraries subscribed to no journals at all.[22] A 2019 piece in the *Guardian* said it succinctly: "paywalls block scientific progress."[23]

Even as some research institutions struggle to get academic research, Elsevier is raking in some of the highest profit margins of any industry in the world.[24] It costs around $600 to publish a scholarly article, but with the prices Elsevier charges, each article makes the company thousands of dollars.[25] Elsevier's profit margin for streaming academic journals is around 19 percent, which is more than double Netflix's profit margin for streaming movies and TV shows.[26] The entire academic research industry's profit margins hover around 30 percent, compared to Walmart's 3 percent profit margins and Toyota's 12 percent profit margin.[27]

Profit margins this high don't happen without exploitation. Elsevier's high-priced fees for publicly funded research are digital versions of classic, exploitative rent-seeking behaviors. Rent seeking happens when companies manipulate existing public resources to extract wealth instead of creating new innovations and products to build wealth. Monopolists like Elsevier can seek rents on already-existing resources because consumers lack alternatives. In one classic example of rent seeking, a feudal lord hangs a rope across a river on his land and hires a toll collector to charge passing boats to lower the rope so they can cross. The lord hasn't improved his land or added any value to it, he's just found a way to make money from something that used to be free. In the digital world, Elsevier can rope off its academic materials and take tolls because people who need the materials have no choice but to pay whatever Elsevier demands.

Publishers profiting from information flows isn't new. It's also not problematic—publishers, like other merchants, deserve to be paid for the goods and services they provide. But historically, we were better able to manage our relationships with publishers. When the companies sold paper journals, publishers' power ended at the point of purchase. Once people bought a journal or book, their own property rights took over. The publisher's copyright still had weight, but not quite as much. Purchasers couldn't make their own copies of the item to sell, but they could share, sell, and give away the copy they'd bought. Even if a publisher like Elsevier preferred if purchasers didn't share their journal with classmates or lab partners, it didn't have much control over what happened to the publication once a purchaser had the paper copy in their hands. But on Elsevier's digital platforms the company never cedes that power to its customers. For one, nobody actually buys any journals or books from Elsevier's digital platforms. Elsevier doesn't run its digital academic information services like a bookstore. Rather, its content platforms are run the way Netflix runs its video streaming company. Instead of selling journals outright, Elsevier invites customers to subscribe to their content services. Customers can stream Elsevier's journals, but they can't buy full ownership of them.

You also never get a physical copy of the material you stream. When academic journal publishing made the transition from paper copies to digital copies on disks and CD-roms, customers could still borrow, share, and reuse the materials they purchased. But when the publishers moved towards "cloud-based" software-as-a-service (SaaS), the publishers replaced physical ownership with platforms on which their materials stay, for the most part, in the companies' servers. The difference between owning and renting information may feel minor in the moment when you've got an article on your computer screen, but it has major implications for access. Buying confers more rights to purchasers than renting. By maintaining full control of the content they sell, the companies can make books and articles come and go from libraries' virtual shelves, "vaporizing" titles whenever they choose.[28] The companies can also embargo new articles and books, even after libraries pay for them, so that subscribers either have to pay extra fees or wait, sometimes over a year, to access the resources.[29] Purchasers have far less control over the materials they pay for. They don't get full ownership, they merely lease streams of information that they may not even be able to download.[30]

Elsevier's digital barricades are felt most in libraries. Libraries have, historically, been the gatekeepers of academic knowledge, and the only institutions with deep enough pockets to afford shelves full of academic journals and books. Like research itself, many libraries are publicly funded to ensure that everyone has access to information. Libraries were always a place where no matter how much money you had, you could stop in and grab a book or journal and copy its pages or take it home with you. While we may still envision academic research on shelves in regal stone libraries on a college campus, the reality is that while research libraries' dapper exteriors are still the same, inside, the materials they provide are, more and more, digital instead of paper. There are a few exceptions, such as Linda Hall Library in Kansas City, Missouri. That library, a brick building smack dab in the middle of the nation, is one of the only free, publicly accessible places to access hard copies of science research articles. But if you don't live nearby, it's a tough place to visit.

You'd think that with all of the technological tools at our disposal, we'd be able to replicate research centers like the Linda Hall library online, making an array of scholarly resources available to the public in digital form, but Elsevier and the rest of the academic research oligopoly hold tight to their copyright assets. They don't seem eager to replace the role of the research library with digital borrowing arrangements such as controlled digital lending. Publishers prevent digital lending with prohibitive licensing agreement terms and lack of funding and infrastructure for digital lending projects.[31] They even sue online lending repositories like the Internet Archive[32] and people who try to "free knowledge" by sharing articles online.

People have suffered severe consequences for infringing on Elsevier's copyrights. In one case, Aaron Swartz, an MIT student, was charged with a list of felonies for downloading content from the paywalled digital library JSTOR.[33] Even though Swartz didn't hurt anyone physically, or even financially (he returned the downloaded materials without incident), prosecutors threatened Swartz with $1 million dollars in fines and up to thirty-five years in prison.[34] In another case, Elsevier sued Alexandra Elbakyan, the researcher who built the paywall-circumventing website Sci-

Hub.[35] A New York court awarded Elsevier $15 million in damages in the case.[36] Copyright infringement violates the law, but prison sentences and multimillion-dollar fines are disproportionate penalties for student activists trying to improve access to science.

Without digital libraries that lend access to the academic research oligopoly's content, the only way to access academic materials without worrying about legal retribution by the likes of Elsevier is by accessing the content through the oligopoly's approved digital ecosystems. When we use those systems, our activities are tracked and policed in ways that were impossible offline. When we do research online, every click, mouse move, and search we enter can be recorded and traced. This digital tracking benefits the data companies in two ways: they can closely guard their copyright assets by policing the traffic and downloads on their platforms, and they can also fold the personal data they collect from tracking subjects into their academic metrics data analysis.

The tracking on these platforms means that there's no place online where we can privately peruse a digital collection. There are also strict limits on what we can do with digital collections. If you pay to access an article on Elsevier's ScienceDirect research platform, you'll be able to view the article on a screen, but you probably can't share copies of the articles with friends or look at them on a different device. In some cases, you may not be able to download them or print physical copies. In addition, when you use ScienceDirect, you'll also be tracked by ThreatMetrix, one of RELX's surveillance products.[37]

Since they are the only sources for the majority of the world's published academic research, the research oligopoly can insert restrictive contract provisions into contracts. Even if their contract clauses are terrible, libraries, especially, have little choice but to sign them if they want access to academic journals. Elsevier's library contracts contain anticompetitive provisions, such as product bundling and nondisclosure agreements. Without alternative sources for the journals their patrons need, libraries are forced into more expensive deals that give them less control over what they're licensing.[38]

Instead of letting libraries buy journals à la carte, the companies force them to buy thousands of journals bundled together, all at once. Librarians have named these multimillion-dollar, multiyear contracts "big deals." These bundling contracts are like all-you-can-eat buffets of content.[39] Having more journals may seem better, but, as your librarian—or anyone with messy bookshelves—knows, cluttered collections aren't ideal.[40] Sifting through tons of material can muddle the research process. This is especially true when many of the items in the collection aren't useful, which is usually the case. When the University of Virginia tracked the use of one of its big deal bundles, Springer Nature, it found that of the four thousand journals in the deal, almost a third of the journals were never accessed. The library's information policy director compared the bundle to a cable TV package: "[T]hey tell you you're getting 250 channels, but if you look inside your heart, you know all you want is ESPN and AMC."[41]

The contracts also last for years. They can't be cut short or reduced, so libraries have to keep paying them even if their budgets change from year to year.[42] Most libraries have limited budgets, and they're not impervious to economic changes caused by external factors such as recessions and pandemics. The big deals assume that libraries' budgets continually increase, but in reality, libraries' fortunes fluctuate. When hardship hits, big deal obligations leave libraries cutting corners and scrimping on other materials because the oligopoly's contracts eat up the lions' share of library budgets.[43] In some cases, libraries have to cancel journals published by smaller companies to afford the big deals.[44]

Bundling contracts like the ones academic research companies use raises antitrust concerns. Bundling deals aren't inherently bad. Sometimes it's more efficient and cost-effective to group things together, like selling shoes with laces already wound through their eyelets or selling a ten-pack of train tickets to regular commuters. But other times, bundling harms consumers by forcing them to blow their budgets on things they don't want. For example, the Supreme Court said movie distributors run afoul of antitrust law when they force television stations to buy packages that include films they don't want.[45] Antitrust experts have argued that the research companies' big deals are similar to that type of movie bundling.[46] In 2018, scholars asked the EU's Competition Authority to investigate Elsevier's bundling practices,[47] but this kind of argument has yet to be heard by a U.S. court. Without intervention, Elsevier and the rest of the academic research oligopoly will probably keep using anticompetitive contract deals to ratchet up prices and restrict libraries' abilities to choose what they're buying.[48]

Nondisclosure agreements and confidentiality clauses are other contract tools the academic research companies use to leverage contract negotiations with libraries in their favor—if librarians can't talk about their contracts, they can't assess what reasonable prices and provisions look like.[49] When consumers buy things, they can usually compare their deals with the deals other people are getting to negotiate the best terms with sellers. For example, people can talk to their neighbors about what prices they're paying for cable TV, or see commercials that describe their package deals. Academic research contracts don't come with the same transparency. Instead, the research companies make unique deals with each institution on the basis of the institutions' wealth and negotiating skills. The companies base their prices on what institutions have been willing to pay in the past, and what their budgets can afford.[50]

When libraries are forced to keep their contracts secret, the academic research companies don't need to pick egalitarian price-points, they can negotiate with every institution without any consistent fee standards. Nondisclosure agreements make it easy for the companies to charge different amounts to different institutions depending on how much the libraries can pay instead of on the market price or value of the materials they're selling. During a debate about access to research, RELX's Deputy Director of Universal Sustainable Research Access David Tempest tipped Elsevier's hand when he offered his rationale for the company's confidentiality clauses, saying that without the provisions, "everybody would drive down, drive down, drive drive drive [down competition], and that would mean that—" At this point, his speech was drowned in the audience's laughter over his accidental admission.[51]

Without an established market price for academic research materials, the contract-to-contract pricing is uneven and unpredictable. For example, in 2009, the University of Georgia paid $1.9 million for Elsevier's "Freedom Collection," but the University of Texas spent $1.5 million for the same product, even though it has a much larger enrollment and almost twice as many PhDs. Similarly, Dartmouth pays $30,000 more than the

University of Virginia for the collection, even though the University of Virginia has four times the number of students as Dartmouth. Brigham Young pays almost $80,000 more for its Sage subscription than the much larger University of Arizona.[52]

Librarians have fought against the nondisclosure agreements. They've anonymously shared contracts online. They've drafted model contracts to use instead of the data companies' contracts and worked to standardize contracts across institutions.[53] They've filed freedom of information act requests to see and compare the secret contracts, working around the nondisclosure promises. Some institutions flat out refuse to enter the nondisclosure agreements.[54] But at the end of the day, most librarians honor the silencing contract clauses to avoid conflict with the companies they rely so heavily upon.

The academic research oligopoly doesn't just strong-arm libraries with contract provisions, they also strong-arm the authors who write the books and journals the companies sell. In a system in which scholars must "publish or perish," academics spend hundreds of hours a year getting their work published in the oligopoly's journals so they can keep their jobs. With all of the pressure from academic hiring committees to publish, companies like Elsevier don't have to pay the authors and editors of their journals a dime—the scholars write, curate, and peer review their journals for free. The exploitation of academics' work also exploits the public, because we fund both the public institutions that hire these academics and the grants that support their work. If we paid to build a road and the construction company the city contracted with didn't pay its engineers and charged us huge tolls to access our road, we'd call it corruption.[55] But when our taxpayer-funded research is similarly exploited, we don't say a word. In academic research, we pay billions for work, and the workers pay too. Then, we all get charged for the end product.

After they hand over their work to the publishing oligopoly, academic researchers sign publication contracts that strip them of their rights to access, use, and share their own work. They give companies like Elsevier the sole right to publish their peer-reviewed research.[56] They allow the companies to embargo their papers, refusing to release their articles to most institutions before a particular date, even though it's ready to share with the public. It's not unusual for researchers, and their home institutions, to hit paywalls for their own work. Our free market system is designed to give people the freedom to contract away almost anything, even the rights to their own intellectual property. Even Taylor Swift can lose the rights to music she "wrote on her bedroom floor."[57] But unlike Taylor Swift, researchers can't remaster their scientific studies and scholarly research. Many studies would be prohibitively expensive and time-consuming to recreate. The oligopoly forces researchers to trade their once-in-a-lifetime intellectual labor for the hope that an institution will see it published and decide to hire them or give them tenure.

The agreements that Elsevier signs with its authors, editors, and peer reviewers save the company billions of dollars. One study estimates that in 2019, volunteer peer reviewers alone provided over a hundred million hours of free labor to academic journals.[58] Researchers and editors don't just work for free, their articles even provide free advertising for other articles in the companies' collections. Every academic study is studded with citations that lead readers to click on other journal articles. Literature reviews that summarize and cite past research are a must-have in most articles fit to publish.

This free labor and advertising helps the academic research industry turn huge profits. In *Paywall: The Business of Scholarship*, a documentary about the academic research market, the filmmakers demonstrated the potential profit of just a few Elsevier articles by multiplying the article's price by the number of times the articles had been cited. (The filmmakers assumed the authors citing the article paid the price to access it.) The results were astonishing.[59] In 1967, Marion Bradford published a method for checking how much protein is in a biological sample in the Elsevier journal *Analytical Biochemistry*. Elsevier charges $35.95 to access Bradford's article, and it's been cited 198,253 times. The movie producers estimate that, so far, the one article alone has paid millions of dollars of dividends to the company. (Of course, Bradford made no money from the publication of his multimillion-dollar paper.) Michael Eisen, a microbiologist at the University of California, Berkeley, called the scholarly publishing scheme a travesty, and said that charging scholars billions of dollars a year to read their own community's research is "a ridiculous transaction."[60]

Ridiculous or not, so long as academia depends on journal prestige to make hiring and tenure decisions, academics will continue to publish in Springer, Elsevier, Wiley, Sage, and Taylor & Francis's most prestigious journals despite the companies' exploitative contract requirements.[61] Most scholars see signing away their copyrights to the oligopolies' journals as a requirement for getting a job in academia. The academic information industry is part of a self-sustaining market built on unfair contracts and free labor.

If it only costs Elsevier $600 to publish an article and Elsevier makes $4,000 from selling it, what happens to the other $3,400?[62] Even accounting for a 30 percent profit margin, thousands of dollars get sucked back into Elsevier's piggybank. There's no evidence that the company shares its windfall with the authors or editors who make the journals, or that it's used to enrich the scholarly community. Instead, those dollars are likely spent in R&D, developing all sorts of data analytics products for academia and beyond.[63] Elsevier's transition from publisher to data analytics company means it's focused not on benefitting scholars but on generating more data assets to sell. In academic publishing, Elsevier's tail wags the dog—whatever Elsevier does, the other academic research companies will also do if they want to compete. So all of the academic research companies are more focused on collecting user data than ever.

The oligopoly companies are acting in concert on data-collecting schemes. They're doing things like forcing users to turn on their data-tracking cookies on their research platforms, blocking people's access to journal articles if they block their cookies.[64] They're also working together, with Elsevier, to develop devices like the "Get Full Text Research" function. The function's sales pitch is that it lets people know where they can access scholarly articles they find online. But Get Full Text Research is really a tool that lets the companies track their customers beyond their research platforms. Get Full Text Research doesn't reside in a particular platform, it sits in the digital infrastructure of any service that allows it, running in the background of all of your online activities.[65] Scholarly communication expert Samuel Moore calls the service a guise to get more data from researchers. He writes that "in return for the convenience of continuous authentication, publishers are able to collect data on users in order to further monetise their behavior. . . ." Moore calls Get Full Text Research part of a larger ontological shift among the oligopoly away from publishing academic research to extracting data from individual researchers.

The German Research Foundation warns that the oligopoly's shift to data tracking in research endangers science. The companies are turning the acquisition of knowledge into a surveillance program. Academia is being turned into a data industry.[66] It's a natural progression for companies like Elsevier that share the same corporate umbrellas as data brokers.

Being both the main suppliers of research *and* the main suppliers of data analytics about research gives Elsevier outsized power to shape science. The research oligopoly controls both the input (funding) and the output (research findings) of the knowledge enterprise. Together, these few companies are merging to form a "supercontinent" that supplies both scholarly discoveries and the academic surveillance data upon which all of academia depends.[67] Putting this much power into the hands of a few private, for-profit businesses creates ethical dilemmas. Privatizing academic knowledge and combining it with predictive data analytics is not ideal for the public interest. A company like Elsevier can control the academic enterprise by using its analytics to decide what gets published. Elsevier's decisions could be based on public interest concerns and geared towards meeting public needs, but it's more likely that a company with shareholders to please will make funding and publishing decisions based on its financial interests.[68]

In the current system, we are putting Elsevier and similarly situated data and content providers in charge of determining how the world solves its toughest problems, from cancer to climate change. Data companies, not experts, make decisions about science, supporting some research projects and stifling others.

The oligopoly's control over research institutions is also problematic because it digitizes historical academic elitism and supremacy. Like all machine-learning software, machine-generated journal impact metrics and researcher ranking systems incorporate the same biases, white supremacy, and systemic racism that permeate academia, favoring the work made by white men at elite institutions.[69] Academic data analytics don't repair the racist and misogynistic decisions made in university tenure committees and college boards, they datafy them. Publications from ivy league schools that have historically shut out Black scholars, female scholars, and other marginalized groups have more clicks and citations than publications from historically Black colleges and universities or colleges serving more diverse student bodies. Harvard publications have higher impact and prestige scores than publications from my public, city-serving institution, the City University of New York. The impact factor problem is self-perpetuating—scholars feel obligated to publish in high-impact journals because hiring and tenure committees view those publications more positively. For example, publishing in the *Harvard Law Review* is more likely to earn you a spot on a law faculty than a publication in *The Journal of Gender, Race, and Justice.*

Infusing academic impact scores into predictive and prescriptive data analytics products doesn't just lift certain journals, it also tilts academic funding in favor of for-profit work being done at elite institutions. If grant funders are using academic metrics from services like Clarivate or Elsevier's Scopus to decide which research proposals to fund, the companies' algorithms will likely put projects at the fanciest labs on the most well-funded campuses with the most well-cited researchers at the top of their lists. Those projects are often led by senior, white, male scholars from wealthy institutions. The algorithms will likely also favor the types of tech and pharmaceutical research likely to make money instead of research that isn't so lucrative. Meanwhile, research done to repair market failures such as environmental degradation or international wealth disparities, and long-term research projects that are less "productive" despite their importance, aren't likely to be prioritized in a system in which profit- and prestige-focused metrics have a lot of weight in funders' decision-making processes.

Academic metrics can also be gamed by researchers and their institutions. As with any other click-based statistics, people can artificially inflate clicks to up impact scores. Institutions have been known to click on their scholars' preprints on SSRN and BePress to make it look like people are reading their faculty members' work. Wealthy institutions that can afford to hire public relations staff have the resources to advertise work and garner clicks in ways that underfunded institutions cannot. Journals can also inflate their own numbers. In 2019, over fifty journals were caught engaging in high levels of self-citation to artificially inflate their journal impact factors.[70] The companies themselves have been caught manipulating metrics. In 2009 Elsevier paid academics to write positive reviews of their journal *Clinical Psychology* on Amazon to boost sales.[71] Inflating clicks and sales games the academic metrics system—more attention raises a journal or article's scores, which leads to more clicks and sales.

Combining research with data analytics doesn't just hurt research, it also hurts the researchers themselves. Data companies' algorithms can determine who gets jobs.[72] Hiring and tenure committees rely on impact metrics to measure scholars' value, using the data products to determine scholars' career trajectories. Metrics weigh so heavily in hiring choices that they change how scholars spend their time. Instead of focusing more on their scholarly pursuits, researchers must spend their time trying to place their papers in high-impact-factor journals to get tenure-track jobs. When metrics decide researchers' futures, the number of publications on their resumes, and the names of those publications, is more important than the substance of their work. In some cases, scholars feel obliged to tailor their work to journals that will raise their "scholarly impact" numbers.[73]

The score-powered system especially hurts researchers in places that can't afford the oligopolies' products. The oligopoly companies own the most "prestigious" journals with the highest-impact scores. When science researchers flock to publish in those high-impact journals, a glut of research ends up under the oligopoly's control. The oligopoly companies are Eurocentric, with headquarters in the United Kingdom and the United States, and most of them are published in the English language. Concentrating academic research under the oligopoly's corporate umbrellas makes research less diverse, and less internationally accessible.

The oligopoly also helps misinformation spread. In a world where scholarly research is paywalled, it's free to hop on YouTube to watch white supremacists spread racist theories about IQ and race. But, to read a scholarly article refuting the racist YouTubers' baseless claims with well-researched facts, you have to pay $37.50 to overcome Sage Publishing's paywall.[74]

Despite the appalling access disparities that academic data analytics companies cause, academics and their institutions cannot escape these companies and their products. The octopus-like tentacles of these types of monopolies dig into so many parts of academia that it's hard to disentangle them. Their products aren't just ingrained in libraries, they're also used in institutional fund-raising and hiring offices. A single university may use numerous, different Elsevier and RELX products. Once an institution adopts a product, abandoning it is often expensive and time-consuming. Dropping Elsevier journals would require library catalogers and collection developers to find, catalog, and create access to alternative digital resources. Academic metrics products collect cumulative data—once you start collecting that data, you'll lose it if you switch to a new product.[75] The high switching costs associated with leaving Elsevier make researchers and institutions more "dependent on publishers than ever."[76]

Elsevier's tentacles are spread across academic institutions. A university's law school likely subscribes to Lexis databases. Its undergraduate library negotiates a multimillion-dollar Elsevier contract, and the recruitment and fundraising offices may use some of RELX's personal data services to decide where to focus the school's recruitment efforts and to build alumni databases.[77] Faculty and hiring committees use academic metrics to decide who to hire and which research projects to support. So many parts of a university might use RELX products that it's hard to even figure out where, and how deep, its tentacles reach into the institution's systems. As one librarian explained, "There is no individual or organization within any university that I am aware of that is responsible for the full suite of research workflow services."[78] The data analytics companies are so ingrained in university systems that it would be hard to separate universities from Elsevier's products and contracts.

If the academic market can't disentangle itself from Elsevier and the rest of the academic research oligopoly, how can we fix the problems the companies cause? One solution that journal editors have tried is to move their operations out from under the oligopoly's control. In 2015, the entire editorial board of linguistics journal *Lingua* resigned when they couldn't agree with Elsevier on fair pricing. The board started an open access version of the journal called *Glossa* as an alternative to the paywalled Elsevier publication. Other scholars are starting new open access, peer-reviewed journals from scratch. Mathematician Timothy Gowers launched his own nonprofit, open access mathematics journal, *Discrete Analysis*.[79] Other open access journals have popped up across science and humanities disciplines. Institutions and funders are also forming coalitions. Research funders have formed alliances to support this type of open access publishing.[80]

But open access isn't free. Someone has to pay to publish, platform, and maintain journals like *Glossa* and *Discrete Analysis*. If we want sustainable, digital Linda Hall libraries, who will bear the costs? While digital publishing is cheaper than print, it still takes time and money to set up and run online journals. Each online journal article costs between $100 and $1,000 to produce and share.[81] The open access movement in academic publishing has been around for decades, but the costs of maintaining open access infrastructure have always made it tenuous. Cornell University's open access archive, arXiv, costs over $2 million a year to run.[82] Even with the membership fees arXiv collects, the digital archive still relies on donations and gifts to cover most of its costs.[83] arXiv doesn't have billions of dollars in profits to keep it afloat like Elsevier does, so if it loses its funders' support, it could cease to exist.

Because it's so expensive to start and maintain digital journals and their archives, librarians and scholars are stuck trying to work with companies like Elsevier to make their existing journals more open. There's a laundry list of open access schemes, from open access journals that aren't peer-reviewed to repositories of preprint versions of paywalled articles.[84] But at the end of the day, Elsevier and the other oligopoly publishers are for-profit enterprises that won't sacrifice profit for public access. In one access scheme, the companies provide access to articles if authors agree to pay an "article processing charge" or APC. With APCs, the companies trade paywall profits for authors' fees, but they still get paid.

Elsevier and its oligopoly counterparts have proven pretty inflexible when it comes to creating affordable open access. The companies wield their copyrights like suits of armor, acting as if their rights to academic researchers' articles are ironclad and impenetrable. But copyright isn't a metal shield, it's a set of laws designed by humans. Copyright laws don't grant absolute power, they balance copyright holder's rights with the public's need for information.[85] Some scholars describe copyrights as bundles of sticks. (One stick is the right to reproduce a copyrighted work, one stick is the right to share the work, one stick is the right to perform the work, and so on.) But copyright owners' control of the sticks isn't absolute. Purchasers, and the public, have some rights to use copyrighted materials too.

There are legal safeguards that are supposed to prevent companies like Elsevier from using their sticks against libraries and researchers.[86] Before digital books and journals became the norm, the first-sale doctrine ensured that once a library bought a copyrighted work, it could share, sell, display, and dispose of the copy it bought.[87] But it's not yet clear how first-sale rights apply to the digital materials that are licensed, not sold, to libraries and researchers.[88] There's also the fair use limitation on copyrights, which gives people permission to use copyrighted work in limited circumstances where the use is deemed "fair."[89] Fair use and first-sale limits on copyrights are meant to preserve purchasers' (including libraries') rights to use and share the materials they buy, even when copyright holders (like the academic publishing oligopoly) would rather limit those rights.

Fair use and the first-sale doctrines were better at balancing ownership rights between analog publishers and purchasers than they are online. Courts are still trying to figure out how to apply copyright rules to digital libraries. Meanwhile, companies like RELX and Thomson Reuters see new digital sharing technologies, as well as the uncertainty in digital copyright doctrine, as opportunities to taper copyright exceptions for digital materials.

The first-sale doctrine is far easier to implement for paper materials than for digital ones. The switch from selling physical materials to licensing access to digital materials helps the companies maintain copyright restrictions even after people "buy" them, because the customers aren't purchasing the items outright. Instead they are merely buying access to digital copies of the items, which remain in the oligopoly companies' servers and under their control. In the current licensing scheme, libraries and researchers can't buy an academic journal article and put it on their shelves or in their backpacks. Instead, they can only stream academic research the same way they stream a show on Netflix or a Spotify playlist.

Under the first-sale doctrine, copyright holders exhaust some of their rights when they sell copies of their work. After a publisher sells a paper journal to a library, the library can lend that copy to patrons, keep the copy for decades, or even throw it in the trash. Once a paper copy of a journal leaves their hands, the copyright holder no longer has absolute control over what happens to that copy. But the first-sale doctrine only kicks in when there's a "sale." If libraries can't buy digital copies, there's no point of sale at which the data company hands over the copyrighted material to its customer. In the digital licensing scheme, companies maintain control of their copies after the point of sale, curtailing library lending and stifling researchers' use by limiting what they can do with the materials they pay for. The copyright holders can restrict downloading, printing, and sharing even after libraries and researchers have paid for full access, the maximum level of rights offered by the companies.

Fair use could also be a sturdier safety net in educational settings, but data companies and other copyright intermediaries have convinced courts to decide what counts as fair use in ways that protect the companies' financial interests instead of consumers' interests.[90] Like today's antitrust enforcement, today's fair use analysis tends to hinge on whether the use in question hurts the economic value of the company's copyright instead of whether the use helps consumers or the public good.[91] In the United States, courts are supposed to decide fair use cases by considering four factors: the purpose and character of the use, the nature of the copyrighted work, the amount and substantiality of the use, and the market effect of the use of the copyrighted material. These factors have historically created some copyright exceptions when materials were used for not-for-profit educational purposes. But over the years, courts have given much more weight to the fourth factor, focusing on the market impact of the copying.[92]

Law professor Brian Frye says that we could treat digital copyright issues more like other property issues instead of giving so much power to copyright holders like Elsevier. He says copyrights should receive the same limited protections as other types of property rights.[93] If we were to treat digital copyrights like real property rights, fair use would be like an easement on the property. We could create access easements to academic research that limit copyright restrictions for the public good, leveling the playing field for public information access.[94] Courts would be able to differentiate between unauthorized use (copyright trespass) and specific permissible uses, like situations when noncommercial academic researchers can't get the materials they need with reasonable ease or efficiency.[95] Especially in cases when academic research is publicly funded, access could be guaranteed, like an informational version of easements to light or air, limiting the data companies' full control of critical public knowledge.[96] Implementing fair use easements and other types of property access schemes for information access could become a way to "push back on owners' efforts to erode fair use rights" in the digital ecosystem.[97]

While we're rethinking how we treat copyrights, we should also rethink how we enforce them, especially for academic research. Elsevier and federal prosecutors have pursued copyright infringers voraciously, pushing for extreme punishments including millions of dollars in damages for copyright infringement and criminal penalties under the Computer Fraud and Abuse Act, a law meant to punish people who hack into government computers or commit cyber espionage. They pursue these penalties even when the copyright infringers aren't profit-seekers or spies but idealistic researchers whose piracy is somewhat justified when paywalls are blocking students all over the world from accessing academic knowledge. After Aaron Swartz died by suicide amidst vicious prosecution over his JSTOR downloads, Representative Zoe Lofgren introduced "Aaron's Law," which would have limited the kinds of activities subject to the Computer Fraud and Abuse Act's harsh penalties. People who merely violate platforms' terms of service agreements wouldn't face the same criminal consequences as people who hack into government systems to spy.[98] Aaron's Law didn't pass, but attorney Tor Ekeland's suggestion that we "reserve criminal sanctions for the cases where it's truly merited, where a significant and real harm occurred" is still an important one.[99]

As people on the front lines of information access struggles, lots of librarians see piracy as a necessary evil instead of a deplorable act. Sometimes, creating access to research is a life-saving imperative. Library experts consider inaccessible academic research to be a market failure that prevents doctors, scientists, and technologists from getting critical information that they need. Piracy is the reparative action when companies like Elsevier block access to critical public information.[100] Aaron Swartz felt he was providing a "banquet of knowledge" to an information-starved public. Alexandra Elbakyan's goal is to "remove all barriers in the way of science."[101] These aren't criminal motives, they're altruistic aspirations.

Congress could ensure access to academic research, and that the academic research companies maintain reasonable prices, choice, and access for those who can't afford to pay for scholarly journals and other reports.[102] There has been some government support for public access to federally funded research in recent years. In 2013, the White House issued a memorandum directing federal agencies that fund research to provide free, online access to that research no later than a year after publication in a peer-reviewed journal.[103] In 2021, Senator Charles Schumer introduced a bill that would codify the 2013 memorandum's open access initiative.[104]

Of course, enforcing antitrust laws to curb the big deal bundling, nondisclosure clauses, and other anticompetitive practices that prevent libraries from negotiating fair deals would also lower costs and barriers to access of academic research. FTC and Department of Justice antitrust enforcement efforts could home in on academic research companies instead of allowing the oligopoly to use publicly funded research to take advantage of consumers. Most of all, antitrust enforcement should disentangle data analytics from the acquisition of knowledge. Scholarly journals shouldn't be mixed up in data brokering and metrics businesses. Academic research is meant to be a public good, not a data-collection tool for private data broker companies. Academic research providers should be focused on supplying high-quality academic journals to the public, not on collecting and crunching researchers' data to make more money.

Until we limit data analytics companies' control of academic research, inequality and piracy will pervade academic publishing. Academic research is a critical public resource, and people will work to get essential information to those who need it whether the laws allow it or not. Elsevier's ScienceDirect has the slogan "making uncommon knowledge common," even as the company does the opposite by putting knowledge behind paywalls. Meanwhile Sci-Hub, Elbakyan's illegal academic research platform, actually enriches the commons by sharing otherwise paywalled research. Articles on Sci-Hub are cited far more often than paywalled articles because people can actually read them.[105] According to Elbakyan, if Elsevier keeps ignoring its own slogan, she and other open access academic research activists are here to "help them fulfill their mission."[106]

4

LEGAL INFORMATION

I N CHAPTER 3, WE SAW how data companies control science and other academic knowledge. Data companies also control legal information. Lawyers, judges, lawmakers, regulators, and anyone else who makes, interprets, or enforces laws in the United States relies on one, or both, of the two major data analytics companies (RELX and Thomson Reuters) for their legal information. Legal information is different from academic information. Instead of being drafted by scholars, legal information is the product of legislative, judicial, and administrative processes. But despite the differences in structure and audience, the data analytics companies treat academic and legal information the same. To the data companies, both types of information are portfolios of copyright assets to profit from, and their legal information platforms supply a wealth of data points for their legal analytics products. The companies use the same exploitative, anticompetitive practices in both markets, including data extraction and pushy contracts and provisions.

Like academic knowledge, legal information is critical public information. Supreme Court opinions, the U.S. Constitution, and other legal writings set the rules for our society. In the United States, legal proclamations are so celebrated that the Declaration of Independence has both its own museum and a Nicholas Cage–focused movie genre. Given their popularity, you may think that everyone would have free-flowing access to our nation's legal pronouncements. If that's your assumption, you'd be surprised to hear that nobody—not even lawyers or lawmakers—gets a full, free copy of our laws. Instead, people collectively pay the data analytics companies millions of dollars every year to access their legal information platforms. And the law isn't cheap: a survey of law firms found that 70 percent of the firms' budgets go to RELX's Lexis and Thomson Reuters's Westlaw.[1]

Though the legal research duopoly seems like a foregone conclusion to those in the profession, legal information access wasn't always a monopolistic enterprise. Just as Elsevier was, originally, a small publishing operation meant to share science, Westlaw and Lexis began as legal information services for small legal communities. West Publishing was started by a pioneering publisher named John B. West, who wanted to print court reports for lawyers in Minnesota. Lexis was the brainchild of the Ohio State Bar Association president James Preston. He wanted to build a legal research system for Ohio lawyers. In books about legal research, both West and Preston are portrayed as patriarchs of the legal profession who wanted nothing more than to improve legal information access for lawyers.

Westlaw and Lexis's origin stories share the folksy, PR-spun feel that big-tech companies invented to humanize their products. People like West, Preston, Steve Jobs, and Mark Zuckerberg are painted as public-serving visionaries with humble beginnings.[2] But like the big-tech companies that Zuckerberg and Jobs built, Westlaw and Lexis have proven to be typical, profit-seeking businesses. John West was a book salesman; he wanted to sell more books. James Preston's database was eventually sold to Mead Corporation, not for its legal databases, but so Mead could get inkjet printing technology from Preston's business partner. Mead wasn't even interested in making a legal information product until consultants told Mead that the databases could be profitable.

The consultants were right—it turns out that digital legal information is a multimillion-dollar industry. West and LexisNexis were able to corner the legal data market by being the first to gather the nation's court opinions en masse. West Publishing, Westlaw's paper precursor, started publishing the nation's court papers in the 1800s.[3] By 1893, West Publishing was "one of the largest publishing houses of any kind in the country."[4] The companies also started buying up the rights to "secondary" law publications—the legal encyclopedias, treatises, and other writings that explain the law. By the late 1900s the companies owned not just the law, but also the gold-standard overviews of legal doctrine.

West Publishing dominated the paper publishing world for decades, publishing law books "by the million."[5] But then databases were invented. While West ruled the paper world, James Preston partnered with Data Corporation, a defense contractor building data systems to organize Air Force procurement contracts and equipment inventory, to make LEXIS, the first electronic legal information service. By the time the internet was up and running, Westlaw and Lexis were far ahead of the competition. They had already captured the legal information market and created infrastructure that would take any competitor tons of money and time to reconstruct. By both inventing the systems that organize the law and becoming the major publishers of case law and statutes, Westlaw and Lexis were impossible to beat.[6] With their plentiful profits, the companies could afford to hire thousands of people, including enough lawyers to run twenty-four-hour-a-day research support hotlines. They could also afford to develop legal research extras, bells and whistles such as digital citators that tell people whether law is still "good" by describing the subsequent history of court opinions, statutes, and regulations. Today, citators are so central to the practice of law that lawyers use their commercial names as verbs: When Marsha Clark failed to find the newest case law in the famous O. J. Simpson trial, Judge Lance Ito threatened her with sanctions for not "Shepardizing" her case.[7] (Shepard's is the commercial name of Lexis's citator.)

In the 1990s RELX and Thomson Reuters acquired Lexis and Westlaw, respectively, and folded the legal information products into their informational empires. Today, RELX's Lexis and Thomson Reuters's Westlaw dominate the legal information market, charging a premium for access to statutes, regulations, and court opinions.[8] The legal research duopoly is so pervasive that when either service has an internet outage, the legal profession goes into disaster mode as their work grinds to a halt. (Just search the phrase "Westlaw outage" on any social media platform to see what I mean. During one outage, Josh Chafetz, a law professor at Georgetown Law, declared, "Westlaw is down. There is no law.")[9] Instead of being readily available to the general public, the best legal information sources and collections are only available to those who pay for Lexis and West-law subscriptions. The companies paywall our public law on their private platforms.

With their market control of legal information, Westlaw and Lexis are more than legal information providers, they also shape the law. They embed their editorial summaries into court opinions and statutes, telling lawmakers how to understand and apply the law. Their key numbers and headnotes organize all of our legal knowledge into categories and themes. They control the citators that dictate what law is "good" and what law is "bad." In some cases, they even choose which case law gets published. Their legal product platforms and search algorithms raise some cases and doctrinal materials and bury others, choosing which precedents lawyers use.[10] Lexis and Westlaw's editors and software were never meant to play a role in stare decisis or lawmakers' decisions, but today, the companies are so pervasive in the legal profession that even typos in their content get baked into the law.[11] When their platforms omit a court opinion, it disappears from our laws because nobody ever cites it.[12]

Just like with academic information, allowing data analytics companies to exert so much informational control turns our critical legal informational resources into fodder for analytics software products. The companies provide the best, and sometimes only, access to our legal materials, and they also run those legal materials through their analytics software and systems to create new predictive and prescriptive information to sell. Their legal data analytics products help the lawyers who can afford them guess how their cases will fare in various courts and intuit what judges and opposing counsel will do on the basis of data pulled from court opinions, news, corporate data, and personally identifiable information.

The more analytics RELX and Thomson Reuters infuse into their legal information platforms, the fewer decisions lawyers, judges, and policymakers will make without the sway of Westlaw and Lexis's automated selections. The platforms provide "data-driven insights" that tell lawyers which cases are likely to win in court. They also predict whether laws are likely to be undermined or overturned. Westlaw uses its analytics software to predict lawyers' research, and it will check your legal briefs and suggest legal authority to infuse into the writing.[13] Lexis's data analytics claim they can help lawyers game court cases by supplying the language that will get them the most favorable outcomes in court and telling them how to use opponents' arguments to strengthen their own.[14]

Automated legal research moves the onus of legal decision making from legal experts to data analytics machines. Where lawyers and lawmakers once selected their own databases and typed in their own Boolean terms-and-connectors searches, now the research platforms select databases and arrange search terms for users. For example, "Lexis Answers" suggests the question you want to ask as soon as you start typing, anticipating your research path, curating and sharing the content it decides you want to see.[15] The data analytics software and algorithms aren't just telling lawyers how to interpret the law and which law to rely on, they're making these choices opaque. Nobody can see how these important decisions about the law are made. The algorithms that sift legal data, deciding which cases and laws are most important, make thousands of choices with every click. One RELX employee calls the company's machine-learning algorithms "blackbox," because they make so many tiny decisions so quickly that they are impossible to observe.[16] Lawyers will rely on RELX's and Thomson Reuters's choices without even understanding the logic behind them.

No research is neutral. This includes legal research. Even in paper collections, someone selects what's included in databases and what's left out. But digitizing and automating legal decisions in Westlaw and Lexis adds another algorithmic layer of bias to historically biased legal decisions. Law historically has been interpreted to favor the decisions of white, cis, wealthy men. Westlaw and Lexis bake those historical, systemic biases into digital legal research platforms. The companies' modern databases are rooted in Civil War–era classifications. It's not surprising that products based on John B. West's 1800s-era legal classification system "reflect a nineteenth-century worldview" that institutionalizes the white, male, heteronormative, upper-class, able-bodied, and politically conservative perspective.[17]

Those historical biases are layered beneath similar biases that flow through AI, machine learning, and search algorithms. Like research, AI is also not neutral. "When you rely on an algorithm, what you are getting is someone's point of view about what's happening in a database."[18] There are layers of bias in these systems—the biases of the tech developers that build them, the biases of the people who supply the data that trains them, and the biases of the editors and designers who curate the data collections. In legal research algorithms, the point of view is a blend of past and present white, male technologists and white, male lawyers. Machine learning systems are known to be infused with the biases of the humans that create them and the "dirty data" that trains them.[19] Like all words and concepts, legal theories and paradigms have various shades of meaning, "depending on one's perspective."[20] We don't see all of the various understandings of legal decrees when we rely on just one or two company's editors to curate all of our primary and secondary legal sources.[21] Westlaw and Lexis's machine-learning systems were trained by (predominately white, male) corporate lawyers who subscribe to the services.

Beyond bias, Westlaw and Lexis's automated systems also make mistakes. Human summaries of the law are more precise than digital decision making, because humans are better at picking through the complex, twisting-and-turning language of court opinions and the dry, technical language of legal codes. Even if software can help make first-round assessments of the law, it's better to have human editors vetting electronically driven legal decisions. Susan Nevelow Mart, director of University of Colorado's law library, found that Lexis's algorithmic headnote system delivered less accurate results than West's human-made system.[22] In situations in which both systems use algorithms instead of human decisions about which cases lawyers should rely on,[23] she was surprised by "how few cases each citation system had in common," because accurate results would have significant overlap.[24] But having humans read and summarize the law is slower, laborious, and expensive work that companies would prefer to swap out for speedy, cheaper algorithms.[25]

These legal data analytics products also sow inequality because they aren't available to everyone. They are expensive tools that only well-monied law firms and corporate counsel are likely to afford. The products aren't made for criminal defense lawyers or public interest organizations. They're geared towards corporate practices, marketed as products that will help corporate lawyers game the law in their favor by creating "strategic advantages" by crafting certain arguments for certain judges and compiling in-depth predictive dossiers about opposing counsel. Because not all lawyers can afford to access these analytics tools, they tilt the legal playing field, giving some attorneys special information to help them win cases that others cannot see.[26]

Running a legal system on only two legal information platforms, and depending on their algorithms, seems like a precarious way to make law, yet the most influential law firms, judges, and government offices are resistant to trying alternative legal research products. Some judges won't even read lawyers' work if it doesn't include Westlaw citations.[27] State governments are similarly finicky about using services besides Westlaw and Lexis. The legal profession collectively spills billions of dollars into the data companies' coffers instead of investing in innovative, new legal information products.[28] The profession's product loyalty begins in law schools. Among the first things law students receive when they matriculate are their personalized Westlaw and Lexis passwords. The schools are required to train the students to use Westlaw and Lexis, and the companies offer regular training sessions to supplement those lessons throughout the year. The companies even insert their own sales reps into the schools' curricula in teaching roles. My own legal research teacher explained that law students pick either the red pill (Lexis-branded red) or the blue pill (Westlaw-branded blue) and then get hooked for the rest of their professional lives.

RELX and Thomson Reuters's legal research duopoly is so lucrative that the companies can afford to lavish the law students in swag. They give legal professionals luxurious prizes to win their favor. Laws limit how drug companies can induce medical professionals to use their products,[29] but there are no similar restrictions for data companies. Lexis and Westlaw have been known to give people designer handbags, iPads, big-screen TVs, and other fancy prizes for using their products. The companies even supply so many pizzas, sandwiches, and other snacks to law students who complete product-training sessions that some students claim they are able to subsist largely on legal research session meals. Beyond prizes, the companies assign personal product reps to every law school and customer's office. The rep's main job is to regularly visit users to make sure they're logging on to their products. Westlaw and Lexis even hire law students at each law school to serve as product ambassadors to their peers.

When two companies run the major legal information platforms, they can use their duopoly power to force consumers to pay above-market prices for access, just like the academic research oligopoly does on their platforms. Paywalls are just as ubiquitous in the legal information market as they are in the academic information market. Putting the law behind paywalls means that sometimes we can't see the laws we're supposed to follow. In a legal system in which ignorance of the law is no excuse for breaking it, making the law visible is especially important.[30] If a government wants people to understand their rights and legal limitations, the government needs to be sure people can read the jurisdiction's rules. For over a century, Supreme Court justices have agreed that "living under a rule of law" means that everyone is entitled to be informed about "what the State commands or forbids."[31]

Beyond needing access to the law to be a law-abiding citizen, people should have access to the law because it belongs to them. Like taxpayer-funded academic information, our tax dollars pay for the government and the laws it makes. The information that comes from the government is "the information of the people."[32] In the 1800s, the Supreme Court declared as much when it upheld the government edicts doctrine, the principle that nobody can privatize the law.[33] Courts have also supported the "citizen authorship" principle, which says the public owns the law because the public pays the salaries of the people who draft legislation. Under citizen authorship, "each citizen is a ruler, a law-maker."[34]

Despite judges' proclamations about public access to the law, legal information hasn't been treated like a public good. The Supreme Court may periodically pay homage to legal information access, but the government hasn't been a good legal publisher. The reason John B. West started publishing court opinions back in the 1800s was to pick up the slack for slow government publishers.[35] Since then, West Publishing's court reporters have always outpaced the official reporters from state and federal courts. West proves that legal materials can be rapidly printed when publishing infrastructure is sufficiently funded and staffed.

The lack of public legal information infrastructure and the lack of financial support endure centuries later. Despite its sprawling .gov websites, the federal judiciary's court opinions sometimes take years to be published and appear online, forcing lawyers to cite Westlaw and Lexis instead. Often, the only way to cite a recent Supreme Court case is to cite it from West or Lexis's Supreme Court reporters. For example, according to Georgetown's law library, as of November 2017, the Supreme Court's official reporter only covered cases through 2012.[36] Some precedent-setting court cases never even get officially published, making Westlaw and Lexis the sole providers of those pronouncements.[37]

It's easy to see that the government hasn't focused on legal information infrastructure when you look at its records-sharing platforms. One often-discussed example of how bad the government is at creating access to the law is its clunky, hard-to-use court dockets system. Public Access to Court Electronic Records (PACER) has hardly been updated since it went online in 1998. PACER has been called as "archaic as a barrister's wig."[38] Private information infrastructure has advanced by leaps and bounds since 1998. Systems like Google Drive and Dropbox let us share pretty much any type of document instantly, in a searchable, printable format, with anyone. Meanwhile, each of our 108 federal courts runs its own PACER system, making cross-jurisdiction searches nearly impossible. Keyword searches are complicated in PACER, and you have to be well-versed at Boolean search operators to find the specific court records you need.

In contrast, Westlaw and Lexis manage to post new court decisions hours after they are issued, complete with annotations and other editorial add-ons. In the paywalled systems, you can easily traverse court materials across jurisdictions. It's difficult to find cases in PACER unless you know a particular case's docket number, which is hard to find. That means that you usually have to do layers of research before you can even use PACER to find the records you need. Lexis and Westlaw are far more efficient and user friendly than the public docket system.

For all of its clunkiness, PACER isn't even free for the public to use. Even though the "PA" in PACER stands for "Public Access," the access system is paywalled. Unless you have an account, you can't use it. In 1988, Congress denied the federal judiciary funding to make the court records available for free, so PACER charges users ten cents a page.[39] Ten cents a page may not sound like much, but PACER users report that it's easy to burn $10 "just by looking up rudimentary information about a single case" because you have to click through so many pages to find what you need.[40]

Without infrastructure and adequate resources for legal information infrastructure, even if the government puts something online, there's no guarantee that it will stay there. The government's online offerings are ephemeral, subject to the whims of whoever is in charge. Entire swathes of government webpages can disappear when political winds or congressional moods shift. Regulations, statutes, and judicial decrees have no guaranteed, permanent online homes. Sometimes the government stalls out on maintaining public data collections, leaving citizen archivists to organize our National Archives[41] or preserve government information at the end of presidential terms.[42] Federal records volunteers are inspiring, but they also expose the government's failure to ensure continuous, stable access to its records. People shouldn't have to rush to save government climate policy records just because an antiscience president gets elected.[43]

According to federal records laws like the Federal Records Act and FOIA, the government is responsible for creating access to its information.[44] But online access to official records doesn't happen for free. Maintaining and organizing online content, and storing it on servers, takes a lot of money and people power. Ensuring access to government information should be a federally funded program, not a volunteer opportunity.

State law access is no better than federal law access. Some states have no online records, some have fee-based access systems, and some states' online legal information systems are far better than anything the federal government puts online. In short, free legal information access in the United States is a jumbled, inconsistent mess. RELX and Thomson Reuters capitalize on governments' chronically confused and underfunded legal information systems. When only Westlaw, Lexis, and the government itself control our legal information, the public is stuck choosing whether to wing it and rely on inconsistent government webpages or whether to pay exorbitant fees for paywalled law databases.

Without sufficient information infrastructure legal researchers aren't the only ones depending on Westlaw and Lexis. States also depend on the data companies to publish their laws. Westlaw and Lexis make the only versions of court opinions for many states.[45] Publishing law is time-consuming and expensive, so courts and legislatures outsource publication to the data companies. Getting from "the governors' pen strokes to the codified set of rules" and to organizing the many decisions handed down from courts each day takes a lot of editorial and maintenance work.[46] Some states cannot afford to assemble their own staff or offices to do that work. For those states, outsourcing is a necessary step in making laws.

In states that do put their laws online, the challenge of maintaining current versions of the law online is so burdensome that governments often won't vouch for the legal information they share. Official government websites can't always guarantee that the laws they post on their webpages are up to date and correct.[47] "Authenticating" laws, vouching for their accuracy, is an important part of publishing the law. Citing bad, outdated law can lead to legal malpractice. Lawyers use Westlaw and Lexis instead of public websites because they know that Westlaw and Lexis are sources that they can cite with some confidence.

Even though publishing the law requires labor, the companies that do it don't have permission to paywall our only access to laws. So how do Lexis and Westlaw get away with doing just that? Everyone agrees that the "raw" bills and opinions are public information that cannot be copyrighted, but Westlaw and Lexis work around those copyright restrictions by inserting bits of proprietary content into their versions of the law. The companies make minor additions to the law's text, infusing it with a few subject headings and some commentary—popping a couple headnotes at the top or footnotes at the end of court opinions and statutes, and hyperlinking citations to other proprietary content.[48] Even though the companies' annotations are small (sometimes less than a sentence), they can confer copyright to material that would otherwise be considered a public resource.[49]

In 2019, the Supreme Court pushed back on the companies paywalling the law. The Court reaffirmed the government edicts doctrine, prohibiting the State of Georgia from keeping its statutes behind a $400 Lexis paywall. The state had sued Public.Resource.Org after it scanned a paper copy of the state's laws and posted them online.[50] Georgia claimed that Lexis's annotations gave the state exclusive copyright to the entire legal text.

Copyright claims like Georgia's had succeeded in the past—in 1986, Westlaw successfully argued that its "star pagination" page number markers were worthy of copyright protection.[51] In 1993, Congress implicitly agreed to let private companies copyright public laws when it declined to pass a law that would have prohibited private copyrights for compilations of state and federal laws.[52] But in *Georgia v. Public.Resource.Org*, the Supreme Court reaffirmed the public's right to access the law. The court opined that Georgia can't copyright its official code even if the text contains some Lexis annotations.[53] Chief Justice John Roberts said private companies publishing official codes are government agents carrying out government work. But the Court's decision doesn't cover every Lexis and Westlaw legal compilation—at least twenty states claim copyright over their official codes, and not all of those copyrights would be denied under the Supreme Court's newest interpretation of the government edicts doctrine.[54]

The data analytics companies' paywalls around legal information are functionally the same as the ones they put around academic information, but the problems that legal information barriers cause are unique. Academic information is critically important for solving human problems, and legal information is critically important for understanding and protecting our rights. Putting paywalls around legal information perpetuates inequality and oppression in different ways than paywalling academic information does.[55] In *Public.Resource.Org*, Justice Roberts describes the injustice of giving the public a lesser, free "economy-class" version of Georgia's law and blocking the best version behind a Lexis paywall. The plain words of legal codes don't always accurately portray what the law is. Statutes are not always easy to understand on their face. Lawmaking is a messy, iterative process, and the end results can be muddled and unclear. Codification is also a complicated process. Sometimes old legal provisions aren't removed even when new provisions and decisions cancel them out. For example, the text of Georgia's code still says that sodomy is illegal even though the state's supreme court declared the law unconstitutional decades ago.[56] People need more than just the words of a statute to truly access and understand the law. You shouldn't have to pay Westlaw $2,570 to be sure your version of the law isn't an "unenforceable relic."[57]

Like scholarship paywalls, law paywalls hurt the people who need legal information the most—people tangled up in the U.S. legal system, whether they're battling it out in court or navigating government bureaucracy to get the services they need. Incarcerated people and detainees whose liberties (and sometimes lives) are in peril need legal information most of all. Most prisoners' legal assistance disappears after sentencing, leaving inmates to manage their own cases.[58] Without lawyers, inmates depend on law libraries to learn about their legal rights. But, in concert with the rest of our libraries, prison law libraries have replaced their paper collections with research platforms run by data analytics companies.

Both Westlaw and Lexis have built special "correctional" legal information platforms for prisons.[59] The correctional product lines seem less focused on information access and more focused on giving guards control over prisoners. They aren't marketed as a resource for prisoners, but as a tool for prison administrators. Unlike the companies' other products, which feature attorneys in power suits and scholars in lab coats, the correctional products show a man in an orange jumpsuit with a seemingly artificial tear tattoo by his eye and spider and snake tattoos on his neck.[60] Instead of being on the most convenient computer systems, correctional products are offered on either kiosks or tablets. Both of these access points are more isolating and physically restrictive than traditional libraries with their rows of shelves to wander and librarians to talk to. "Kiosks" are computer monitors covered in shatterproof glass and locked inside steel boxes that prisoners can access in a fixed location. Tablets are similarly locked, but they're portable, so they "decrease the need for prisoner movement" because prisoners don't have to leave their cells to use them.[61]

The kiosks and tablets don't just restrict movement, they also restrict information in comparison to the libraries they replace. The kiosks and tablets aren't the same as human librarians and more user-friendly law books. Westlaw and Lexis are so complicated that law schools offer special classes to train people about how to use them. Prisoners don't get those lessons on how to use the platforms. They also don't always get access to secondary sources that explain what the laws mean and how they work. Lexis and Westlaw's correctional platforms often contain little more than the case law and statutes for a single jurisdiction even though they replace paper collections that contained an array of secondary sources including legal encyclopedias and how-to guides. Like the rest of the public, prisoners usually need those secondary sources to understand their cases. Before they can file a habeas petition to argue that their detention is unlawful, they have to know what a habeas petition is. Inmates' cases can also involve both federal and state law, so they might need to access the law from multiple jurisdictions to make their case, not just one. If prisoners in a Florida jail can only access Florida State law, they may not be getting the legal information they need.

Perhaps the worst thing about Westlaw and Lexis's correctional products isn't their meager offerings but the surveillance systems that RELX and Thomson Reuters embed in them. The companies put their data-collection and analytics tools in their correctional products so prison administrators can spy on inmates. Paper books don't have eyes, but the data companies' prison products are loaded with tools to track their users. The spyware reports everything an inmate does online back to prison guards and administrators. Lexis's correctional product also polices prisoners' online activities, "promptly shut[ting] down" any "suspicious activity."[62] The companies create click-by-click tracking lists of prisoners' searches in their product, as well as any attempts to use any webpages beyond theirs.[63]

In 2019, the Netflix series *Orange Is the New Black* featured Lexis's correctional facility product in episodes about ICE detention centers to illustrate their limited utility for people swept up in ICE's deportation system. In the show, detained women tried to use Lexis to get information to prevent their own deportations. The Lexis terminals were one of the women's only information sources. The detainees waited anxiously for their turn on the computers. Whether they could even sit at the terminals depended on "the mood of ICE agents on a power trip."[64] As they waited, they were treated abysmally, held in large, bullet-proof "fish tanks" or rooms stripped of everything except rows of bunk beds. They were fed rotting food and left without anything to fill their days except the memories of the families and lives they might never see again.

Putting Lexis on the show was meant to illustrate how America's most vulnerable prisoners cannot get access to justice. Offering Lexis instead of real assistance was cruel. Lexis didn't seem to notice that it was portrayed as part of a human-rights abusing system. The company bragged about the show's product placement, even though using Lexis in the show wasn't meant to compliment the company.[65] Lexis was built into the scene because one of the show's writers was a former attorney who noticed some Lexis kiosks on a tour of California's largest ICE detention facility. The writer knew that a person with no legal training, who may not speak English, wouldn't be able to navigate such complex legal software. They saw the provision of Lexis terminals to immigrant detainees as a tragic irony.[66] Oblivious to the terribleness of ICE detention, Lexis playfully chided a detainee for calling Lexis "Google for old legal cases," even as the woman frantically searched Lexis's paltry correctional offerings trying to find information that would save her from being deported. The company spun the immigrants' suffering into an ad: "[W]e do so much more than just 'old legal cases[!]' We offer a wide suite of products designed to glean insights from the vast amounts of data available in our legal system—that includes new and ongoing cases, too." Lexis's post about the show ends with a paragraph telling readers to "Click here to learn more about the Lexis Analytics Suite." You can be sure that few, if any, people in ICE detention can access this fancy "analytics suite" of products. This callous advertising for Lexis seems especially cruel when you consider that RELX has a $16.8 million contract with ICE to supply the agency with surveillance data that the agency uses to arrest and detain women like the ones portrayed in *Orange Is the New Black*.[67]

People still use Lexis and Westlaw despite their high prices and questionable ethics because their legal research duopoly is practically impenetrable. Lawyers and legal researchers are stuck with Lexis and Westlaw, no matter what they do, even if the quality of their products isn't as good as it could be. The problem with monopolies is that you can't stop using them even if you don't like what they're providing, because there are no other options in the market.

You can see the same declining quality in RELX's and Thomson Reuters's legal information platforms as we saw in Elsevier's academic information products. The companies are more focused on growing their legal data analytics business and less focused on providing quality, well-vetted content. They are offering more dubious information products that aren't great for consumers. Unedited trial court records, unpublished opinions, and law blogs don't necessarily contain good legal analysis, but they do contain plenty of data points for analytics systems to crunch. This glut of "other content" is similar to the unvetted content on different types of information platforms, but unlike news and entertainment, the law shouldn't be presented as a never-ending news feed. When content lacking precedential value and expertise appears next to official legal materials and expert analysis, it's hard for people to figure out what legal analysis is accurate. There's no label for blog posts specifying that it's one lawyer's opinion, and there's nothing differentiating trial court documents from binding court opinions.

Lawyers and librarians have noticed the declining informational quality on Westlaw and Lexis. Westlaw's current approach to publishing has been called "the waste-basket method," because it tosses in whatever legal material it can find, even if it's junk.[68] The "platform-everything-you-can" ethos erodes the law by muddying legal precedent with superfluous content. Legal research blogger Jean O'Grady called out Lexis's declining legal research product, accusing the company of adding data features to its platform instead of improving the legal information offerings. O'Grady writes, "It is a rather sad commentary that Lexis appears to view their flagship legal research product Lexis Advance as a sinking ship which must be held afloat by their other product lines—mostly products which Lexis did not develop but acquired over the past few years. Are Lex Machina, Law 360, Ravel and Intelligize really commercial pontoons keeping Lexis Advance afloat?"[69]

Despite their anticompetitive market domination, the federal government has done little to curb Thomson Reuters and RELX's control of legal information in the United States. After Thomson bought West in 1996, the Department of Justice ordered the company to divest some of its assets to Lexis to prevent Thomson from monopolizing legal information.[70] As the government has done in other informational market sectors such as the government data brokering market, it equipped RELX and Thomson Reuters to be a legal information duopoly.

Without government intervention, other companies can't compete. The duopoly companies can sue their competition out of business, burying them in legal fees. Alan Sugarman, a lawyer who tried to compete in the legal information market, described West as a cutthroat company that's "incredibly litigious . . . suing people right and left."[71] In the 1990s, when Sugarman fought West's copyright claims in court, the judge called it a David versus Goliath battle: a legal information giant against Sugerman's small startup business.[72] Sugarman ultimately won the case,[73] but the victory didn't matter for his company, HyperLaw. The legal dispute sucked up all of Sugerman's financial resources. West's litigation effectively shut HyperLaw down. Almost thirty years later, Westlaw sued another legal information startup, ROSS, out of existence. Thomson Reuters claimed ROSS violated its copyrights by downloading Westlaw data.[74] Although ROSS was likely to win in court, the litigation costs were so high that ROSS was out of business within a year. In the startup's farewell message, ROSS said the spurious lawsuit strangled their fledgling business.[75]

Lawsuits aren't the only weapons the companies use to stifle competition. They also swipe other companies' innovations. When I worked at Bloomberg Law, a legal research website started by financial data analytics company Bloomberg L.P., I saw firsthand how the companies can smash startups. Within months of cool new product features being released on Bloomberg Law, the duopoly would fold the same features into their products. Westlaw and Lexis were so powerful and well-equipped with product developers that they could quickly incorporate all of our new innovations as features on their platforms. Years later, I wasn't surprised to read that Bloomberg L.P. insiders call the Bloomberg Law project "Bloomberg's Vietnam."[76]

The legal research duopoly can also stifle open access efforts in the legal information sector. The companies pay firms to lobby against laws and policies that would improve free access to the law. Thomson Reuters and RELX's business models—making people pay for government information—are antithetical to government transparency, so the companies fight laws that would improve access to legal information. Together, RELX and Thomson Reuters spend hundreds of thousands of dollars convincing lawmakers to vote against laws intended to improve PACER and other public legal information projects. In 2019, Thomson Reuters spent over $300,000 lobbying against the Electronic Court Records Reform Act,[77] a law that would make PACER materials free to the public.[78] RELX similarly spent over half a million dollars lobbying Congress to vote against public PACER access and to vote against privacy laws that would have stifled the company's data brokering business.[79] In 2020, the companies funded efforts to kill another public PACER bill.[80]

RELX and Thomson Reuters also put the same types of anticompetitive contract provisions they use in academic product contracts into legal product contracts. Westlaw and Lexis contracts bind consumers with burdensome nondisclosure agreements and expensive product-tying deals. Like academic law librarians, law librarians cannot discuss their contract terms.[81] Thomson Reuters has even tried to force librarians to sign nondisclosure agreements *before* negotiating contracts to keep negotiations secret.[82] Contractual silencing helps RELX and Thomson Reuters charge customers different prices for the same product on the basis of what they think the customer will agree to pay. After all, nobody knows the market value of legal information if nobody knows how much anyone else is paying for it. This type of price discrimination pushes each customer to pay the maximum amount they can afford, instead of creating an equal pricing scheme. In 2016, after Lexis wrote licensing agreements with such broad nondisclosure clauses that libraries could not discuss *any* aspect of their contracts with their professional colleagues, the American Association of Law Libraries asked Lexis to narrow the language. Lexis said no.[83]

The companies' nondisclosure agreements are so effective that law librarians are afraid to discuss their Westlaw or Lexis contracts. When a library science student circulated an anonymous survey asking librarians about their Westlaw and Lexis contracts, only twelve of the seventy-five recipients responded.[84] Most of the librarians who didn't answer declined because they were afraid of breaking their nondisclosure agreements. These nondisclosure agreements don't just scare librarians, they also make it hard for the public to see how much of their tuition and taxes are flowing to Westlaw and Lexis. Many of the institutions that use legal information—courts, academic institutions, government agencies stocked with lawyers—are public. Because of the nondisclosure clauses, students have to file freedom of information requests to see how much of their tuition is going to the data companies.[85] Even when Georgia and Public. Resources.Org fought it out in court, the state didn't reveal the details of its deal with Lexis.[86]

Product-tying "big deal" contracts are another anticompetitive tool that RELX and Thomson Reuters use in both legal information and academic research products. Westlaw and Lexis contracts combine critical primary legal resources (the laws themselves) with secondary fluff like case briefs and other editorial content, forcing people to buy both unless they want to pay even more exorbitant "à la carte" prices for individual databases. The companies make it hard for consumers to carve out smaller contracts for just the materials they need.[87] Legal professionals and schools spend thousands of dollars on bloated law products pumped full of unnecessary data analytics tools. UCLA alone spent $340,000 on Westlaw and $250,000 on Lexis between 2015 and 2020, and significant chunks of law firm budgets go to Westlaw and Lexis subscriptions.[88]

Lexis and Westlaw have such firm strongholds on legal information that to break up their duopoly, we'd have to re-envision legal information access in the United States. Luckily, a group of legal scholars and practitioners are already working on projects that envision different, alternative legal information access models. An international coalition called the Free Access to Law Movement (FALM) is thinking about how to provide free, online access to legal information.[89] Cornell Legal Information Institute (LII) was the first open access product of the FALM movement. Today, Cornell LII serves over thirty million unique visitors each year as one of the main unpaywalled, comprehensive sources of legal information in the United States.

FALM members treat legal information like "digital common property" that should be accessible to everyone—the government edicts doctrine for an electronic era. U.S. law reflects FALM principles both in cases like *Georgia v. Public.Resource.Org*, and in public records laws like the Federal Records Act,[90] the Presidential Records Act,[91] and of course, the Freedom of Information Act.[92] These laws are meant to ensure that the federal government preserves, and provides access to, government records.

If we were serious about implementing the government edicts doctrine, we'd turn FALM principles into government policy, not just judicial dicta or aspirational (unfunded and unenforced) legislative language. Right now, FALM is a nongovernment movement. Cornell's LII and all of the other LIIs that serve as our primary, public legal information platforms cost money and require constant, consistent maintenance.[93] There needs to be a legislative mandate to create the legal information infrastructure and designate the staff needed to build and maintain it, and there needs to be a sufficient budget to put up authenticated versions of legal information and update that information regularly.[94]

Regarding information technology, the U.S. has always scraped by, budget-wise, investing a minimal amount of money and resources in informational infrastructure. The government has neglected to build national public centers for legal information, even though centralized, easy-to-navigate access to our laws is a basic public service that the government should provide.

There are laws that are meant to ensure access to government records, like the Federal Records Act (FRA) and the Freedom of Information Act (FOIA). They could be expanded and updated to cover electronic versions of our primary legal materials. The FRA tells the government how to manage its records.[95] It creates requirements for how government offices collect, preserve, and dispose of federal records. It works in tandem with the FOIA, which ensures access to the same records. Together, FRA and FOIA are like a lock-and-key system for our federal records: FRA secures federal records by ensuring they will be properly preserved and not thrown away, and FOIA is the tool the public can use to release the records and ensure government transparency. These government information preservation and access laws fall short because they only apply to agency records.[96] FOIA requires agencies to give the public agency records, but there's no law requiring anyone to provide laws, regulations, and court opinions.

The FRA and FOIA also fall short because they are outdated. The laws were written in the 1950s and 1960s, and they haven't been thoroughly overhauled for digital publishing, even though today most federal records are "born digital," created electronically and never printed to paper. Congress recognizes the waning utility of paper records. It advances bills that would banish paper versions of major federal publications, like the Federal Register,[97] and it moved FOIA records repositories from their physical library spaces to online "electronic reading rooms" decades ago.[98] But even though Congress has moved government publishing online, it hasn't sufficiently funded the government's online information infrastructure. Congress seems keen to eliminate the government's paper publications but less willing to invest in improving the government's digital publications.

Congress hasn't seriously entertained laws that would ensure online access to authenticated, up-to-date case law and statutes. The American Association of Law Libraries has convinced some states to adopt versions of the Uniform Electronic Legal Material Act (UELMA),[99] which guarantees access to authenticated legal information, but no federal law obligates U.S. courts and legislative bodies to provide continuous access to authenticated legal materials.

An updated FRA could expand the definition of "federal records" to cover the laws, including congressional and judicial records. The law could also require online preservation and consistent access to regulatory, judicial, and legislative records instead of just preserving agency records in paper *or* electronically. Because FOIA shares its definition of "federal records" with the FRA, changing the scope of what's considered a federal record in the FRA would also expand FOIA access to the same records. Amending the definition of federal records to something like "Records include all recorded information, regardless of form or characteristics, made or received by a federal agency, and *all sponsored bills and Acts of Congress, and opinions issued by U.S. Federal Courts*—" would go a long way towards creating access to the law.

If we wanted to fully implement the government edicts doctrine, we'd also push back when companies claim copyright to our laws. We'd make it impossible for data companies to privatize the law and keep it in walled gardens, away from the public. Instead, we'd treat legal information like a common, public good. Legal information access wouldn't be an exclusive experience that only some people can buy, like seeing Beyoncé at Coachella. It isn't enough to revive the government edicts doctrine, we need to see that it ensures digital access to every U.S. jurisdiction's court opinions, statutes, regulations, and constitutions, as well as the secondary explanations that we need to make sense of those legal declarations.

We'd also make sure the government was putting out open source versions of the law if we were serious about improving access to the law. If we wanted to invite more competition in the legal information market, we'd require courts and legislatures to provide copies of their judgments and legislation in "the best computerized form that they can produce" to anyone who wants to publish it.[100] If the law was open source, legal tech startups could innovate and compete in the legal information market, and the public could get copies of the law for free.

Until we change the law, we should welcome new legal information startups and stop enforcing the fallacy that Westlaw and Lexis are the only options for legal information access. We can support FALM organizations and new legal information platforms instead of clinging to the legal information duopoly's products. We can urge courts to accept "universal citations" instead of ones based on Westlaw or Lexis publications.[101] The legal profession is steeped in tradition and slow to change, but we can make decisions, as individuals, about where to search for our legal information and we can push for public access to the laws we have a right to access.

5

FINANCIAL INFORMATION

C HAPTERS 3 AND 4 COVERED "publisher-grade" information—
information written by scholars, lawmakers, or other experts. Financial data is somewhere in between the unstructured personal
data dossiers that the data analytics companies sell and that "publisher-
grade" information. The term "financial data" can mean different things:
people use the phrase to describe data about our personal finances, and
they also use it to describe data about financial opportunities. This chapter
focuses on the latter type of data: information and data about companies,
industries, and stock market trends—the types of information that help
people make savvy investments.[1] Data analytics companies sell the raw
financial data (stock prices, market trends, data derived from companies'
annual reports), but they also sell financial information, compiled and
aggregated into "insights" that tell investors where to put their money and
help investors and banks avoid financial risks. Companies like Bloomberg
L.P., LexisNexis, and Refinitiv Eikon—which was until recently a Thomson Reuters company—claim to "connect the world's decision makers
to accurate information on the financial markets and help them make
faster, smarter decisions"[2] and to prevent financial risks by "identify[ing]
fraudsters."[3]

The data analytics companies provide the same kind of gauzy descriptions of their financial data products and services as they provide for their other "risk" products. Instead of clearly explaining what their financial products do or how they work, companies like RELX and Bloomberg L.P. say that they will "let you make critical business decisions with confidence and speed" without describing which decisions they mean, or how their products make those decisions. Because good financial information is hard to find, people who make financial decisions pay a premium for financial data analytics products. These data products are as integral to finance professionals as the companies' legal information products are to lawyers. Just as "there [was] no law" when Westlaw went down, financial operations all over the world "ground to a halt" when Bloomberg went offline for a few hours in 2017.[4]

While people treat resources such as Refinitiv and Bloomberg like crystal balls that foresee the financial future, the companies make their financial insights the same way they make their other risk insights—they process a slurry of data and information scraped from SEC filings and other public records or drawn from stock price updates and financial news through their machine-learning and algorithmic software and systems. Their data analytics claim to list the riskiest investments and identify emerging industry trends using data-crunching technology, telling financiers what to do, but they are vulnerable to the same shortcomings as the other data analytics products.

As we've seen, in these massive data analytics systems, there are no errorless sets of data or perfectly unbiased algorithms. Financial data isn't some magical exception to the biases and data quality problems that pervade the other data analytics products. Truly, we don't know how reliable the financial data analytics products are. They are created inside the companies and they don't go out for peer review like academic research. Nor are they externally issued official decrees from the government, like laws are. And unlike personal data dossiers, financial data dossiers aren't about humans, they are about markets that can't complain when their data dossiers are mistaken. In fact, the financial data products are so heavily used by major financial forces that we probably can't even tell when financial data analytics are wrong. Even if their predictions are flawed, the analyses are adopted by so many banks and investing firms that they're self-correcting—they become truthful as they're followed by all of the forces that shape the market. The financial information products aren't powerful because they're right, they're powerful because they tell the financial sector what to do, and the financial sector listens. They're not just predictive, they're self-fulfilling financial prophesies.

We rely on financial information to make decisions about how to invest our money, whether it's choosing a retirement plan or avoiding risky investments. Like picking a restaurant in an unfamiliar town or buying a car, we can't make good financial decisions in a vacuum. We need information about the options and help in picking the best one. People who have more access to financial data ultimately make greater financial gains. As famous investor Peter Lynch explained, "If you don't study any companies, you have the same success buying stocks as you do in a poker game if you bet without looking at your cards."[5]

In a world where finance seems like alchemy, it's difficult to figure out which financial information is safe to rely on when you're trying to save or invest your money. Back in the 1700s, economist Adam Smith described finance as an "invisible hand" that distributes wealth. Financial information and data help make the "invisible hand" visible by predicting markets' ebbs and flows and providing rationales for why they're happening. That's why people call financial information services like Bloomberg L.P.'s the lifeblood of the financial world.[6]

The gulf between what financial data subscribers and the general public know about finances is an "information asymmetry," or an "information failure." Information asymmetries perpetuate inequality in economic transactions. Financial information asymmetry is like other social asymmetries: creating inequality and hardship for some in order to benefit a few others.[7] Money is a social construct, a system humans made to determine who gets what. While some social functions like convening meetings or ordering goods and services have been simplified online, monetary systems have grown more complex through datafication.

Over the last hundred years, finances have become less connected to tangible, material goods and more "informationalized."[8] We started investing not in tangible objects, but in intangible corporate profits by purchasing stocks and bonds. Then the stock market moved from physical trading floors to datafied, online trading. The relationships between humans, financial instruments, and goods themselves has become increasingly distant and unclear. Today, stocks seem more like obscure, virtual financial ideas instead of physically tangible dollars or stock certificates. Law professor Julie Cohen explains that digitization has made the idea of money both "increasingly notional" and "increasingly detached from the real-world activities that it was designed to enable."[9] This detachment has put an informational wedge between most people, who have varying degrees of resources and sophistication, and the rarified world of stockbrokers, hedge funders, and other Wall Street financiers with a wealth of financial information on their desktops.[10] That complexity has only increased information asymmetry—people with access to financial information products are the only ones who can figure out what's going on as the financial industry becomes more abstract.

Financial data analytics that explain the value of stocks and investments might seem cutting edge, but financial data services aren't new. We've been transmitting financial data since stock prices were sent by telegraph and printed out on paper strips. The ticker symbol codes we use to identify publicly traded companies are a relic of a centuries-old financial data system, made to fit on telegraph tape, the earliest mass-communication technology for financial information. As in the legal information industry, there used to be mom-and-pop financial data companies that compiled and provided structured access to SEC filings and corporate overviews.

Financial data also isn't rare. There's plenty of information about companies and market trends online. But the best financial information is consolidated within the walled gardens of just a few data analytics enterprises. As in the other informational markets, many of the specialized financial information services have been acquired by the data analytics companies. Data companies like RELX and Thomson Reuters were among the first to develop robust financial data collections. Just as RELX's Elsevier cornered the academic market by being the first to publish academic journals and platform them online, and RELX's Lexis was the first to develop case law databases, Lexis was also first to provide a digital search-and-retrieve system for the SEC's digital financial disclosure system, EDGAR (Electronic Data Gathering, Analysis and Retrieval).[11] In addition to getting in early, RELX has been able to acquire a host of smaller financial data companies.[12] Lexis sells financial information and also uses its financial data company acquisitions to bolster its "risk" business, building tools that root out fraud and other financial malfeasance.

Bloomberg L.P. similarly cornered the financial data market by being the first to sell a real-time financial data service to finance firms. In the 1980s, Michael Bloomberg used his investment banker know-how to invent a computer terminal to help people simplify and make sense of financial information.[13] Today, Bloomberg has carved out its niche, dominating the financial information market. The company's double monitors and chunky, rainbow-colored-keyboards are the "sun" that powers the financial solar system, a fixture in Wall Street firms.[14] These products are the only way to "mainline real-time market data."[15]

The prices for these financial data platforms are steep, costing thousands of dollars a month.[16] Bloomberg is for wealthy bankers, not for the public. Its extra features—restaurant reviews, vacation advice, and entertainment news—are "optimized for the 1% of the 1% looking to blow some of the wealth they have just extracted from their fellow man."[17] Financial institutions and corporations pay billions of dollars, collectively, to get premium financial information.[18] The investment in information is worthwhile, because financial information is especially hard to parse. Unlike with other information markets, it's not hard for the public to find free financial information online. There is plenty of financial information floating around, but a lot of that information is speculative, unverified, and out of step with the information that the market movers are getting on their subscription services. The information is also packed with financial and legal jargon that makes it hard to understand.

Access to financial information is so important that we've had laws guaranteeing it for over a century. Like legal information, financial information is not supposed to be subscription-only. States passed laws requiring businesses to share financial updates as early as 1911. The laws were written in an era when new printing innovations and transportation methods were making it easy for speculators to pass through towns, luring people to invest in fraudulent ventures, and mailing mass-produced allur-ing ads for speculative investments to people's homes.[19] The state laws were called "blue sky laws" because they were meant to enlighten consumers presented with risky schemes having "no more basis than so many feet of blue sky."[20] Kansas was the first state to pass a blue sky law. It's little surprise that, in the same era, Kansas was depicted as a place where the Wizard of Oz could roll through town selling crystal ball fortunes and fake elixirs to farmers and their families.[21]

In the 1930s, financial disasters led the federal government to pass sim-ilar financial disclosure laws. Without access to substantive financial in-formation, unfounded gossip caused bank panics and intensified financial depressions.[22] National events made people worry about money: farmers couldn't sell their crops,[23] gold prospectors' booms were turning into busts as surface gold dwindled,[24] and "paper railroads"—speculative railroad plans without proper funding—left investors empty handed. As people heard rumors about missing gold, failing railroad deals, and bankrupted farmers, they began to worry about their own investments. Stories swirled about banks folding and business ventures in peril, and people stopped trusting the financial system. Without knowing whether their accounts and investments were safe, everyone rushed to withdraw their funds from financial institutions. The Great Depression, the biggest economic crash in U.S. history, was spurred by a "contagion of fear."[25]

1930s-era legislators sought to prevent market upheaval by making fi-nancial information publicly accessible. New securities laws were meant to prevent financial panics by providing the public with plenty of financial information.[26] The first securities law the federal government passed, the Securities Act of 1933, was nicknamed the Truth in Securities Act.[27] The Act required publicly traded companies to publish financial disclosures.[28] The Securities and Exchange Act of 1934 ensured more market transpar-ency, creating the SEC, an agency tasked with making sure public com-panies and markets operate transparently.[29] Today, the SEC is one of our most powerful financial information agencies.

Economists have identified the phenomenon of financial "information cascades," herd-like behavior in which groups of people react to outside information by taking an identical action, simultaneously and swiftly.[30]

Like animal herds stampeding when they hear a loud sound, people will stampede banks to withdraw their money when they hear worrisome financial gossip, or pour their money into shady investments when they hear about potential windfalls. In one recent information cascade, commenters on the social media platform Reddit convinced droves of people to dump millions of dollars into stocks from failing businesses including GameStop and AMC Theaters. Spurred by word of mouth, millions of people invested their money on the basis of posts from armchair financiers trying to imitate hedge funds.[31] Ill-informed investors lost their lifesavings when stock prices crashed.[32]

The best way to stop information cascades is with corrective information. Once people know which banks and investments are safe, they can regain trust in financial institutions and the financial system starts working again. That's why today's policymakers use information campaigns to restore confidence in banking systems when they struggle.[33] Investing and banking are trust exercises—we hand over our savings to institutions with the promise that they'll protect our finances. It's no surprise that, during historic financial downturns, people hid their money under mattresses and in coffee cans. They even carried their entire savings in their wallet instead of participating in banking systems.[34] Financial disclosure laws don't just protect consumers from fly-by-night business ventures, they also protect our faith-driven financial system from collapsing.[35]

Since the 1930s Congress has infused even more financial information access into our laws, reacting to modern information cascade-driven crises and also to situations in which corporations hid important information from the public. For instance, Congress made more financial transparency requirements after companies such as Enron and WorldCom caused financial catastrophes by hiding their bad financial realities from investors.[36] After the 2008 mortgage crisis, which happened because people weren't told about the risks associated with their home loans, Congress created the Consumer Financial Protection Bureau (CFPB) to help consumers understand financial instruments and investments.[37]

Agencies like the CFPB recognize that financial information access isn't just a matter of protecting the financial industry—it is also important for protecting consumers. Bad financial actors can use the lack of free-flowing public financial data as a tool to hide scams and to grift from the public. Bad hunches and hot financial tips can come from "stream[s] polluted at the source."[38] People who can't access financial information are easy marks for predatory financial schemes.

Financial information access is also a necessary part of repairing systemic discrimination that pervades financial systems. Financial information inequality is part of systemic financial discrimination. The same redlining practices that historically deprived Black people from home ownership are now used to deprive people of color from access to credit and investments. When Congress passed the Equal Credit Opportunity Act in 1974, it recognized that not only do investors vary, the ways they are treated by lenders and investment banks vary.[39] It is harder for minority entrepreneurs to invest in ventures and to start their own successful businesses because they can't access the financial information resources they need.[40]

Unfortunately for consumers, the financial information guarantees in securities laws have been weakened over time. Financial institutions have used their lobbying and legal powers to bend statutory language and regulatory interpretation to withhold information.[41] Companies have also figured out ways to hide information in their financial disclosures. Their SEC disclosures have snowballed into hefty tomes. Between 1950 and 2004, Fortune 500 companies' annual reports grew from around 16 pages to over 165 pages.[42] Ford's 2019 10-K is 182 pages long.[43] Much of the content in these hundreds of pages is irrelevant, redundant, and trivial. Filings like these leave readers sorting through haystacks of financial jargon to find the nuggets of actionable information.[44] The lawyers who draft financial disclosures don't help make these disclosures more clear. Companies have been known to paint positive pictures of their finances for investors even as they're sinking in bad deals and rising debt.[45] The government mandates companies to disclose investment risks to the public, but company lawyers have found ways to describe risks that make them seem less worrisome or embarrassing. It's easy for people without more interpretive tools to miss seeing the companies' true financial pictures by reading SEC reports.[46]

The voluminous company records also don't help us invest more wisely. Most of us can't read through two-hundred-page financial reports, making sense of all of the financial jargon and legalese, to figure out which companies to invest in, even if we're given a list of good options. But experts say that to make reasonable investments, people must read and comprehend "all the noise and signals in the marketplace that encapsulate formal disclosures, economic data, market trends, senseless speculation, and irresponsible rumors."[47] This means that, without the help of specialized information services, most of us aren't reasonable investors equipped to participate in financial markets.

Companies' financial information hasn't just grown more voluminous, it's also grown more complex. Historically, the United States has supported complicated, speculative investments because they can be used to finance big projects like railroads and wars. The nation's most ambitious projects were built on financial risk and national investments. This acceptance of risky investment schemes has become embedded in our digital ecosystem.[48] As with other types of information, digitization and datafication have made financial information far more complex than its analog predecessors. Today's financial data is not as straightforward as printed balance sheets and stock price updates in the daily paper.[49] Investment portfolios and market trends are depicted on complicated spreadsheets, line charts, and other jargon-filled interactive data visualization tools.

Datafication has also made investing itself more complex. Financial institutions have been able to use data analytics products and forecasting models to create more complicated "exotic" financial instruments and schemes (versus traditional "vanilla" schemes). The subprime mortgage crisis showed how opaque, complex financial instruments can hurt consumers. Loan companies and investment bankers invented obscure financial instruments to sell people's debts. By the early 2000s, lenders were routinely bundling mortgages, credit card debt, student debt, and car loans into securities to sell to investors.[50] As debt became more profitable for rich investors, lenders convinced more and more people to take on risky mortgage arrangements. Mortgage delinquencies soared, the housing market crashed, and people lost their homes and the money they'd invested in them.[51] While many of us can explain the mortgage crisis in broad, sweeping terms (like my own explanation in this paragraph), few of us understand how the actual asset-backed securities that caused the crisis work.

Datafication has also made investing harder to keep up with. Investing has gotten much faster in our digital ecosystem. The financial system we built in a pre-internet world has sped up to a pace that the naked eye cannot follow. Without the high-speed, real-time data platforms, most people can't track financial investments. People with the right kind of data access can make lightning-fast stock trades, and they can see market changes before the general public sees them.[52] Online trading has become such a rapid-fire activity that it is virtually impossible for someone who lacks the best data and technology to get ahead in financial dealings. In 2012, financial journalist Scott Patterson predicted a new financial hierarchy based on who owns the most powerful data systems[53]—a decade later Patterson's prediction has come true.[54] Digital trading tools have created a "shadow banking sector" that only some people can see.[55]

Financial information is so fast-moving and complex that merely putting SEC filings or stock prices online doesn't make financial information "accessible." The SEC's EDGAR system posts information online, but it doesn't make the information any easier to sift through or understand. Unlike the judiciary's PACER system, EDGAR is free to use, but it contains over ten million records—an overwhelming amount of information for even the most skilled investor.[56] EDGAR contributes to a digital financial information glut. It doesn't break down hundred-page filings into easy-to-parse pieces or compare companies to one another with the click of a button. It doesn't warn about negative filings or bump the best investment bets to the top of the list. It's hard to search and slow to update.[57] EDGAR may provide a "common pool of knowledge" but it doesn't fulfill its goal of guaranteeing that "individual investors are not at an informational disadvantage to institutional investors and securities offerers."[58] EDGAR's public access can't compete with the subscription financial information services. On EDGAR, "The common user and particularly the retail investor are overwhelmed by the deluge of information, not empowered."[59] The differences between free resources like EDGAR and subscription platforms like Bloomberg and Refinitiv divide financial information access into a two-tiered scheme: one tier for the public, and another for wealthy people who can afford Lexis, Refinitiv, or Bloomberg L.P. services. Like clothing, automobiles, and other types of goods, financial data ranges from high-end, designer data to low-end, "off-the-rack" information. Nonprofessional investors who invest their own money are "retail investors" who get their information "off the rack," from public sources like cable news stations, social media and free other online content, and newspapers.

In contrast, the designer financial information services aggregate data across SEC filings with the push of a button. They can instantly provide up-to-date marketwide summaries and outlooks, comparing multiple companies clearly and easily. People with Bloomberg access can zip from one complex financial calculation to another, "running down a hunch and preparing to make a killing," by correlating data charts and news reports, splicing different pieces of information to find patterns and perceive changes, and exploiting information advantages "with overwhelming financial force."[60] If you have a Bloomberg or Refinitiv terminal, you can see up-to-the minute trading data and get explanatory overviews about companies and markets.

For investors without those informational resources, finances can seem as random as weather patterns seem to nonmeteorologists. It's hard to predict what markets will do, and it's hard to decide how to invest our money, without good, reliable information. Without equal access to financial information, people have wildly different perspectives on financial risks. Factors such as status, family history, ethnicity, religious and cultural beliefs, and historical racial discrimination color peoples' understandings of how finances work and shape their reasoning about what is a good deal and what is a bad deal. In an information vacuum, people are prone to making investment decisions based on their guts, Superbowl ads, and superstitions.[61] It's more likely to be "dumb money" (a term economists associate with retail investors) than "smart money" (the name given to institutional investors and market experts)—in 2012, the SEC said that most U.S. investors lack basic financial literacy.[62]

Not only do people not understand the markets, they also don't understand their own level of risk compared to the risk of the people they get their financial advice from. Financial risk for one person may not be a risk for someone else, depending on job status, geographical location, and debt history. Expertise also varies from person to person. Some laypeople are experts in certain financial areas, but not others. For instance, airline pilots familiar with the costs of jet fuel may be able to make predictions about aviation industry finances after seeing how many passengers are boarding their planes. They may regularly read airline trade magazines. This body of knowledge makes the airline pilot more savvy about aerospace markets than others. But that same pilot might know comparatively little about foreign markets, agriculture commodities, and other investment schemes.

None of us can understand the intricacies of every financial market without more information. We need help to navigate the complex, intertwined world of supply chains, global trends, and industry-specific quirks and practices that make markets rise and fall. Financial information services provide that help. They're maintained by "armies of research analysts, sophisticated forecasting models, and high-speed trading platforms."[63] People who can afford financial information services can wield their informational power like a "magic sword that turns mere wheeler-dealers into Masters of the Universe who execute trades with extreme prejudice." Data companies give users real-time market data for "anything anyone anywhere has ever done a deal in," breaking news and regulatory filings, industry reports, gossip, rumor, innuendo, propaganda, and "everything else that might possibly conceivably in some imaginable universe affect the price of something worth buying or selling."[64] People who can't afford to pay $24,000 a year or more for customized, tailor-made financial information have less reliable, less up-to-date information.

On the other side of the financial information scheme, "retail" financial information is often outdated by the time it's reported. By the time financial news appears on TV or gets printed in a paper, it's hardly a hot tip. Journalistic sources aren't the same as financial information sources. It takes time to edit, vet, and publish information on a public forum, and by the time a retail investor finds the results, it's old news. The public also gets limited information about businesses' financial futures from TV and other sources because CEOs can't give too much actionable, "forward looking" advice to the public.[65] Researchers who studied publicly available media on the Chinese stock market found that "[t]he actual information content of CEO interviews on CNBC is very low."[66]

Retail financial news information can also be less neutral than the data-based calculations and information that the subscription platforms sell. Analytics companies' products offer data-based information, not rosy personal outlooks from overenthusiastic reporters and pundits' opinion-based chit-chat. In financial information services, users can see minute-by-minute numbers and trends with few, if any, informational strings or ads attached. On the other hand, financial news provided by media conglomerates, peoples' blogs, and social media accounts can be biased by the motivations of their authors and publishers.

A twenty-four-hour news station's primary goal isn't to give great financial tips, it's to maintain constant viewer attention. They primarily want to entertain, not inform. CNBC wants to keep people tuned in to their station so companies keep paying for ads. They exaggerate and prolong financial news stories to hold your attention. Financial newscasters want to "keep you at the edge of your seat" with financial cliffhangers, so you return for more. Creating financial drama makes consumers overreact to "every little hiccup in the market," churning their portfolios and making speculative investments instead of investing for the long haul and accumulating wealth.[67]

Turning financial information into entertainment can decrease its quality. "Fake news" pervades financial papers and shows.[68] Televised pundits can substitute their opinions and guesses for facts, giving the public bad information without repercussion. CNBC pundit Jim Cramer told his viewers to invest in internet companies right before the dot-com bubble burst,[69] and he promised people that "Bear Stearns is not in trouble" and told them, "Don't move your money from Bear" right before the investment bank collapsed.[70] Despite the misinformation he spreads, Jim Cramer is entertaining, so CNBC keeps his show on the air.

Another informational problem with for-profit media companies creating financial news is that the media companies are beholden to advertisers. When TV stations depend on certain companies' ad revenue, reporting on those companies could be biased. If publishing depends on advertising, the two—advertising and reporting—can become intertwined. Advertisers can find ways to infiltrate media. Product placement pervades modern televisions shows and movies.[71] That same advertising sentiment can also sink into financial news sources and television shows. For instance, research shows that CNBC gives more airtime to CEOs whose companies buy more ads.[72]

Sometimes free financial information is actually advertising with little, if any, truth or value. Financial services companies like The Motley Fool

plant clickbait on news websites to lure customers with get-rich-quick promises. Stories with headlines like "This Stock Could be Like Buying Amazon
in 1997" exaggerate financial promises to prey on people with less market
savvy and experience.[73] These investment advice ads are especially fraught
for people vulnerable to scams and clickbait, including older adults.[74]

As the public takes its chances using retail-grade financial information,
financial data analytics platforms have created a safe, walled-garden space
for companies and investors to play with financial data and instruments.[75]
In the mortgage crisis, investment bankers were able to create and test out
risky securities on private financial data platforms, beyond the regulators'
purview.[76] By doing this type of experimenting and dealing on nongovernmental, third-party platforms, financiers can escape public oversight.
When Congress passed the first financial information access laws in the
1930s, legislators said that there can't be honest markets without honest
publicity because dishonest marketplace practices thrive on "mystery and
secrecy."[77] Third-party financial information platforms have re-created
secret financial spaces in our digital ecosystems. The only people who can
watch what happens on subscription-access financial platforms are the
other subscribers.[78]

Walled-garden financial information platforms also help isolate
wealth, preventing its spread to those not able to afford entry. The wealthy
have walled off their enclaves since the beginning of time. Robert Moses
purposely made bridges on Long Island, New York's Southern State Parkway so low that buses from the city couldn't get to the posh, suburban
beaches, and the rules of tennis were purposely obscure so only royalty
could follow them.[79] Today's digital walls cordon off spaces where wealthy
people can accrue more wealth without interlopers. Financial data platforms are digital gated communities. Less open access to financial information means that "relatively little lending takes place outside of close-kin
networks."[80] In some ways, the data analytics companies have figured out
how to paywall not just access to information about money, but access to
money itself.

This walled garden is, perhaps, the most harmful aspect of the private
financial information companies. Access to financial data can improve our
fortunes and drive upward mobility. People with more financial information have more financial opportunities. In one especially sinister example,

as a U.S. senator, Kelly Loeffler was able to use special information from congressional meetings with health experts about the Covid pandemic. She dumped millions of dollars worth of stocks in companies doomed by the pandemic and invested in teleworking companies like Citrix and DuPont, a company that makes protective gear and body bags.[81]

On the other side of the wealth spectrum, people excluded from the walled garden have fewer financial opportunities and successes. A 2017 study found that in the United States, "financial knowledge is a key determinant of wealth inequality."[82] People who can pay for financial information live wealthier lives. They get to retire earlier, and they have more money when they retire. In a nation where only 14 percent of families are directly invested in the stock market, most peoples' only connection to stock markets is through their retirement accounts.[83] Wealth inequality spiked when workers' unions replaced their professionally managed pension plans with plans that forced people to make their own investment choices.[84] Workers who could afford to invest in financial literacy or hire financial experts had more information, so they amassed more wealth. They ended up "holding very different amounts of retirement wealth" than their less informationally enriched counterparts.[85]

Walled-garden financial information platforms helped a few people with a lot of information to consolidate most of the nation's wealth, taking advantage of flash trading, cryptocurrency gambits, exotic financial instruments, and hedging schemes that were impossible without fast-moving, plentiful financial data. Financial opportunities in the United States are plucked up by just a fraction of Americans, who tend to be older, affluent, and white.[86] The wealthiest 10 percent of U.S. households own 87 percent of all stocks and mutual funds.[87] While the majority of Americans' finances are invested in their homes, the top 1 percent of wealthy people can invest much more broadly across the market.[88]

With all of the inequality they sow, financial data analytics platforms haven't gotten much government attention or oversight. There has been a lot of congressional work to make financial information more transparent, but that work has focused on ensuring corporations disclose their own financial outlooks, not on ensuring access to financial data created by third parties. In the 1930s, Congress turned consumers' information-seeking burdens into companies' information-sharing obligations. The federal government does require third-party financial information providers that also give advice and ratings, like stockbrokers, financial advisors, and credit bureaus, to disclose certain types of information. For instance, credit rating companies have to disclose their methodologies to the public.[89] But Congress hasn't accounted for third-party financial data analytics companies walling off premium financial information from the public. Without transparency requirements for data companies like Bloomberg L.P., Refinitiv, and LexisNexis over the years, information asymmetry has increased, as their analytics methods have remained as mysterious as ever, even though Congress has updated its 1930s-era disclosure laws and the SEC has passed supplementary regulations plenty of times.

Meanwhile, investors have become so reliant on commercial financial information products that the data companies can provide space for questionable schemes and practices. There are regulations to prevent insider trading (using nonpublic financial information to make decisions about buying and selling stock). But there are no rules that make it illegal for financial information companies to disclose information before it goes public.[90] That means data companies can control the flow of financial information in ways that even the publicly traded companies themselves can't. In 2013, Thomson Reuters was investigated by the State of New York after it prereleased consumer sentiment data to the University of Michigan and other clients who paid extra for early information.[91] The company said that the practice of providing "exclusive" information is a normal practice, infusing news reporting logic (where "exclusives" and "scoops" *are* normal practice) into its financial data service, where "exclusive" early information gives certain people insider information to help them game investing systems.

The data analytics companies can also spy on their investment bank users, invading their customers' privacy to glean business information content. In the same year that Thomson Reuters sold information before it went public, Bloomberg News reporters were caught snooping on investment bankers' activities on their Bloomberg terminals.[92] Bloomberg reporters spied on JPMorgan Chase executives as they used their Bloomberg terminals to learn more about what the bank was up to and to predict what might happen in financial markets on the basis of that information.

As a first step to improving public access to high-quality financial information, economists and accountants have suggested that companies' financial information should be regarded as a public resource, in the same way that legal information is supposed to be treated.[93] Like our laws, our financial markets are shaped by the public's investments, and financial information belongs to all of us. Even though most of us don't buy and sell stocks directly, the dollars that flow into our retirement funds, the loans we take, and our other financial activities determine how the markets behave. Our labor and our purchasing decisions fuel the companies and make them accountable to us. The companies' financial information isn't created with our tax dollars, but the markets depend on our labor and spending. Also, because transparency is so important for preventing market failures, such as crashes, bank runs, depressions, and bubbles, it benefits everyone to prevent financial crises by supplying access to financial information.

Financial information should also be publicly accessible to balance the information asymmetries between banks, billion-dollar corporations, and people. The financial chasm between the 1 percent of us who run huge companies like Amazon or Facebook and the vast majority of us who work paycheck to paycheck has been laid bare in the last decade. Wealth inequality is so stark that companies are as powerful as the government. Corporations like Starbucks and Apple have economies larger than entire nations. Walmart's economy is the tenth-largest in the world, larger than Spain's and Australia's economies.[94] With their financial power, private companies have become so entrenched in policymaking that people wonder, "Are we sure the United States isn't just Raytheon, Boeing and Chevron in a trenchcoat?"[95] If these companies are forming our policies and rules, we deserve to see what they are doing. Financial information access helps us understand what powerful companies are up to.[96]

But putting SEC filings on EDGAR is insufficient to truly create access to financial information. To make sure that financial information is accessible to everyone, we can't assume that everyone understands companies' financial summaries. The current financial disclosure laws assume investors can understand and act on the disclosed information as soon as they get it. Courts use a "reasonable investor" standard to decide whether financial information access is sufficient, but a diversity of investors has a diversity of perspectives, so what is financially "reasonable" varies widely from case to case.[97] Investors are not homogenous. As business law professor Tom C. W. Lin puts it, "In the sea of investors, not all investors are minnows. There are minnows swimming with sharks, whales, and a host of other species."[98] Even with rules that ensure nobody is getting early information, certain investors will invariably have more access, more information, more fluency, and more capabilities than other investors. They also have more access. Professor Lin writes, "The chief executive officer of Apple would not meet with the average investor who is concerned about the company's policies, but he would meet with a sophisticated activist investor like Carl Icahn if that investor expressed similar concerns."[99]

In an ideal financial information ecosystem, private companies wouldn't run the only user-friendly financial data systems. Bloomberg L.P., LexisNexis, and Thomson Reuters financial data products would run alongside a robust public financial data platform. Our government could dedicate budget and infrastructure to transform EDGAR into a dynamic system that would let the public parse and analyze SEC disclosures. Alternatively, Congress could authorize spending for a public version of Bloomberg, Refinitiv, or some other financial data platform. As another law professor, Professor Henry Hu, explains, the same tech innovations that cause financial information to be more complex could also make them more accessible.[100]

Modern SEC disclosure could provide more of the functionality that private data companies already provide. All investors should be able not just to see SEC filings—they should be given the tools to understand what the filings mean. Economic historian Robert E. Wright says that if there's one thing history has made clear, it's that reducing information asymmetry in financial markets is imperative to ensure more widespread economic growth.[101]

6

NEWS

THE LAST MARKET THIS BOOK will cover is the news information market. Like personal data, scholarly research, legal information, and financial data, the news is simultaneously a special type of critical information that has its own standards and practices, and material that can be reduced to digitized content stored in data companies' files. News, timely information about things happening in the world,[1] is both an essential public information resource and fodder for data analytics software and tools. Like legal and scholarly research, news content is an information-rich ingredient that can be combined with other datasets to create predictions and advice for all sorts of consumers.

News information lies at the foundation of informational content in every society. Even before there were written words and printing presses, people would convey news information through dances and songs.[2] Telling people about current events has always been a primary informational goal. Since ancient times, humans have broadcasted news ranging from social concerns ("Did you hear how poorly Aristogeiton treated Zobia?"[3]) to pressing dangers ("There's a lion!"). Countries all over the world support robust public news systems.[4] Public news systems (so long as they are unbiased)[5] are central parts of information infrastructures in healthy democracies.[6] People tend to trust public news sources over private ones. For instance, British people are more likely to call the BBC their main news source regardless of their political leanings.[7] National Public Radio (NPR) and the Public Broadcasting Service (PBS) are the most trusted news sources in the United States.[8]

News is such a fundamental type of information that it's a "hugely profitable" information sector.[9] It's no surprise that the data analytics companies have long been in the news business. Reed (the "R" in RELX) started as a newsprint company,[10] and both Thomson Corporation and Reuters Group were also news enterprises.[11] Today, Thomson Reuters runs Reuters news, a large-scale international news agency with hundreds of journalists reporting from at least two hundred locations. RELX doesn't have its own news company, but it partners with specialty news services such as legal news provider American Lawyer Media.[12] RELX also maintains Nexis, a huge digital archive that contains over four hundred thousand news sources going back almost half a century.[13] The company claims that Nexis is the "largest set of aggregated news sources available."[14] Whether that claim is true or not, any high school or college debate team can tell you that the news offerings are robust—LexisNexis is debaters' go-to resource for finding relevant news articles for every conceivable world issue or policy topic.[15]

The transition from paper to digital information systems has changed the news information market like it's changed the other informational markets. But changes in the news industry have felt more drastic than changes in the legal or scholarly information markets.[16] When we switched from getting academic journals and case law in print to accessing those materials on digital platforms, the changes happened without much fanfare—publishers added a new database here and created a fancier search function there, until most of their informational products were only available online and they stopped calling themselves publishers and renamed themselves as data companies.

In contrast, the transformation from print news to digital media has felt more extreme. Journalists themselves use words like "disaster" and "carnage" to describe the collapse of news companies.[17] In less than a decade, the U.S. newspaper industry lost more than 50 percent of its employees. Those losses were concentrated in smaller cities, towns, and rural communities, leaving hundreds of those communities without access to local news. Remaining news companies have become prey for hedge funds that buy them and sell them for parts, and hosts for clickbait companies that use the companies' platforms to disguise their ads as news information.[18] Consolidated, international news giants put local public news services out of business, leaving barren "news deserts" in places they decide aren't financially worth serving.[19]

One reason the transition from paper, radio, and TV news sources to digital ones has been so destructive is that the U.S. government hasn't maintained its support for public media infrastructure online. The government used to subsidize paper, radio, and televised news services. One of the first things George Washington did when he established the U.S. postal system was to make sure that newspapers would be sent at a discounted rate. Washington saw access to news as crucial for an informed electorate.[20] For centuries, the federal government continued Washington's support for public news, subsidizing newspaper postage rates by overcharging for letter postage or by borrowing from the U.S. treasury. But when Congress transformed the United States Postal Service into a self-funding agency, the subsidies for newspaper delivery shrank.[21]

Support for other public news sources similarly waned over time. Public radio and television started with financial support from the federal government with the goal of providing free educational and news information to the public. The Public Broadcasting Act of 1967 established the Corporation for Public Broadcasting to ensure that local public news and educational programming would be available on every television in the United States.[22] NPR was launched soon after, providing educational, noncommercial radio broadcasting at the low end of the FM radio dial.[23] But as the federal government embraced the Chicago School's free market approach to public services in the 1970s, government support for public news dwindled. The government encouraged private companies to replace public news programs with privately run news services.

Public news was federally protected to prevent the very types of information monopolies described throughout this book, and without those protections, news monopolies flourished. In the 1930s, before government intervention in the news market, radio was quickly overtaken by media monopolists. After radio's mass privatization, only 2 percent of the radio market was run by nonprofit broadcasters.[24] Legislators saw how swiftly the radio waves were taken over by a single company and wanted to prevent that type of market dominance. When televisions became common, Congress continued to protect space for nonprofit news sources on the new device. Congress passed the All-Channel Receiver Act of 1962, which required television manufacturers to make TVs that could receive UHF channels for public service media access,[25] and companies were only allowed to own a limited number of television stations.[26]

Subsidized news from paper, radio, and television sources made news access the norm in the United States. For decades, the federal government kept renewing its support of public news access. President Lyndon Johnson compared public, nonprofit media to the marketplace in ancient Greece, saying that public media was a modern way to guarantee that public affairs would take place "in view of all the citizens."[27] Public news was a go-to source of information during some of the nation's most politically fraught moments. People all over the nation tuned in to their local public television stations to get news about the Watergate Scandal from Robert MacNeil and Jim Lehrer, and National Public Radio covered Vietnam War protests as they unfolded, providing the public with access to historic civil unrest.[28]

But the heyday of government-supported news access stopped with the internet. Instead of bringing a public access ethos into the digital broadcasting era, President Bill Clinton weakened rules that protected public media access and local news. The Telecommunications Act of 1996 overhauled the Communications Act of 1934 under the guise of encouraging the growth of internet enterprises. When the law was passed, Clinton's FCC allowed single companies to take over multiple media sources in a single region instead of protecting local news providers.[29] These policies were meant to spur financial success among new digital companies by removing limits on where, or how much, they could consolidate and grow their media enterprises.[30] Clinton wanted U.S. companies to take advantage of new ventures like digital radio and television, unfettered by limitations written into pre-internet laws.

The 1996 law opened up opportunities for digital companies to expand, but it sacrificed smaller, nonprofit news companies to promote that expansion. The government put its faith in the private companies dominating the "free market," dropping interventions and safeguards that supported public media. The same federal government that subsidized newspaper delivery and supported public news offerings on radio and television to promote a national "marketplace of ideas" didn't subsidize or support public access to news information online.[31]

The 1996 law failed to recognize that informational monopolies were just as likely to overtake news markets in the 1990s as they were in the 1920s. When the government stopped treating news and educational media as a public good, massive telecommunications consolidation ensued.[32] Without regulatory limits, a few media corporations quickly became national media giants. In 1983, over fifty corporations ran America's televised news media, but by 2000, only five corporations owned most U.S. news media stations: Time Warner, Disney, Murdoch's News Corporation, Bertelsmann of Germany, and Viacom.[33] There are also only five major newspaper companies in the United States: the *New York Times* is owned by the publicly held New York Times Corporation, the *Washington Post* is owned by the publicly held Washington Post Company, and the *Chicago Tribune* and *Los Angeles Times* are both owned by the Tribune Company. Hearst Publications owns twelve newspapers including the *San Francisco Chronicle*, as well as magazines, television stations, and cable and interactive media.[34]

Meanwhile, National Public Radio is straining to stay afloat as corporate underwriting wanes. The company is being forced to cancel shows and pare down reporting. At this point, the government only supports 1 percent of NPR's funding, leading people to wonder whether it can even be considered "public" radio.[35] Without government support, declining ad revenue is the most serious threat to news.[36] Between 2000 and 2015, print newspaper ad revenue dropped from $60 billion to $20 billion a year. In 2020, NPR predicted that pandemic losses would cut $12 million to $15 million in ad revenue from the radio service's budget. PBS similarly struggled without guaranteed access to U.S. airwaves. By 2009, the UHF stations that Congress fought for in the 1960s were no longer protected, and most television stations had been replaced by digital television services. Now *Sesame Street*, one of our most beloved PBS programs, is only available on the subscription service HBO.

This type of informational paywalling is like the paywalls data companies put around legal and scholarly information. When private, for-profit companies control critical information we rely on, they'll charge a premium for it knowing that many of us will have no choice but to pay to get the information we need. News paywalls are ubiquitous on the platforms we've talked about in this book. It's no surprise that Reuters is planning to make its news service a paywalled, subscription-only platform.[37]

Privatizing news products moves the locus of control for news information from journalistic institutions to private tech and data companies. It's the same phenomenon that's happened in the other informational markets: private companies swoop in and take over information infrastructure that the public fails to adequately support. When the government didn't provide high-quality access to academic research, financial information, and law codification, the data companies figured out how to privatize and monetize the public information resources. Likewise, when data companies control news, they don't treat it like a public good. They treat it like a source of profit.

When private companies run news access, there's also no guarantee they'll preserve news for the public records when their business folds. When the online news website Gothamist closed up shop, the paper's stories disappeared and years of reporting were gone, erased from the internet.[38] Even the stories' authors couldn't get access to their own work. When news is privatized, access is never guaranteed. Stories that were once public can be privatized in news archives by companies like LexisNexis, EBSCO, and ProQuest that "hoover up a digital feed from the news organization, store the information in a database, and then license packages of such databases to libraries."[39] To data companies, news is just another form of "content" meant to make viewers buy subscriptions and log on to their services.

Unfortunately, as with financial information, legal materials, and scientific research, when high-quality information is paywalled, low-quality information is all the public can see. Free news tends to be less reliable because high-quality news is expensive. Fake news is cheap. "It costs money to produce good writing, to run a website, to license photographs. A *lot* of money, if you want quality."[40] Good reporting requires trained journalists, financially supported media platforms, and enough money for investigation, fact-checking, and other journalistic tools and resources.

Consolidating news sources under for-profit umbrellas isn't just inconvenient and polarizing, it's dangerous. Local news providers cannot compete with national newspaper companies, digital radio giants, and huge twenty-four-hour news companies like CNN, MSNBC, and Fox.[41] But national, for-profit news corporations don't cover local stories and events. Sometimes, local news updates are necessary to warn people about public catastrophes.

When weather risks like tornadoes loom, or toxic spills happen, getting quick, local news is imperative for public safety. On January 18, 2002, a small city in North Dakota experienced firsthand how risky life can be without local news. At around 1:00 a.m., a freight train carrying hazardous anhydrous ammonia slid from fractured tracks west of Minot, North Dakota, sending clouds of toxic gas into the air. As the clouds drifted towards the city, emergency responders needed to warn people of the looming chemical catastrophe and tell them not to go outside. But six of Minot's seven local radio stations had been sold to Clear Channel, a Texas-based radio corporation that owned dozens of radio stations across the country. The Clear Channel stations ran largely on autopilot with only one news reporter assigned to provide news to all of them.[42] Since the train derailed in the middle of the night, Minot's radio stations were playing automated programming from San Antonio. Police couldn't get ahold of people at any of the stations. Nobody was at Clear Channel to transmit the warnings. Without radio warnings, disaster response was confusing and chaotic, and over a thousand people were injured, according to some reports.[43] In Minot, killing local radio put local lives in peril.

At the same time local radio, news, and television stations are disappearing, more unvetted news reports than ever are floating around online. The rise of social media platforms as a major conduit for the news has made accessible, neutral news access all the more important. People are getting their updates about current events from Facebook and Twitter.[44]

But social media posts do not have to satisfy journalistic standards. In fact, social media companies are insulated from liability for posting fake news—Section 230 of the Communications Decency Act protects internet service providers and information content providers from liability for the content that ends up on their websites.[45] Media companies can be sued for libel and other breaches of public trust, but Section 230 shields tech platforms from those consequences.[46] The congressmen who sponsored the law were convinced that companies hosting bulletin boards and communication centers online are more like libraries than media companies. Just as libraries don't have to account for what authors write inside the books in library collections, tech platforms shouldn't have to be accountable for what their posters write on their online services.[47] Social media platforms like Facebook, news aggregators like Google, and content providers like YouTube don't have to vet or verify the "news" information people put on their websites.[48]

As more and more people get their news from these online platforms, the companies have worked hard to weasel out of accountability for the fake "news" that their websites disseminate. Even though the companies have the largest news platforms and aggregators in the world, they insist that they're "technology platforms" and not "media companies." Facebook CEO Mark Zuckerberg insists that his company isn't media because it "builds the tools" for sharing news but doesn't produce the content.[49]

At a glance, Section 230's logic may seem sound, but when you really stop and think about it, social media sites aren't that different from traditional media. Newspaper companies also don't produce content. They provide a platform for reporters' stories. Similarly, public radio stations don't make their own content, they air syndicated programming from NPR and other sources. Companies like Facebook and Google also edit and curate news content; their employees and algorithms choose what appears on people's news feeds. The companies sometimes step in and moderate news content that they view as unacceptable. They block misinformation about the Covid pandemic or place warnings on false election reports when they feel like it.[50] Tech platforms can cherry pick the news they want to vet, but the full-time social responsibility of being news providers is a burden the companies are unwilling to bear. They can shape political sentiment by changing the flow of news on their users' feeds. They let people pay extra to push their stories to the tops of people's screens. Facebook has used its power to tweak its news feed, decreasing access to media like articles from progressive magazine *Mother Jones* and allowing false, political propaganda and right-wing stories to permeate its platform.[51]

Given their behavior, social media companies aren't universally regarded as mere "libraries" of news. Internationally, officials disagree with the premise of Section 230—German justice minister Heiko Maas says Facebook "should be treated as media even if they do not correspond to the media concept of television or radio."[52] But in the United States, Section 230 gives data and tech companies "power without responsibility."[53]

The more that news is privatized, and the more that media companies consolidate, the more that people will rely on social media for news regardless of whether the social media companies consider themselves news providers. Community sharing groups on social media websites such as Facebook or NextDoor are filling in as news sources in communities where local newspapers, radio stations, and television programming have disappeared. Thousands of towns and counties use the websites' group pages to share local news.[54] The Beaver County, Pennsylvania, news alerts group has forty thousand members, which includes about a quarter of the county's population. Bismarck, North Dakota's "People Reporting News" group has twenty thousand members. The groups help spread news about local events and problems, from potholes to crime prevention, but posts on the group webpage lack journalistic standards. Without editors and fact-checkers, people can muddy reports with unfounded gossip and racist rumors. As Deanna Romigh, one of the Beaver County page's curators says, "Do I want to spread fake news? No. We all just want to know what's going on." But even with their good intentions, self-reporters like Romigh can make unchecked mistakes. Like scholarship and legal information preservation, journalism isn't a volunteer enterprise—it costs money and takes lots of time to provide quality, vetted news products.

There are thousands of local news groups like Beaver County's on Facebook, covering news for towns that lack consistent local public news access. Some are rife with misinformation that puts community members in danger. A seven-thousand-member group in Klamath, Oregon, spread rumors that led to an armed standoff. Jennifer Grygiel, a social media scholar, faulted a lack of legitimate local news for the proliferation of these online groups. Without access to news, people might only be able to get newsworthy information "by posting gossip and having the police correct it." Grygiel predicted that makeshift online news groups will flourish as police and government replace press releases with social media posts.[55]

Like social media platforms, data companies are focusing more on content quantity, and they're growing less concerned with content quality. For-profit news sources depend on attracting viewers, and advertisers, to make money. When news is for profit, it's reported with the hope of attracting an audience. As they focus on data analytics and for-profit platforms, data companies strive to put out as much content as they can to lure information-hungry customers to their products. The companies want to keep people's content feeds churning. They're prioritizing populating search results and social media feeds with more stories rather than assessing what information is high quality and worthy of disseminating.

Treating news as entertainment creates twenty-four-hour news cycles in which everything is dramatized as "breaking news," even if it's actually quite mundane. Polarizing people are invited to stir up entertaining content for those who tune in. High-drama, high-impact news may be good for viewership numbers, but it's often hyperbolic and not entirely true. In most of our other informational markets, fact-checking and information-vetting happens at some point along the supply chain—peer reviewers and editors pore over the content of academic journals, and judges and their clerks closely examine their court opinions. Just as academic scholars depend on peer review to ensure the veracity of their reports, journalists subscribe to a set of ethics and standards to ensure their reports are truthful, accurate, and objective.[56] But while news is similarly vetted by journalists, when it appears on platforms run by data analytics and social media companies the vetted stories are harder to identify—some sources are legitimate news sources that honor traditional journalistic standards, but others are biased or just plain incorrect.

There are also plenty of biased sources and propaganda spreaders parading around as news media. Fake news sources fill information voids that remain when most high-quality news sources are paywalled. Commentators pretending to be news reporters spread conspiracies, exaggerations, and misleading information. In the financial information market, we observed how easy it was for just a few people on Reddit to cause an information cascade that caused millions of readers to invest in risky stocks. Similar informational contagion happens when fake news about political leaders, pandemics, and climate change is broadcast to the public. People lose trust in institutions and their claims when it's easy to access free, fake news but hard to get neutral, fact-checked news. Information from sources like InfoWars, a far-right website that supports conspiracy theories about everything from the 9/11 attacks to chemtrails and the shooting at Sandy Hook Elementary School are, disproportionately, the ones shared on social media.[57] Without access to verified, well-researched journalism, sources like these have become "disinformation superspreaders."

If local news stations are taken over by companies that infuse news reports with political dogma, then even local news coverage becomes more politically biased.[58] Companies like Sinclair Broadcast Group control hundreds of local TV news stations and force reporters to read out rightwing political content as if its regular news. There is no way to tell that the reporters, who look official in their usual business attire and news desks, are reading biased, "forced read" scripts full of political propaganda.[59] Politicized reports from corporate news sources like Fox News and Sinclair have influenced Americans' views about laws, wars, and national policies. News reports even convinced people that a hurricane threatened the State of Alabama because Donald Trump drew a pretend storm path on a map with a marker.[60]

Companies like Sinclair are also taking over online newspapers. A Republican political operative is buying up websites with names like *Maine Business Daily*, *Ann Arbor Times*, and *Des Moines Sun*—titles that sound a lot like newspapers. These platforms pretend to be news claiming to platform "objective, data-driven information without political bias," but they are controlled by politicians and PR firms that pay people to write stories that promote Republican officials and plans or smear the Republicans' rivals.[61] There are over a thousand websites like these filling voids left by vanishing local news sources.[62] Reporters call these websites "pink slime" news, comparing their content to the low-quality meat by-product used as filler in processed beef.[63] By 2020, pink slime news networks had more than twice as many sites as the nation's largest newspaper chain, Gannett.[64]

People who get their news from sources like Sinclair television stations, from listening to right-wing talk radio shows, or from reading online sources like Breitbart fall into information bubbles. Their entire worldview becomes warped as they are fed a continuous fake news slurry. During the coronavirus pandemic, conservative talk radio listeners were treated to deceptive marketing for fake coronavirus cures.[65] A voting machine company sued Fox News for libel when its news personalities wouldn't stop repeating lies about how the companies' machines helped President Joe Biden "steal" the election.[66] Despite the lawsuits and lies, these sources are flourishing online, proliferating in social media feeds, podcasts, YouTube videos, and other online platforms.

Another unsavory practice that news providers have in common with other informational markets is that they infuse their information platforms with consumer surveillance. The same type of data surveillance that happens in RELX's and Thomson Reuters's walled-garden information systems happens on companies' news websites. If you peruse the *New York Times* online in the United States, you'll be tracked by over fifty different companies, including data brokers like Oracle.[67] *Mother Jones* and other magazines and newspapers sell subscriber lists to political fundraisers.[68] Online newspapers sell the space at the bottom of their websites to companies that generate "promoted stories" that are merely clickbait, enticing news readers to click on their stories so they can gather data about the readers.[69] As public news access and paper news printing die out, this type of data surveillance and collection becomes inevitable for people who want to read, hear, or watch news reports.

Some of the best suggestions for saving public information access and building public information infrastructure have focused on saving the news information industry.[70] Before it was privatized, public news services provided good models for information access in the United States—our public television and radio services, as well as our subsidized newspaper deliveries, made it so that anyone could access news so long as they were near a television, radio, or newspaper. News was a basic provision, like electricity, waterworks, or phone lines. But today we lag behind countries such as the United Kingdom, Norway, and Sweden in our financial support of public news infrastructure.[71] If we returned to treating news information like a critical public resource, we could ensure that there's accessible information infrastructure to guarantee access to the news online.

Lawmakers have considered different ways to support news access in an informational landscape where news is largely produced and published by a few for-profit media companies. New Jersey's governor budgeted state funds for supporting local journalism.[72] When Verizon shut down its Fios1 local news channel, New York state legislators proposed a law that would require cable companies operating in the state to carry independently produced local news channels that featured news, weather, and public affairs programming.[73] Federal lawmakers have floated the "Saving Local News Act," which would make news organizations tax-exempt.[74]

All of the various legislative and regulatory interventions for the news industry are different, but their basic rationale is the same—the lawmakers agree that news is a public informational good that should be supported by the government if markets fail to provide it efficiently and effectively to the public.[75] Private tech and data companies are not the best news providers. They're focused on selling data products and attracting clicks and log-ins. They are not focused on providing trustworthy, objective news to the public. Their for-profit models muddle public-interest-focused news reporting with the political and entertainment motives of their owners, and they refuse to be classified as media companies instead of tech platforms so they won't be legally bound by libel laws or journalistic standards. These conflicts are probably why privatized news wasn't always the preferred norm in U.S. media.

Because the internet has revolutionized information markets, we can't fix news information access by simply pumping more money into subsidizing newspaper delivery or funding public television like we did decades ago. New communication technologies require us to reinvent public news for the digital age.[76]

One popular suggestion is to have billion-dollar big-tech platforms subsidize digital public news systems. Just as the New York law would have cable providers guarantee cable news, we could require internet service and platform providers to guarantee online news by taxing online advertisers, big-tech companies, or internet service providers.[77] Mark Zuckerberg himself has suggested that tech companies like Facebook should underwrite local and public news. In 2019, his company pledged a $300 million commitment to help local news publishers build their readership and to support local reporting.[78] Companies like Google and Facebook make billions of dollars a year on surveillant advertising (advertising that uses our private data to track us online and target ads towards us on the basis of our digital habits).[79] It would make sense to divest some of that advertising money, made by exploiting our data, back to public services that would benefit us. Ethan Zuckerman estimates that even a tiny 1 percent tax on surveillant advertising could create a $1–2 billion annual fund to support digital public service media.[80]

We could also build a collective, collaborative digital news infrastructure to host news reporting online. That way, we wouldn't have to rely on social media platforms or paywalled news sources to get news information. Instead of having to use privatized research services, a public database could contain publicly accessible news and information resources. The information system would have an intuitive, simple, open search function so you could find information with ease and without bias. Public news could have a "true universal search, uncorrupted by paid advertising" and be guided "by the desire to create the greatest possible access to knowledge rather than by economic considerations."[81] This news commons could build off of other news cooperatives like the Associated Press. The Associated Press is an independent, nonprofit news cooperative with U.S. newspapers and broadcasters fulfilling the cooperative's mission of informing the world through objective, accurate journalism.[82] We could support existing news cooperatives, or we could create similar structures that work in harmony with those co-ops.

Even though collecting big-tech tax subsidies and building digital news cooperatives wouldn't be drastically different from the government's prior public news projects like newspaper subsidies or the Corporation for Public Broadcasting, these types of projects may not have as much public support today as they did then. A neoliberal approach to information access has eroded our ideas about public information access. Victor Pickard, an American media studies scholar explains that "Americans harbor a surprising recalcitrance toward public subsidies for journalism. Many believe that if the market doesn't support a news outlet—or if it doesn't receive a wealthy benefactor's support—then it deserves to wither."[83]

In the past, we treated communication infrastructures as public utilities.[84] Regulating the news industry to ensure public access to the news in every community worked—the government provided plenty of oversight and resources to ensure that everyone could get news and educational programming and information, and we had robust news access in various forms and formats. Pickard suggests revisiting a 1912 public newspaper experiment in Los Angeles, where the *Los Angeles Municipal News* was designated a "people's newspaper," and guaranteed annual subsidies.[85] The paper was killed by commercial interests in the city, but it lives on in the dreams of public news advocates. In the age of digital information, publicly owned papers could be built on existing municipal websites. Governments could support their local news sources online like Los Angeles did over a hundred years ago with their physical newspaper.

Even if a public digital newspaper model isn't the be-all, end-all public news solution, we should build some sort of public news infrastructure. Media experts agree that public radio and public television need to rapidly and radically reorient towards "digital-first local news."[86] In online platforms, access to high-quality, verified news reports are more important than ever. After an especially tense NPR interview with his secretary of state, President Trump retweeted the question, "Why does NPR still exist?" NPR reporter Steve Inskeep replied with a tweet-length declaration: NPR "exists to tell the truth" and "Citizens support NPR to inform themselves and all citizens." Inskeep concluded with the most enduring, basic rationale for supporting public news: "The truth should be universal."[87]

CONCLUSION

ENVISIONING PUBLIC INFORMATION
AS A PUBLIC GOOD

> *The path forward is clear: Fuck the algorithms, dismantle*
> *the tech monopolies, and build infrastructures of care and*
> *justice where these systems of social control once stood.*

—Nantina Vgontzas and Meredith Whittaker[1]

NOW THAT WE'VE SEEN THE various ways data analytics companies are mucking up our information circulation system, it's time to talk honestly about how to resolve the problems these companies cause. Until now, the data analytics companies have done a good job of obscuring the immensity of their informational power by maintaining each of their product lines in separate silos, and by obscuring what their data products do by giving them vague names like "special services" and "risk solutions." In turn, we, as consumers, have treated each of the companies' markets as separate entities, not as pieces of the same problem. If we deal with each of the data companies' product lines—personal data, academic information, legal information, financial information, and news—as if they are separate, we will never get to the heart of the problems data analytics companies cause. When you look at the whole of these companies, you can see how they are blocking information access and exploiting people's private information across the entire informational spectrum, running all of the materials they warehouse through increasingly powerful data analytics systems.

If we want to ensure intellectual freedom, the ability to seek information without barriers to access, there are some notions that apply no matter which category of information we're talking about. We should treat information that's created by the public, and that's essential to public decision making, like a public resource. In contrast, we should treat private information as private, not as a resource that can be exploited by data companies. We should fund and maintain public information infrastructures just as we maintain public roads and water systems. We should do better to oversee the companies that steward public information, and we should prevent informational oligopolies that make it harder for the public to get the information it needs and that share our private data without our consent.

The internet was recently described as "a big endless, money-making party" that the general public isn't invited to.[2] But internet companies shouldn't be able to take over public information resources, turning our private information, our laws, the research we fund, and the news and financial information we need into their portfolio of profitable assets. Data analytics companies shouldn't have carte blanche to turn our information into high-priced data products.

As tech systems like Amazon's online superstore, Facebook's social media platform, and Google's search engine ossify into sturdy, immovable features of internet life, it's not too late to prevent data analytics companies from solidifying their roles as digital information barons. We can still loosen their grasp on our digital information markets and create a human-centered data ecosystem that focuses on what's best for people, not data companies. After all, people are not the government's customers, they are constituents. By participating in government; paying taxes and tuition; sharing news, financial, and medical data; and consenting to companies collecting our data exhaust, we are not buying information infrastructure, we *are* information infrastructure. We deserve to be treated as participants in the data infrastructure, not mere subjects of its whims.

Digital life should be more like the real, physical lives we want for ourselves and others. We shouldn't be accepting data corporations' ideas of what the world should look like. Instead we should be determining "what technologies we want and need for digital media to have a productive role in democratic societies."[3]

Our digital ecosystem could align with the ethics and practices we envision. We should reclaim the digital world, including our data and informational resources, for the public, building digital infrastructures that specifically serve and protect public interests.[4] Data and information flows could be equal access. They could protect human dignity and embody democratic principles. If we are entitled to essential public information, then how can we ensure it's available to us? How can we prevent companies like RELX from privatizing our informational resources and becoming our only online data and information source, a Facebook-Amazon-Google-esque data giant?

When it comes to Gilded Age–style barons, we can learn from past experience. As antitrust expert Tim Wu explains in his book *The Curse of Bigness*, by allowing tech and data giants to dominate digital industries in our current informational revolution, we are re-creating the kind of Gilded Age problems that pervaded the industrial revolution.[5] More than a century ago, several monopolies took over markets by capitalizing on technical advancements like new mining enterprises, telephones, and electrical lighting. Today, a few companies are similarly concentrating wealth and power by capitalizing on new digital technologies that generate, store, and process data. The downside of repeating the "curse of bigness" in the digital era is that ceding that much power to profit-focused companies is bad for people who aren't running those companies. But the upside is that the United States managed to overcome Gilded Age monopolists—and if we did it once, we can do it again. We can borrow some of the antitrust tools we used to quell steel, oil, and railroad cartels in manufacturing markets, and to ensure access to public telecommunication services like phones, radios, and televisions.

If we want to create effective public data infrastructure, the first thing we have to do is to stop treating technology and data like they are mysterious sorcery. Data technologies may be new, but digital problems are just the same old problems translated into binary code. Amazon is a mall controlled by one company. Facebook is a privatized community square. Google is an all-in-one digital post office, printing service, and office supply center. But instead of treating these online businesses like the brick-and-mortar companies that preceded them, we treat them like they're exceptional. When regulators fall prey to the myth of "technological exceptionalism," they hesitate to intervene in tech work because they think tech companies are "doing too much good, chang[ing] too fast, and too complicated for the US government to write rules around."[6]

Tech companies, including data analytics companies, want regulators to believe that their work is so cutting edge, and so vital, that it's unregulable. But modern communication technologies weren't the first ones, and they won't be the last. We were able to regulate past technologies such as printing presses, telephones, radios, and photographic cameras, even though the companies that sold these old technologies also claimed their products were unregulable.[7] Even the most complicated tech is developed by humans, created in manufacturing processes controlled by humans, and used by human consumers. [8] Human creations can be regulated by humans. The amount of "good" a company is doing is something people get to decide, not something the companies get to decide for us.

Tech and data companies shouldn't set the course for tech and data regulation. Mark Zuckerberg's "move fast and break things" credo may be profitable for him, but it sacrifices the careful work of creating fair systems for governing things that are important to the public. If you move too fast, without thinking about the human consequences, your social media platform may end up interfering with democratic elections,[9] prolonging pandemics,[10] and even inciting genocide.[11] Instead of letting tech companies fix problems fast, humans should move deliberately and with care as we decide who controls all of our news, science, law, financial, and private information and how they exercise the power that that control imparts.[12] Sometimes the right choice might be to not build a technology or data system at all.[13]

Even though slow and deliberate is a better approach for building infrastructure, we have failed to intervene on Facebook and other companies' fast-moving, thing-breaking developments. Federal, state, and local governments treat tech developers like wizards instead of regular, profit-seeking companies. Tech exceptionalism and industry capture may seem like ridiculous reasons for the U.S. government's failure to intervene on the ever-expanding data and tech monopolies, but there are few other rationales to explain the government's inaction. It's not like there haven't been dozens of legislative bills, regulatory proposals, and lawsuits filed in response to the problems that digital companies are causing. Hundreds of legal experts, information science researchers, and other humanities scholars have drafted research papers suggesting all sorts of legal reforms and interventions to improve competition and consumer protection online. The problem isn't a lack of curiosity or concentrated study, it's a lack of movement to change the law. We haven't even been able to advance comprehensive data privacy legislation while other nations have already successfully implemented their data privacy laws.

One of the main things we could do to create more equitable data systems is to prevent data analytics companies from taking over entire information markets. Fostering competition in information markets will give consumers choices about where and how they get information. Without competition, data analytics companies are engaging in the sorts of anticompetitive behavior that antitrust laws were meant to prevent.[14]

Both the breadth and the depth of data analytics companies' market dominance are stunning when you see them from a bird's-eye view, across the product-specific market silos. It's easy to see why monopolies were depicted as octopuses in the Gilded Age. Data analytics companies' tentacles are wrapped around multiple information markets and dug deep into government offices' decision-making and informational processes. They are so embedded into all of our social systems—educational, financial, legal, governmental—that their tentacles already feel inextricable from our daily lives.

The companies' grip on information markets hurts all of us. When the data analytics companies monopolize all of our essential information markets, we are all stuck with their mediocre content and incorrect predictions, because there aren't any other competitive sources for information. The companies have so much data that it gives them a "god's-eye view" of the world. They predict what will happen next in almost any context. They claim they can foresee crimes, loan defaults, health outcomes, insurance risks, and national security breaches.[15] But in every market they occupy, the data analytics' companies' algorithms are imperfect and their data contains errors. As we've seen in every chapter of this book, no data company thoroughly vets its data collections. The data companies get so much data at such high speeds that they can't manage quality control. Personal data, new academic articles, published court opinions, legislative updates, and corporations' financial reports are constantly flowing into their information warehouses. A steady deluge of unvetted information will likely contain errors. When you run mediocre data through biased algorithms, the predictions can be incorrect.

The octopus-like nature of data analytics companies also hurts consumers by blurring the lines between informational markets that should be separate. Especially when data analytics are involved, there are problems with combining our personal data dossiers with information about the law, information about health and science research, and financial data. Lawyers and health care workers are entrusted with people's private legal problems and ailments, and they have a duty to keep those things private. Legal and medical practitioners shouldn't have to worry that using a data analytics system is violating their clients' and patients' confidentiality. There should be protective barriers between research and data analytics. We need to preserve intellectual freedom, which includes protecting the freedom to seek information without fear of surveillance. We also need to be able to get critical, essential information without having to contribute to systems of surveillance in exchange for that information access. We need to slice apart the tentacles, separating data analytics companies so that they aren't simultaneously our main information sources and major data brokers. We shouldn't have to trade our private information as a cost of doing research.

So how do we deal with these data analytics octopuses? Antitrust actions are rarely straightforward, and antitrust solutions are rarely the same. Because each market is unique, picking the best way to protect consumers in a given market involves case-by-case, fact-based analysis. In the case of information markets, preserving competition and protecting consumers requires preventing multimarket information empires. A functional information system would have private information companies, but it would also be able to swiftly deliver essential public information to the public without sacrificing personal privacy.

Open Access

The most popular solution in libraries and academic communities is "open access." I put the phrase open access in quotes because it means different things to different people. To some, open access is literal, and a dramatic departure from our neoliberal, privately run information infrastructure—it's a free, open access to every resource without reservation. To others, open access is hardly a switch from the systems we have in place—it's a collaboration with data companies in which consumers pay a price to release paywalled materials to the public. Whether people subscribe to an ideal vision of open access, or a traditional "open" infrastructure constructed within the existing parameters of private data companies, creating open access information infrastructure would give all of us more access to critical informational resources (although the latter option does not free us from the companies' surveillance).

A not-for-profit, open access option would prevent some of the conflicts of interest we experience when we use data companies' products and platforms. When RELX and Thomson Reuters combine research platforms in the same company as government data brokers, our subscription fees likely fund "risk" product research and development. We shouldn't have to pay data analytics companies that make surveillance products for police and predictive products for insurance companies, employers, and landlords in order to get information we need.

An alternate system wouldn't just free us from funding government surveillance and sketchy risk products—it wouldn't need to collect users' data at all. If information platforms aren't trying to make a profit, users' data isn't a valuable resource to sell. Instead of valuing personal data, the public systems can value privacy. Stewards of public data infrastructure will also be less motivated to police or track users to protect copyrighted materials. If resources are openly available and not part of the platform owners' personal copyright troves, there will be little reason to track the platform's users. And if there are plentiful private open access resources online, we won't have to spend as much time using surveillant data products.

A public information infrastructure could take on information preservation goals that private data companies do not strive for. Even though information access is a necessary ingredient of our lives, data companies sell information as just another marketable good. Privatizing and monetizing data strips data of its social value. The data companies don't provide and preserve information resources if it's not financially valuable. When private companies are in charge of important records, there's no guarantee that they will preserve information, even if it's important to the public. People rush to archive historically relevant materials like presidential tweets and insurrection videos because they can't be sure that Twitter, YouTube, and other private platforms will save the historically significant posts.[16] Open infrastructure could be built to support collective, consistent stewardship of the data pipeline where we can participate in information preservation choices.[17]

Open access infrastructure can also guarantee that everyone has consistent, continuous access to essential information. In the current, data-company-driven scheme, people who can't afford to pay are denied the information they need. Fee barriers to information access harm poor people and institutions that lack ample budgets.[18] For instance, data companies give community college students stripped-down, paltry academic journal collections instead of the services they provide to wealthier, more elite academic institutions.[19] Community college students are "hemmed in" by invisible informational boundaries these companies create. They can't see the full spectrum of academic research and findings that exist. Public data systems could prevent this type of digital inequality by ensuring that people have equal information access.

The open digital information system must be built with historic, physical systems of oppression in mind. Making "open" infrastructure won't fix our access problems unless the infrastructure is separate from data analytics companies' systems and also unmoored from institutional oppression and personal biases that our digital systems are based upon. Access does not guarantee equality.[20] We must ensure that we don't insert biases and inequities into our digital information infrastructure. April Hathcock, a librarian at New York University, urges people building open access systems to consider "Who is being left behind?" in the systems they build.[21] Our information access infrastructure should be formed with attention not just to who is being included, but to how we can eliminate barriers to entry for those who would otherwise be left out.

This type of truly open access is possible, even if the data companies own a bulk of the resources we want to liberate. Open access to privatized resources isn't unfounded. We provide open access to all sorts of privately managed public resources. Private companies maintain most of the U.S.'s physical infrastructure, running pipelines, power stations, and railways.[22] Even though corporations run the major arteries of our physical world, they can't put walls in the middle of public roadways or siphon away our public water supplies. We expect that everyone will be able to use essential public infrastructure when they need it. When the private owners of a ferry pier in Greenpoint, Brooklyn, decided to stop letting New York City's public ferry system use their stop, people were outraged that their commuting paths were obstructed. It was both comical and infuriating that one day, instead of providing a ride to work, the ferry conductor shouted "Sorry, we don't stop here anymore!" as the ferry floated past the pier full of waiting customers.[23] We aren't accustomed to this type of private intervention on our public transportation systems.

The way we treat public resources online is a departure from how we treat public resources in the physical world. In the physical world, we're shocked when public transportation leaves people behind because private companies playing critical roles in public systems have to guarantee public access to essential public infrastructure. We generally don't let electric companies keep people from having the power they need to heat their homes, and we don't let waterworks condition peoples' ability to have a drink or take a bath on their willingness to install surveillance devices on their faucets. When we set up a public ferry system and pay companies to maintain it, we expect it to be open, consistently, for public use. Yet we allow the private companies that run our digital infrastructure wall off information and take our personal data in order to use essential public information resources.

One of the main sticking points in public information infrastructure is deciding who should cover the costs to build and operate it. People who use public infrastructure systems usually pay a fee to access them. Part of the reason the NYC ferry riders were pissed off when their ride floated away without them was that they'd paid $2.75 per ticket. While $2.75 isn't a hefty price for a trip across the East River the ferry-riding public doesn't have to pay higher prices because the ferry system is subsidized by city funds.[24]

At the end of the day, public infrastructure is often a balance between private companies that want to profit from their creations and the public, who want affordable access to the same creations (which, incidentally, are subsidized with their tax dollars and usage fees). We can't ignore the fact that, like Brooklyn's ferry system, the information infrastructure costs money, and that the data companies are currently the parties footing the bill for many of those expenses. The operating budgets of companies like RELX are not zero. There are costs associated with collecting, processing, indexing, and maintaining digital collections, not to mention making them user-friendly with searchable databases, hyperlinks, and other bells and whistles that help people use online research systems. Since online access to information isn't free, we have to decide who should pay to build and maintain the access systems.

If cities help pay for their local transportation system, and the federal government subsidizes highways,[25] who should subsidize our digital information infrastructure? What about companies like RELX who make billions of dollars by privatizing our public information? Should they promise to help build and maintain public access to information?

Data Companies as Public Utilities
In the past, we forged a path between completely public and completely privatized resources, making certain goods and services "public utilities," private companies that would maintain the infrastructure for some public services, enjoying monopoly power in whatever market they operate in (supplying electricity, gasoline, railways, and so on). In exchange for that monopoly power, the companies would guarantee consistent and stable public access, as well as accept a considerable amount of regulatory oversight. To be treated like a public utility, a company must provide an essential, non-differentiated public commodity (like electricity or water) and operate in a capital-intensive public infrastructure. Data analytics products aren't good candidates to be public utilities because they don't fit that description.

One reason that data companies' information troves aren't like other public utilities is that data and information themselves aren't infrastructure. They're the substances that fuel the digital infrastructure, aka the internet. (The government has been going back and forth over whether to treat the internet like a public utility for years.)[26] Another reason data companies' data and information troves aren't like public utilities is that they aren't the same as electricity or water. Each piece of information is unique, while those other resources are fungible and interchangeable.

Even if the data companies' products aren't public utilities, per se, the government can still intervene to regulate them as the major providers of essential public resources, and to guarantee public access to essential, critical information. There is a balance to be had somewhere between private data companies fully privatizing and paywalling our informational resources and magical—but impossible—zero-cost public information resources. Almost a hundred years ago, we found that balance with other telecommunication tools, like the radio.[27] When the radio became popular, a few companies quickly figured out how to privatize public airwaves.[28] The government intervened to prevent our airwaves from being overtaken by a few radio station giants like NBC and CBS, by passing the Radio Act of 1927.[29] The Act created a system in which the government held radio frequencies instead of the private companies. The government divvied out radio frequencies to private companies by giving the companies operating licenses for radio frequencies when the private companies demonstrated that their radio station would satisfy the "public interest, convenience or necessity."[30] The government considered content providers like television and radio stations to be commercial enterprises with "public character."[31] To keep their broadcasting licenses, companies had special duties to provide access to important, timely information about news and public affairs as "public fiduciaries."[32]

Data analytics companies may not be like public utilities, but they are similar to radio companies. Both radio companies and data companies broadcast information to the public. But right now, data companies aren't required to provide public access, and they have no obligations to satisfy the public's interest. The government could treat data companies more like the content providers that came before them, and insist that the companies provide public access to critical public information as a condition for receiving, and profiting off of, the government's legal, financial, and research data.[33] Under "net neutrality," if the internet was considered a common carrier, it could be treated like airwaves or phone lines, with licenses and access requirements for sources of critical public information that would ensure at least some public access to public information. People have also suggested that we create a Corporation for Public Broadcasting–styled scheme for digital infrastructure (a "Corporation for Public Software"), which would be subsidized by the government, not paid for by the companies themselves.[34]

Other people have suggested that, instead of getting financial support for data infrastructure from the government, or from the data analytics companies who profit from data infrastructure, we should fund our own open access system. End users including researchers and libraries could redirect the fees they pay data analytics companies towards building and maintaining public information resources instead. This collective model of open access is my least favorite conception of "open." First, it forces the wrong people to pay for data infrastructure. In a collectively funded digital publishing cooperative, participants would have to foot the bill for platforming data companies' products and creating shared public digital repositories for essential public information.[35]

Second, collective open access projects are a logistical nightmare. Collective repositories across different institutions and organizations would require collective coordination and support from hundreds of funders, dozens of publishers, and libraries. A collective open access repository would also be tough to fund because when resources are put online for free, they tend to attract "free riders," people who use the shared resources without contributing to them. If people can enjoy open access with or without paying for it, it's likely that many researchers and research institutions will forgo helping to pay for the infrastructure. For instance, while most of us use Wikipedia, most of us probably don't respond to their pleas for donations at the top of the website, even though Wikipedia needs funding to stay afloat.

A more straightforward way to guarantee open, public infrastructure would be to build a government-funded digital library instead of relying on piecemeal support from participating libraries. The government could collect funding for public digital infrastructure by properly taxing private big-tech and data companies. Tech companies have been able to avoid paying their share of taxes.[36] If the government closed the tax loopholes tech companies use to avoid paying into public systems, that money could pay for public digital infrastructure.

Our physical libraries are already subsidized by local, state, and federal funds.[37] Government funds support the physical infrastructure of public libraries, as well as the information professionals that curate and run those spaces. Like our public library systems, digital library platforms could be common, shared spaces, staffed by information experts.[38] Physical libraries create public spaces to access knowledge and gather information. Public digital libraries could do the same. A few privately funded online efforts, like HathiTrust, a free repository that's run by well-funded research institutions like the state universities of Michigan and California, and the Internet Archive, a free digital library supported by a variety of research foundations, provide models for online library spaces that digital public libraries could follow.

Funding library-like online spaces would require sufficient financial, infrastructural, and legal resources. Our governments historically have underfunded digital information infrastructure. When the government provides information to the public, it does so with outdated, insufficient online tools and platforms. In every situation, the information resources the government provides aren't anywhere near as good as the ones on data companies' websites. The government's current attempts at information access can't replace the superior paywalled services. Systems like EDGAR and PACER are notoriously outdated and hard to use. They run on outdated technology, and the government doesn't hire the numbers of catalogers, editors, and information experts necessary to create enduring, up-to-date information infrastructure. Our major public science database provides abstracts of published articles and books, but the government doesn't subsidize access to the full text articles themselves.[39] Other countries are considering paying to set paywalled materials free, or passing laws to ensure their access.[40] To break access barriers, the United States government should follow through with its Obama-era directive to give access not just to article abstracts, but to the full articles.

Beyond funding and infrastructure, the government must update our copyright laws to ease the way for open infrastructure online. Right now, copyright laws don't account for digital ownership. Copyright holders have taken advantage of the gaps in the law. Instead of conveying full ownership to purchasers copyright holders license limited rights of access to purchasers.[41] Digital open access platforms can't get the rights for digital materials that they need in order to share and lend digital information on their platforms like traditional paper libraries do. HathiTrust and the Internet Archive have both been sued for copyright infringement by groups representing publishers that own sweeping collections of copyrights to millions of written materials.[42]

The easiest way to overcome the grey area of digital copyright law is to clarify and update consumers' rights in digital information ecosystems. Law should guarantee that library-like online platforms can lend materials, and law should also ensure that digital information purchasers can enjoy at least some of the intellectual property rights that physical ownership conveys.

Regulation

Without intervention, data companies aren't going to save the day. Like the rest of big tech, for-profit data analytics companies can't operate information infrastructure in the public interest. Their loyalty is to shareholders or other company stakeholders, not to the rest of us. Data companies' problems are baked into their defining practices and designs. Just as "The problem with Facebook is Facebook,"[43] the problem with data companies is data companies—their business model is based on hoarding, paywalling, and crunching as much information and data as possible. Their very existence is based in data exploitation, surveillance, and informational inequality. Fixing the problems data companies cause is not as simple as updating a single law. Changing the legal parameters of data analytics' companies' roles requires a large, orchestrated round of legal changes including copyright reform, reinvigorating old antitrust doctrine, closing up constitutional law loopholes, and designating resources for government data infrastructure and access. That type of legal revolution isn't likely to happen any time soon.

So we must strive to implement incremental changes to our information infrastructure. One incremental change we should push for is separating data brokering businesses from other parts of our critical information infrastructure. The companies that funnel our personal data to the police, ICE, and the FBI should not be the same companies that we depend on for our critical information resources. They should be walled off as their own entity, and treated like state actors bound by constitutional obligations such as the Fourth Amendment's warrant requirements. As long as we treat RELX's and Thomson Reuters's data brokering companies like just another information product, they will continue to work around legal protections meant to shield people from data surveillance, including the Privacy Act of 1974 and the Fourth Amendment. These companies' "risk" and "special services" products have become "arms of the government" and they should be treated as such.[44]

Another incremental shift we could make is to treat data companies like "information fiduciaries," the way radio and television stations are treated.[45] In fiduciary relationships, one party must rely on, and trust, a more powerful party. The law forces the more powerful party to act in ways that will benefit the less powerful party. We are so dependent on data companies for essential information that they could be treated like fiduciaries. Data companies could be assigned certain duties, including confidentiality, care, and loyalty.[46] We would be the beneficiaries of the companies' legally enforceable duties. While creating information fiduciary standards wouldn't wrest informational power from the data companies, it would, perhaps, put some responsibilities into our relationships with these sprawling data corporations.[47]

Interventions like separating data brokering from other types of information businesses and making data companies informational fiduciaries may not be the sweeping informational reforms we need, but they are steps away from the status quo in which we let tech companies govern themselves, which isn't doing much, if anything to improve our information infrastructure. We've been waiting for digital markets, and the companies that operate within those markets, to react to consumer outcry over privacy breaches, subpar information (like fake news and online scams), and paywalls, but so far the companies have been largely impervious to consumers' concerns.

We can't reverse digitization—there's no putting the technology cat back in the bag, nor should there be. Digital innovations are awesome and helpful. Data visualization is neat. Social media is a way to connect with people all over the world. I met my partner and other friends online, and I bet some of you did too! Online purchasing is convenient and could be environmentally friendly and geographically equalizing if done properly.

The goal isn't to stop tech or data innovations, it's to make sure that data and tech supply chains are sustainable and just. If we stay the course, data analytics companies will keep creating an unhealthy informational reality. Without intervention, our informational reality will only grow more bleak.

We've seen what happens when we ignore companies' bad behavior. In the 1960s when companies were allowed to pour all of their toxic sludge into waterways and incinerate whatever they wanted, rivers caught fire and cities were choked with smog. Even as their practices were making people sick, the manufacturers causing the harm insisted that they couldn't make consumer goods any other way. The companies said that if they were subject to regulation, there would be no more affordable cars or electronics. And yet, when the president created the Environmental Protection Agency and passed the Clean Air Act and the Clean Water Act, which forced industry to curb pollution, the industries survived and we all got healthier environs.

American industries were innovative enough to work with regulators before, and they'll be able to do it again. But as Senator Sherrod Brown says, we'll need to challenge the industries if we want results.[48] We have to reign in data cartels not with small, tech changes but with big, structural evolution.[49] Siva Vaidhyanathan urges us to imagine building entirely new information systems. His message is optimistic, envisioning a better digital future: "We know what's wrong. We have only begun to imagine how it could be better." Data infrastructure problems are not too big for us to fix.[50]

The internet doesn't have to be an informational labyrinth of dead-end paywalls blocking critical public information, and privacy-stealing platforms where companies prey on our personal data. With the right blend of governance, oversight, and support, we can open up science, law, and financial data and information to all. With more active antitrust interventions, information projects could flourish without inevitably being procured or tamped out by the data analytics companies. By enforcing consumer protection rules and rethinking privacy rights, we can prevent data analytics companies from siphoning and selling our personal data, and their personal data-based risk products without our consent. With more funding and resources, we can make and maintain public information infrastructure. Just as we provide public transportation, public libraries, public parks, and other public services and structures, we can build public data and information resources in our online ecosystem. If we treat essential information as a public resource, and if we stop treating private data as an extractive industry, we can all "swim in the ocean of knowledge."[51]

NOTES

Preface

1. Sam Biddle and Spencer Woodman, "These Are the Technology Firms Lining Up to Build Trump's 'Extreme Vetting' Program," *The Intercept*, August 7, 2017, https://theintercept.com/2017/08/07/these-are-the-technology-firms -lining-up-to-build-trumps-extreme-vetting-program/.

2. Joe Hodnicki, "Does WEXIS Use Legal Search User Data in Their Surveillance Search Platforms?" Law Librarian Blog, July 16, 2018, https://perma.cc /MQ2V-HDXG.

3. The representative even sent an email to students accusing me of purposely and repeatedly "spreading incorrect information." Email on file with author.

4. https://perma.cc/9UQR-YVXE. See also Joe Hodnicki, "AALL's 'Extreme Vetting' Removes Post on Professional Ethics for Suggesting Collective Action by AALL Readers," December 13, 2017, https://perma.cc/26PZ-7LZB.

5. Guaranteeing access to information is so central to our modern existence that we've dedicated a whole field of study, information science, to setting standards for collecting, storing, retrieving, and using information. We've also coined the concept "intellectual freedom" as a foundational ethical principle that governs our information flows. Intellectual freedom doesn't have a strict definition, but it's the idea that people should have the freedom to research, and access, information free from censorship and surveillance. Office for Intellectual Freedom, *Intellectual Freedom Manual*, 8th ed. (Chicago: ALA Editions, 2010), 12.

6. The two groups that filed FTC reports are Public.Resource.Org and SPARC (the Scholarly Publishing and Academic Resources Coalition). Lisl

Dunlop, John O'Toole, and Sam Sherman, "Submission to Federal Trade Commission on Behalf of Public.Resource.Org," Axinn, October 29, 2021, https://law.resource.org/pub/us/case/ftc/Public%20Resource%20FTC%20Submission.pdf; "Opposing the Merger Between Clarivate PLC and ProQuest LLC, SPARC, October 22, 2021, https://sparcopen.org/wp-content/uploads/2021/10/SPARC-FTC-Letter-in-Opposition-to-the-Clarivate-ProQuest-Merger.pdf.

Chapter 1

1. "Thomson Reuters," *Encyclopaedia Britannica*, https://perma.cc/QS2U-K4KE (accessed March 6, 2022).

2. "Explore Elsevier's History," Elsevier, https://perma.cc/UJC2-CXQG (accessed March 6, 2022).

3. Robert M. Jarvis, "John B. West: Founder of the West Publishing Company," *American Journal of Legal History* 50, no. 1 (January 2008–2010): 1–22; "The LexisNexis Timeline," LexisNexis, https://www.lexisnexis.com/anniversary/30th_timeline_fulltxt.pdf (accessed March 6. 2022).

4. "Thomson Reuters."

5. Google alone made at least $4.7 billion by serving as a platform for news in 2018, according to a New Media Alliance Study; see Marc Tracy, "Google Made $4.7 Billion from the News Industry, Study Says," *New York Times*, June 6, 2019, https://www.nytimes.com/2019/06/09/business/media/google-news-industry-antitrust.html.

Large law firms pay millions of dollars apiece for annual subscriptions to Lexis and Westlaw's legal information services. The online legal services industry, which likely includes legal information services, is an $8.8 billion industry. "Online Legal Services in the US—Market Size 2003–2026," *IBISWorld*, November 25, 2020, https://www.ibisworld.com/industry-statistics/market-size/online-legal-services-united-states/.

"Fintech," the datafication of the financial industry, has a market valued in the hundreds of billions of dollars. A single annual subscription to one Bloomberg terminal, the holy grail of financial data portals, is $24,000 a year.

Scientific content publication is a multibillion-dollar industry. Kyle Siler, "Demarcating Legitimate and Predatory Scientific Publishing: The Influence of Status on Institutional Logic Conflicts," Innovation Studies Group, Copernicus Institute of Sustainable Development, Utrecht University, October 1, 2018, preliminary draft, file:///Users/sarah/Downloads/LegitSciBoundaries_June3018-20 18-10-01T20%2021%2020.185Z.pdf.

Data brokering is a $200 billion industry; see *What Are Data Brokers—And What Is Your Data Worth?* FX Blog, March 16, 2020, https://www.webfx.com/blog/internet/what-are-data-brokers-and-what-is-your-data-worth-infographic/.

6. Mihai Andrei, "Why Nestlé Is One of the Most Hated Companies in the World," *ZME Science*, February 1, 2021, https://www.zmescience.com/science/nestle-company-pollution-children/; Philip Mattera, "Nestlé: Corporate Rap Sheet," last updated June 29, 2021, Corporate Research Project, https://www.corp-research.org/nestle.

7. Justin Peters, "Why Is It So Expensive to Read Academic Research?" *Slate*, April 5, 2016, https://slate.com/technology/2016/04/the-lawsuit-against -sci-hub-begs-the-question-why-are-academic-journals-so-expensive-anyway .html.

8. Luís Cabral and Lei Xu, "Seller Reputation and Price Gouging: Evidence from the COVID-19 Pandemic," *Economic Inquiry* 59, no. 3 (July 2021): 867–879, https://doi.org/10.1111/ecin.12993.

9. Amazon, "Price Gouging Has No Place in Our Stores, *Amazon Company News*, March 23, 2020, https://www.aboutamazon.com/news/company-news/ price-gouging-has-no-place-in-our-stores.

10. Megan Cerullo, "Face Mask Prices Surge as Coronavirus Fears Grow," *CBS News*, February 27, 2020, https://www.cbsnews.com/news/amazon-corona virus-face-mask-price-gouging-shortages/.

11. Elsevier, "Elsevier Gives Full Access to Its Content on Its COVID-19 Information Center . . ." March 13, 2020, https://www.elsevier.com/about/press-re leases/corporate/elsevier-gives-full-access-to-its-content-on-its-covid-19-informa tion-center-for-pubmed-central-and-other-public-health-databases-to-accelerate -fight-against-coronavirus.

12. "Novel Coronavirus Information Center," *Elsevier Connect*, updated October 4, 2021, https://www.elsevier.com/connect/coronavirus-information-center.

13. There are many examples of this bullying in the library context. Library vendor relations have declined with the rise of data cartels and their "big deals," huge purchasing requirements placed on libraries and kept secret with nondisclosure agreements. Jamie Baker, library director at Texas Tech University School of Law, describes how vendors "corner" libraries, forcing them to rely on their products at unfair, unsustainable prices, though much of the material they sell was produced for free by governments and academics. Jamie J. Baker, "Law Library Lessons from the UC/Elsevier Split," *LLRX*, March 29, 2019, https:/ /www.llrx.com/2019/03/law-library-lessons-in-vendor-relations-from-the-uc -elsevier-split/.

14. Christian Fuchs, "Labor in Informational Capitalism and on the Internet," *The Information Society* 26 (2010): 179–196, 187.

15. Paul McFedries, "Tracking the Quantified Self," *IEEE Spectrum: Technically Speaking*, August 2013, 24.

16. "Trends in Book and Journal Spending in ARL Libraries, 1986–2006," Western Illinois University Library, http://www.wiu.edu/library/images/arlprices .jpg (accessed Decmber 19, 2021).

17. Don't get me wrong, digital publishing is not free. It still costs thousands of dollars to publish and maintain an online journal. But studies show that the profit margins that companies like RELX are making are exponentially larger than other emarkets such as ebooks, etc.

18. Dennis W. Carlton, *Market Definition: Use and Abuse, Competition Policy International* (Spring 2007): 3, 7; *United States v. Aluminum Co. of America*, 148 F.2d 416, 430 (2d Cir. 1945).

19. When a company occupies around 80 percent or so, its market share

reaches monopoly levels, according to antitrust law. *Colo. Interstate Gas Co. v. Natural Gas Pipeline Co. of Am.*, 885 F.2d 683, 694 n.18 (10th Cir. 1989); *United States v. Dentsply Int'l, Inc.*, 399 F.3d 181, 187 (3d Cir. 2005).

20. Allen R. Myerson, "The Garbage Wars: Cracking the Cartel," *New York Times*, July 30, 1995, https://perma.cc/3G8E-KYY6.

21. Stacey Vanek Smith, "The Maple Syrup Cartel," Planet Money Podcast, April 10, 2019, https://www.npr.org/transcripts/711779352.

22. J. B. MacKinnon, "The L.E.D. Quandary: Why There's No Such Thing as 'Built to Last,'" *The New Yorker*, July 14, 2016, https://www.newyorker.com /business/currency/the-l-e-d-quandary-why-theres-no-such-thing-as-built-to -last; Robert Smith, "How a Swiss Cheese Cartel Made Fondue Popular," Planet Money Podcast, April 23, 2015, https://www.npr.org/2015/04/23/401655790/how-a -swiss-cheese-cartel-made-fondue-popular.

23. David Segal, "Record Fine for Vitamin Cartel," *Washington Post*, May 21, 1999, https://www.washingtonpost.com/archive/politics/1999/05/21/record-fine -for-vitamin-cartel/57235454-9cc1-4609-a613-20c114f10301/.

24. Paul Lewis, "Why OPEC Is Not a Cartel," *New York Times*, March 11, 1983, Section D: 1, https://www.nytimes.com/1983/03/11/business/why-opec-is -not-a-cartel-news-analysis.html.

25. Adam Smith, *Wealth of Nations* (London: W. Strahan and T. Cadell, 1776). The quote was put in a modern context in Andrew Simms, "Adam Smith Was Right . . . Businesses Can't Help Colluding," *Independent*, December 8, 2007, https://www.independent.co.uk/voices/commentators/andrew-simms-adam-smith -was-right-businesses-can-t-help-colluding-763811.html.

26. Ben H. Bagdikian, *The New Media Monopoly*, 2nd ed. (Boston: Beacon Press, 2004), 5.

27. The U.S. Federal Trade Commission has permitted RELX and Thomson Reuters to split the law enforcement data broker market and the legal informa- tion market. They use RELX to prevent Thomson Reuters monopolies and vice versa, by making the companies split their data products. This division of market control sets up duopolies in the markets. See 2008 FTC press release, https:// perma.cc/WB5W-8QXA, re: the data broker market, for example.

28. Udo Keppler, Standard Oil Political Cartoon "Next!" 1904, Library of Congress (LC-USZCN4–122).

29. *Standard Oil Co. of New Jersey v. United States*, 221 U.S. 1 (1911); *U.S. v. AT&T*, 552 F. Supp. 131 (D.D.C. 1983).

30. Diana L. Moss, "The Record of Weak U.S. Merger Enforcement in Big Tech," American Antitrust Institute, July 8, 2019, https://www.antitrustinstitute .org/wp-content/uploads/2019/07/Merger-Enforcement_Big-Tech_7.8.19.pdf.

31. Zephyr Teachout, *Break 'Em Up: Recovering Our Freedom from Big Ag, Big Tech, and Big Money* (New York: All Points Books, 2020).

32. Naomi R. Lamoreaux, "The Problem of Bigness: From Standard Oil to Google," *Journal of Economic Perspectives* 33, no. 3 (Summer 2019): https://www .aeaweb.org/articles?id=10.1257/jep.33.3.94.

33. Moss, "Record of Weak U.S. Merger Enforcement in Big Tech."

34. Eric J. Savitz and Max A. Cherney, "The White House Wants to Rein in Big Tech. Here's How," *Barron's*, August 20, 2021, https://www.barrons.com/articles/white-house-big-tech-51629428885; Marcy Gordon, "Break Them Up? 5 Ways Congress Is Trying to Rein in Big Tech," *Associated Press*, June 25, 2021, https://apnews.com/article/amazoncom-inc-technology-business-government-and-politics-5929d1293a67e7336471429e91cbab83.

35. Alex Wichowski, "The U.S. Can't Regulate Big Tech Companies When They Act Like Nations," *Washington Post*, October 29, 2020, https://www.washingtonpost.com/outlook/2020/10/29/antitrust-big-tech-net-states/.   Elsevier's profit margins are bigger than Apple's, Google's, and Amazon's. Stephen Buranyi, "Is the Staggeringly Profitable Business of Scientific Publishing Bad for Science?" *The Guardian*, June 27, 2017, https://www.theguardian.com/science/2017/jun/27/profitable-business-scientific-publishing-bad-for-science.

36. David Lazarus, "Shadowy Data Brokers Make the Most of Their Invisibility Cloak," *Los Angeles Times*, November 5, 2019, https://www.latimes.com/business/story/2019-11-05/column-data-brokers.

37. Stuart A. Thompson and Charlie Warzel, "Twelve Million Phones, One Dataset, Zero Privacy," *New York Times*, December 19, 2019, https://perma.cc/M2HK-GU7U.

38. Alex Barker and Patricia Nilsson, "Mutinous Librarians Help Drive Change at Elsevier," *Financial Times*, February 11, 2020: 11.

39. "Thomson Reuters' Brain," *Twin Cities Business*, November 11, 2009, https://tcbmag.com/thomson-reuters-brain/.

40. Ron Schmelzer, "The Vital Importance of Data for AI: Interview with Rick McFarland, Chief Data Officer—LexisNexis Legal & Professional," *Forbes*, June 25, 2021, https://www.forbes.com/sites/cognitiveworld/2021/07/25/the-vital-importance-of-data-for-ai-interview-with-rick-mcfarland-chief-data-officerlexisnexis-legal--professional/?sh=219ca89356b6. Clarivate's 2020 annual report describes the way data analytics companies process raw data to form structured, predictive information. Clarivate Annual Report 2020, 11, https://www.sec.gov/ix?doc=/Archives/edgar/data/1764046/000176404621000074/clvt-20201231.htm.

41. *What Is the Difference Between Data and Information?* Computer Hope, December 30, 2019, https://perma.cc/ZNZ4-JWTU.

42. "Powering Decision Making: Technology Careers at RELX Group," RELX, https://perma.cc/PR5F-T89Q (accessed September 27, 2021); Thomson Reuters, "Thomson Reuters Labs," https://perma.cc/3B86-JA6Q (accessed September 27, 2021).

43. Ian Freed, "Using Machine Learning to Analyze Taylor Swift's Lyrics," *Codeacademy*, September 19, 2018, https://news.codecademy.com/taylor-swift-lyrics-machine-learning/. For curious readers, the algorithm found that Swift's music made a transition to more "dance" topics with her switch from country to pop genres, and that Swift's music was especially vengeful in 2014, when she was at odds with both Kanye West and Katy Perry.

44. Liam Kane, "Agile Data Science—Part 2, The Burndown," October 28, 2027, https://perma.cc/6CJC-4X7E.

45. Jathan Sadowski, "When Data Is Capital: Datafication, Accumulation, and Extraction," *Big Data & Society* 6, no. 1 (January 2019): 8, https://journals.sagepub.com/doi/10.1177/2053951718820549.

46. LexisNexis, "Taking Analytics to Court: Technology Advances Are Driving a Higher Form of Litigation Intelligence," https://perma.cc/S5LC-HRHL (accessed September 27, 2021).

47. According to BCGEU, a Thomson Reuters shareholder, Reuters news accounted for only 10.7 percent of Thomson Reuters's total revenue. BCGEU called this a "drastic and alarming drop from a business that contributed over 50% of total revenues a decade earlier." Letter to Norges Bank on file with the author, April 28, 2020; BCGEU, "Calling on Thomson Reuters (TSX, NYSE: TRI) to Properly Assess Risks of Working with ICE," BCGEU Investor Brief, May 19, 2020, https://perma.cc/YS3F-9JFC: Thomson Reuters Annual Report 2019, https://perma.cc/5GPS-SL8F.

48. MSCI recategorized RELX as a business services company instead of a media group. Ronald Van Loon, "RELX Group: A Transformation Story," RELX, accessed September 27, 2021, https://perma.cc/Q9WY-LY8Y.

49. Fuchs, "Labor in Informational Capitalism and on the Internet," 189; Jonathan Zittrain, *The Future of the Internet—And How to Stop It* (New Haven: Yale University Press, 2008).

50. *International News Service v. Associated Press*, 248 U.S. 215, 250 (Brandeis Dissent) (1918).

51. Carl Malamud, "Who May Swim in the Ocean of Knowledge?" *The Wire*, March 2, 2018, https://perma.cc/223Q-YXFN.

52. Bart G. J. Knols, "Costing Lives," *Index on Censorship* 41, no. 3 (September 2012): 119, https://doi.org/10.1177/0306422012456482.

53. Thomas C. O'Bryant, "The Great Unobtainable Writ: Indigent Pro Se Litigation After the Antiterrorism and Effective Death Penalty Act of 1996," *Harvard Civil Rights-Civil Liberties Law Review* 41, no. 2 (Summer 2006): 299.

54. Nathan J. Robinson, "The Truth Is Paywalled but the Lies Are Free," *Current Affairs*, August 2, 2020, https://www.currentaffairs.org/2020/08/the-truth-is-paywalled-but-the-lies-are-free/.

55. Sharon Ringel, "Digitizing the Paper of Record: Archiving Digital Newspapers at the *New York Times*," *Journalism* (June 14, 2021): https://doi.org/10.1177/14648849211023849.

56. Karan Deep Singh, "As India's Lethal Covid Wave Neared, Politics Overrode Science," *New York Times*, September 14, 2021, https://perma.cc/8Y3J-84UC.

57. Ronald Van Loon, "(Part 2) RELX Group: The Transformation to a Leading Global & Analytics Company," LinkedIn, October, 26, 2017, https://perma.cc/3AXT-QRR3.

58. The U.S. National Archives actually calls its aggregated electronic records "big buckets." The agency introduced its big bucket archiving system, which

consolidates paper and electronic information into broad categories ("buckets"), with the name "flexible scheduling" in 2004. National Archives and Records Administration, "Strategic Directions: Flexible Scheduling," January, 2014, https://perma.cc/VX53-URSY.

59. Van Loon, "(Part 2) RELX Group."

60. Paul Hellyer, "Evaluating Shepard's, KeyCite, and BCite for Case Validation Accuracy," *Law Library Journal* 110, no. 4 (2018): 449–476.

61. Ivan Oransky, "25,000: That's How Many Retractions Are Now in the Retraction Watch Database," Retraction Watch, April 2, 2021, https://perma.cc/DJR7-8WP4.

62. Shea Swauger, "My request finally came in! It's 41 pages long. Here's the cover letter they sent," Twitter, December 13, 2019, https://perma.cc/24HF-F54X.

63. Jason Koebler, "Detroit Police Chief: Facial Recognition Software Misidentifies 96% of the Time," Vice, June 29, 2020. https://perma.cc/PP4J-2WE8.

64. Thomson Reuters, "Scouring Social Media: Leverage Web Data for Valuable Intelligence," CLEAR Webinar, https://perma.cc/4YWF-7R7F.

65. Elizabeth Leigh, "LexisNexis Adds Social Media Tool to Accurint Investigative Product; Haywood Talcove Comments," *ExecutiveBiz*, October 15, 2013, https://perma.cc/LK5D-FX7S.

66. Cora Currier, "Lawyers and Scholars to LexisNexis, Thomson Reuters: Stop Helping ICE Deport People," *The Intercept*, November 14, 2019, https://theintercept.com/2019/11/14/ice-lexisnexis-thomson-reuters-database/.

67. Lexis participates in health data analytics, partnering with hospitals, healthcare systems, and health care data analytics companies. LexisNexis Risk Solutions, "Improve Healthcare Outcomes Through Consumer, Provider and Claims Data Analytics," https://perma.cc/4XZM-23KB (accessed March 6, 2022); Electronic Health Reporter, "Carrot Health and LexisNexis Risk Solutions Announce Social Determinants of Health Collaboration," May 25, 2021, https://perma.cc/MCY8-AH6E.

68. Megan Kimble, "The Blacklist: Screened Out by Automated Background Checks, Tenants Who Face Eviction Can Be Denied Housing for Years to Come," *Texas Observer*, December 9, 2020, https://www.texasobserver.org/evictions-texas-housing/.

69. McKenzie Funk, "How ICE Picks Its Targets in the Surveillance Age," *New York Times Magazine*, October 2, 2019, https://perma.cc/GJR9-BV7A.

70. Sam Biddle, "LexisNexis to Provide Giant Database of Personal Information to ICE," The Intercept, April 2, 2021, https://theintercept.com/2021/04/02/ice-database-surveillance-lexisnexis/.

71. Sarah Lamdan, "When Westlaw Fuels Ice Surveillance: Ethics in the Era of Big Data Policing," *New York University Review of Law & Social Change* 43, no. 2 (2019): 255–293.

72. The American Library Association has urged antitrust intervention with Elsevier. Ana Enriquez, "Keeping Up with . . . Antitrust and Competition Law," American Library Association's Association of College and Research Libraries,

https://www.ala.org/acrl/publications/keeping_up_with/antitrust (accessed December 19, 2021).

73. Katharina Pistor, *The Code of Capital: How the Law Creates Wealth and Inequality* (Princeton, NJ: Princeton University Press, 2019).

74. *The Telecommunications Act of 1966*, Pub. L. No. 104-104, 110 Stat. 56, 47 U.S.C., Ch. 5.

75. Daniel Greene, *The Promise of Access: Technology, Inequality, and the Political Economy of Hope* (Cambridge, MA: MIT Press, 2021).

76. Sadowski, "When Data Is Capital," 5.

77. The "big three" music labels are Sony BMG, Universal Music Group, and Warner Music Group. The "big five" academic publishers are Reed-Elsevier, Wiley-Blackwell, Springer, Taylor & Francis, and Sage, and the "big five" trade book publishing houses are Hachette, HarperCollins, Macmillan, Penguin Random House, and Simon & Schuster. See Heather McDonald, "How the Big Four Record Labels Became the Big Three," The Balance Careers, July 29, 2019, https://www.thebalancecareers.com/big-three-record-labels-2460743; Vincent Larivière, Stefanie Haustein, and Phillipe Mongeon, "The Oligopoly of Academic Publishers in the Digital Era, *PLOS One*, June 10, 2015, https://journals.plos.org/plosone/article?id=10.1371/journal.pone.0127502; University of Montreal, "Five Companies Control More Than Half of Digital Publishing," June 10, 2015, https://phys.org/news/2015-06-companies-academic-publishing.html; and Valerie Peterson, "The Big 5 Trade Book Publishers," The Balance Careers, May 30, 2019, https://www.thebalancecareers.com/the-big-five-trade-book-publishers-2800047.

78. Tech Inquiry, Thomson Reuters, https://techinquiry.org/explorer/vendor/thomson%20reuters%20(grc)%20inc./ (accessed November 12, 2021); Tech Inquiry, RELX, https://techinquiry.org/explorer/vendor/relx%20plc/. (accessed November 12, 2021).

79. Jack Corrigan, "There's Only One Under-30 IT Specialist Working in Agencies for Every Four Who Are Over 60 Years Old," *Nextgov*, December 1, 2017, https://perma.cc/RH57-MLFK; Euroreporter, "#USA—How the Revolving Door in Washington Spins Between Government and Industry," July 29, 2020, https://perma.cc/NT34-ST75.

80. Bradford Grossman, "LexisNexis Special Services Inc Hires James Onusko as Head of Federal Strategy," *WashingtonExec*, July 31, 2019, https://perma.cc/8R6M-4STK.

81. "LexisNexis Special Services Appoints William G. Gross to Board of Directors," *PRNewswire*, April 26, 2021, https://www.prnewswire.com/news-releases/lexisnexis-special-services-appoints-william-g-gross-to-board-of-directors-301276765.html.

82. RELX Group: Summary 2020 Cycle, Open Secrets, https://perma.cc/4C2U-KM47 (accessed March 6, 2022).

83. Barker and Nilsson, "Mutinous Librarians Help Drive Change at Elsevier," 11.

84. Kenneth Frazier, "The Librarians' Dilemma: Contemplating the Costs

of the 'Big Deal'," *D-Lib Magazine* 7, no. 3 (2001): http://www.dlib.org/dlib/marcho1/frazier/03frazier.html.

85. When the author worked at Bloomberg Law, Westlaw and Lexis regularly incorporated Bloomberg Law tools into their own products, including Bloomberg Law's folder system and user-friendly webpage design.

86. Eric Segall, "The Justice Souter Speech Every Law Student Should Read," *Dorf on Law* (blog), August 19, 2020, http://www.dorfonlaw.org/2020/08/the-justice-souter-speech-every-law.html.

Chapter 2

1. The legal definition of the term "data broker" remains unsettled. Justin Sherman, "Federal Privacy Rules Must Get 'Data Broker' Definitions Right," *Lawfare*, April 8, 2021, https://www.lawfareblog.com/federal-privacy-rules-must-get-data-broker-definitions-right.

2. "The LexisNexis Timeline." LexisNexis, https://www.lexisnexis.com/anniversary/30th_timeline_fulltxt.pdf (accessed November 10, 2021).

3. From our RELX LexID's and Thomson Reuters CLEAR profiles.

4. Wolfie Cristl's in-depth report about the data broker industry describes the various types of data brokers. "Corporate Surveillance in Everyday Life: How Companies Collect, Combine, Analyze,Trade, and Use Personal Data on Billions," Cracked Labs, June, 2017, https://crackedlabs.org/dl/CrackedLabs_Christl_CorporateSurveillance.pdf.

5. This is a term Lexis uses in its risk product ads. "Reduce Fraud Risk at Account Opening," LexisNexis, https://risk.lexisnexis.com/products/lexisnexis-fraud-intelligence (accessed November 12, 2021).

6. Hannah Webha-Bloch, "Transparency After Carpenter," *Washburn Law Journal* 59, no. 1 (Winter 2020): 23–33.

7. Cristl, "Corporate Surveillance in Everyday Life."

8. Logan Danielle Wayne, "The Data-Broker Threat: Proposing Federal Legislation to Protect Post-Expungement Privacy," *Journal of Criminal Law and Criminology* 102, no. 1 (Winter 2012): 253–282; McKenzie Funk, "How ICE Picks Its Targets in the Surveillance Age," *New York Times*, October 2, 2019, https://www.nytimes.com/2019/10/02/magazine/ice-surveillance-deportation.html.

9. Chris Hoofnagle, "Big Brother's Little Helpers: How ChoicePoint and Other Commercial Data Brokers Collect and Package Your Data for Law Enforcement Enforcement," *North Carolina Journal of International Law and Commercial Regulation* 29, no. 4 (2004): 595–638.

10. Cathy O'Neil, *Weapons of Math Destruction: How Big Data Increases Inequality and Threatens Democracy* (New York: Crown, 2016).

11. David Lazarus, "Shadowy Data Brokers Make the Most of Their Invisibility Cloak," *Los Angeles Times*, November 5, 2019, https://www.latimes.com/business/story/2019-11-05/column-data-brokers.

12. "Hank Asher, Entrepreneur, Technology Visionary, and Philanthropist, Dies at 61," *Reuters*, January 12, 2013, in the Internet Archive, https://web.archive

.org/web/20150924173144/http://www.reuters.com/article/2013/01/12/fl-hank
-asher-tlo-idUSnBw9vHVLda+11c+BSW20130112.

13. Hoofnagle, "Big Brother's Little Helpers," 624.

14. Michael Shnayerson, "The Net's Master Data-Miner," *Vanity Fair*, December, 2004, https://www.vanityfair.com/news/2004/12/matrix200412.

15. Some government agencies sell our personal data to bolster state budgets. In 2017 alone, Washington State's Department of Licensing made $26,371,232 selling driver and vehicle records to data brokers, including LexisNexis and companies that work with Thomson Reuters. Funk, "How ICE Picks Its Targets in the Surveillance Age."

16. Hoofnagle, "Big Brother's Little Helpers," 624.

17. Reed Elsevier Group, Plc bought Asher's company for $775 million. "Reed Elsevier's LexisNexis Acquires Seisint for $775 Million," Spectrum Equity, July 2004, https://www.spectrumequity.com/news/reed-elseviers-lexisnexis-acquires
-seisint-for-775-million.

18. "The LexisNexis Timeline."

19. Sam Biddle and Spencer Woodman, "These Are the Technology Firms Lining Up to Build Trump's 'Extreme Vetting' Program," *The Intercept*, August 7, 2017, https://theintercept.com/2017/08/07/these-are-the-technology-firms-lining
-up-to-build-trumps-extreme-vetting-program/.

20. "FTC Challenges Reed Elsevier's Proposed $4.1 Billion Acquisition of ChoicePoint, Inc.," Federal Trade Commission, September 16, 2008, https://
www.ftc.gov/news-events/press-releases/2008/09/ftc-challenges-reed-elseviers
-proposed-41-billion-acquisition.

21. "About LexisNexis," LexisNexis, https://www.lexisnexis.com.hk/about
-us/overview; "Who We Serve," Thomson Reuters Special Services, LLC, https:/
/www.trssllc.com/government-2/ (accessed November 14, 2021); "LNSSI: Industries We Serve," LexisNexis, https://www.lexisnexisspecialservices.com/who-we
-are/industries/ (accessed November 14, 2021).

22. "Criminal Investigations & Analysis," LexisNexis, https://risk.lexisnexis
.com/law-enforcement-and-public-safety (accessed November 11, 2021); "Ensure safety," Thomson Reuters, https://www.thomsonreuters.com/en/products-services
/government.html#safety.

23. LNSSI is a suite of risk products specially designed to "arm government agencies with superior data, technology and analytics to support mission success." LexisNexis Special Services, Inc., "What We Do," https://www.lexisnexis
specialservices.com/ (accessed December 10, 2021).

24. Maryam Saleh,"As Trump Announces Mass Immigration Raid, Documents Show How ICE Uses Arrest Quotas," *The Intercept*, July 3, 2019, https:
//theintercept.com/2019/07/03/ice-raids-arrest-quotas/; Simon Egbert and Matthias Leese, *Criminal Futures: Predictive Policing and Everyday Police Work* (Abingdon, UK: Routledge Studies in Policing and Society, 2021).

25. Tyler Wall, " 'For the Very Existence of Civilization': The Police Dog and Racial Terror," *American Quarterly* 68, no. 4 (December 2016): 878, https://muse
.jhu.edu/article/641464.

26. Caitlin Dewey, "How the NSA Spied on Americans Before the Internet," *Washington Post*, August 23, 2013, https://www.washingtonpost.com/news/the-switch/wp/2013/08/23/how-the-nsa-spied-on-americans-before-the-internet/.

27. Rachel Levinson-Waldman describes how The PATRIOT Act's section 215 authorized law enforcement to obtain "any tangible thing" related to an investigation. "What the Government Does with Americans' Data," The Brennan Center for Justice, at New York University School of Law, 2013, p. 8, https://www.brennancenter.org/sites/default/files/2019-08/Report_What-Government-Does-With-Americans-Data.pdf, discussing the *USA PATRIOT Act*, Pub. L. No. 107-56, § 215, 115 Stat. 365 (codified as amended at 50 U.S.C. § 1861(a)(1) (2012)).

28. Jihan Abdallah, " 'Under the Prism': Muslim Americans Reflect on Life Post-9/11," *Al Jazeera*, September 11, 2021, https://www.aljazeera.com/news/2021/9/9/under-the-prism-muslim-americans-reflect-on-life-post-9.

29. Christopher M. Ferguson, "The IRS's Big Plans for Big Data," *The CPA Journal*, October 2021, https://www.cpajournal.com/2021/10/26/the-irss-big-plans-for-big-data/.

30. *EPIC v. U.S. Postal Service et. al*, No. 21-2156 (D.D.C., filed Aug. 12, 2021).

31. "LNSSI: Industries We Serve," LexisNexis; "Welcome to Accurint," https://www.accurint.com/hr.html (accessed November 11, 2021).

32. Chris Mills Rodrigo, "Majority of Independent Shareholders Vote to Review Thomson Reuters' ICE Contracts," *The Hill*, June 9, 2021, https://thehill.com/policy/technology/557591-majority-of-independent-shareholders-vote-to-review-thomson-reuters-ice; "Who We Serve," Thomson Reuters Special Services, LLC.

33. "Risk," RELX, https://www.relx.com/our-business/market-segments/risk (accessed November 14, 2021); RELX Annual Report and Financial Statements 2020, https://www.relx.com/~/media/Files/R/RELX-Group/documents/reports/annual-reports/2020-annual-report.pdf.

34. Charlie Warzel, "The Internet's Original Sin: Shoshana Wodinsky Explains Bad Ads," *Galaxy Brain*, September 23, 2021, https://warzel.substack.com/p/the-internets-original-sin.

35. Brian Hochman, *The Listeners: A History of Wiretapping in the United States* (Cambridge, MA: Harvard University Press, 2022), 229–230.

36. Vinay Patel, "Racially Motivated Spying Pretext: Challenging the FBI's New Regime of Racialized Surveillance," *Columbia Journal of Race and Law Forum* 11, no. 1 (February 2021): 1–31.

37. Andrea L. Dennis, "A Snitch in Time: An Historical Sketch of Black Informing During Slavery," *Marquette Law Review* 97, no. 2 (Winter 2013): 279–334; Patel, "Racially Motivated Spying Pretext."

38. Jenn Stroud Rossmann and B. R. Cohen, "The Roots of Digital Racism Date Back to 19th Century Railroads," *Fast Company*, October 19, 2021, https://www.fastcompany.com/90683997/the-roots-of-digital-racism-date-back-to-19th-century-railroads.

39. Ruha Benjamin, *Race After Technology* (Cambridge: Polity Books, 2019), 116.

40. Funk, "How ICE Picks Its Targets in the Surveillance Age."

41. Thomas S. Mullaney et al., eds., *Your Computer Is on Fire* (Cambridge, MA: MIT Press, 2021).

42. Safiya Umoja Noble, *Algorithms of Oppression: How Search Engines Reinforce Racism* (New York: New York University Press, 2018).

43. Elizabeth Brico and Marta Monteiro, "When Data Discriminates," *Weapons of Reason*, April 17, 2019, https://medium.com/the-ai-issue-weapons-of-reason/when-data-discriminates-4791f14c5906.

44. Steven Rich, "Here's a brief thread on decontextualized data and why it's bad, through the lens of the data collected by my car insurance company for the purpose of determining a discount based on how I drive," Twitter, December 26, 2020, https://twitter.com/dataeditor/status/1342877187251310592.

45. Joseph Cox, "How the U.S. Military Buys Location Data from Ordinary Apps," Motherboard, Vice, November 16, 2020, https://www.vice.com/en/article/jgqm5x/us-military-location-data-xmode-locate-x.

46. David Lazarus, "Is a Supermarket Discount Coupon Worth Giving Away Your Privacy?" *Los Angeles Times*, January 21, 2020, https://www.latimes.com/business/story/2020-01-21/ralphs-privacy-disclosure.

47. Jessica Saunders, "Predictions Put into Practice: A Quasi-Experimental Evaluation of Chicago's Predictive Policing Pilot," *Journal of Experimental Criminology* 12 (2016): 347–371, https://doi.org/10.1007/s11292-016-9272-0; Jeremy Gorner and Annie Sweeney, "For Years Chicago Police Rated the Risk of Tens of Thousands Being Caught Up in Violence. That Controversial Effort Has Been Quietly Ended," *Chicago Tribune*, January 24, 2020, https://www.chicagotribune.com/news/criminal-justice/ct-chicago-police-strategic-subject-list-ended-20200125-spn4kjmrxrh4tmktdjckhtox4i-story.html.

48. Funk, "How ICE Picks Its Targets in the Surveillance Age."

49. Alice Holbrook, "When LexisNexis Makes a Mistake, You Pay For It," *Newsweek*, September 26, 2019, https://www.newsweek.com/2019/10/04/lexisnexis-mistake-data-insurance-costs-1460831.html.

50. "What Information Do Data Brokers Have on Consumers, and How Do They Use It?" Testimony of Pam Dixon, Executive Director, World Privacy Forum, Before the Senate Committee on Commerce, Science, and Transportation, December 18, 2013, http://www.worldprivacyforum.org/wp-content/uploads/2013/12/WPF_PamDixon_CongressionalTestimony_DataBrokers_2013_fs.pdf.

51. "LexID," LexisNexis, https://risk.lexisnexis.com/our-technology/lexid (accessed November 11, 2021); "Thomson Reuters CLEAR," Thomson Reuters, https://legal.thomsonreuters.com/en/products/clear-investigation-software (accessed November 11, 2021).

52. "LexID"; "Cast a Wider Net with Our Powerful Public Records Search," LexisNexis, https://www.lexisnexis.com/en-us/products/public-records/powerful-public-records-search.page (accessed November 14, 2021).

53. In 2014, the Federal Trade Commission chairwoman, Edith Ramirez,

said that today's data brokers "often know as much—or even more—about us than our family and friends." In "FTC Recommends Congress Require the Data Broker Industry to Be More Transparent."

54. Ian Goldberg et al., "Privacy-Enhancing Technologies for the Internet," Institute of Electrical and Electronics Engineers COMPCON Proceedings, 1997, https://ieeexplore.ieee.org/stamp/stamp.jsp?tp=&arnumber=584660.

55. Terry Gangcuangco, "LexisNexis Risk Solutions Links Disparate Customer Data for Motor Insurers," Corporate Risk and Insurance, February 7, 2018, https://www.insurancebusinessmag.com/us/risk-management/news/lexisnexis-risk-solutions-links-disparate-customer-data-for-motor-insurers-91463.aspx; "NICB-LexisNexis Strategic Partnership," National Insurance Crime Bureau, May 22, 2017, https://www.nicb.org/news/news-releases/nicb-lexisnexis-strategic-partnership; "LexID® for Healthcare," LexisNexis Risk Solutions, https://risk.lexisnexis.com/products/lexid-for-healthcare (accessed November 14, 2021).

56. Doug Wyllie, "New LexisNexis Service Keeps Tabs on Social Media," *Police1 by Lexipol*, January 30, 2014, https://www.police1.com/police-products/investigation/investigative-software/articles/new-lexisnexis-service-keeps-tabs-on-social-media-KfCucEkc3UnXtP5Z/.

57. "Records, Computers, and the Rights of Citizens," U.S. Department of Health, Education & Welfare, p. 20, https://www.justice.gov/opcl/docs/rec-com-rights.pdf (accessed April 24, 2022).

58. David E. Pozen, "The Mosaic Theory, National Security, and the Freedom of Information Act," *Yale Law Journal* 115, no. 3 (December 2005): 628–679.

59. Andrew Quodling, "Shadow Profiles—Facebook Knows About You, Even If You're not on Facebook," *The Conversation*, April 13, 2018, https://perma.cc/M2K3-XZXS.

60. "What Investigators Can Learn from People Who Want to Disappear," Thomson Reuters, December 3, 2019, https://legal.thomsonreuters.com/blog/what-investigators-can-learn-from-people-who-want-to-disappear/.

61. Goldberg et al., "Privacy-Enhancing Technologies for the Internet."

62. Adam Stone, "LexisNexis, Bode Technology Team to Accelerate DNA-Based Investigations," *WashingtonExec*, December 16, 2019, https://washingtonexec.com/2019/12/lexisnexis-bode-technology-team-to-accelerate-dna-based-investigations/#.YACST15Om8W.

63. Russell Brandom, "Exclusive: ICE Is About to Start Tracking License Plates Across the US, *The Verge*, January 26, 2018, https://www.theverge.com/2018/1/26/16932350/ice-immigration-customs-license-plate-recognition-contract-vigilant-solutions.

64. "Forensic Logic Launches COPLINK X, The Next-Generation Information Network for Law Enforcement," *PR Newswire*, July 16, 2019, https://www.prnewswire.com/news-releases/forensic-logic-launches-coplink-x-the-next-generation-information-network-for-law-enforcement-300885164.html; "Thomson Reuters and Palantir Technologies Enter Exclusive Agreement to Create Next-Generation Analytics Platform for Financial Client," Thomson Reuters,

April 12, 2010, Internet Archive, https://web.archive.org/web/20120508172659/
http://thomsonreuters.com/content/press_room/financial/2010_04_12_palantir
_technologies_agreement.

65. U.S. Const. amend. IV.

66. Kit Kinports, "Culpability, Deterrence, and the Exclusionary Rule," *William & Mary Bill of Rights Journal* 21, no. 3 (March 2013): 821–856.

67. *Hester v. United States*, 265 U.S. 57 (1924).

68. *Coolidge v. New Hampshire*, 403 U.S. 443 (1971).

69. The 1970s-era third-party doctrine cases deal with old-fashioned information collection such as whiskey distillers' bank records from the days when banking was an in-person affair and police used phone companies' data from pen registers, devices that capture phone numbers called from a particular phone line. *United States v. Miller*, 425 U.S. 435 (1976); *Smith v. Maryland*, 442 U.S. 735 (1979).

70. *United States v. Jones*, 565 U.S. 400 (2012) (Sotomayor, S., concurring).

71. *Carpenter v. U.S.*, 585 U.S. ___ (2018); 138 S. Ct. 2206; 201 L. Ed. 2d 507.

72. In *United States v. Gratkowski*, 964 F.3d 307 (5th Cir. 2020), the Fifth Circuit Court of Appeals ruled that the third-party doctrine applies to information on the bitcoin blockchain, comparing information to bank records, which are subject to the Fourth Amendment exception.

73. Gilad Edelman, "Can the Government Buy Its Way Around the Fourth Amendment?" *Wired*, February 11, 2020, https://www.wired.com/story/can
-government-buy-way-around-fourth-amendment/.

74. The Constitution Project, "Recommendation for Fusion Centers: Preserving Privacy & Civil Liberties While Protecting Against Crime and Terrorism," 2012, p. 5, https://archive.constitutionproject.org/pdf/fusioncenterreport.pdf.

75. LexisNexis Risk Solutions, "Prevent and Solve More Crimes with Data-Driven Insights," https://perma.cc/U8B7-Q833 (accessed April 24, 2022); LexisNexis Special Services, Inc., Public Safety Data Exchange (PSDEX), https://
www.lexisnexisspecialservices.com/what-we-do/big-data-solutions/public-safety
-data-exchange/ (accessed April 8, 2018).

76. Laws like The Privacy Act of 1974, 5 U.S.C. § 522a, provide people with access to their records and the right to request corrections when records are incorrect.

77. Alice Holbrook and Nerdwallet, "When LexisNexis Makes a Mistake, You Pay for It," *Newsweek*, September 26, 2019, https://www.newsweek.com/2019
/10/04/lexisnexis-mistake-data-insurance-costs-1460831.html.

78. Shea Swauger, "My request finally came in! It's 41 pages long. Here's the cover letter they sent," Twitter, December 13, 2019, https://twitter.com/
SheaSwauger/status/1205591704973103104.

79. Swauger, "My request finally came in!"

80. Lazarus, "Shadowy Data Brokers Make the Most of Their Invisibility Cloak."

81. Elise Schmelzer, "How Colorado Law Enforcement Quietly Expanded

Its Use of Facial Recognition," *Denver Post*, September 27, 2020, https://www
.denverpost.com/2020/09/27/facial-recognition-colorado-police/; JPrivate, "Cops
Use Lexis Nexis Facial Recognition to Identify Your Family and Friends," *Tenth
Amendment Center Blog*, May 20, 2019, https://blog.tenthamendmentcenter.com
/2019/05/cops-use-lexis-nexis-facial-recognition-to-identify-your-family-and
-friends/.

82. Virginia Eubanks, *Automating Inequality: How High-Tech Tools Profile,
Police, and Punish the Poor* (London: Macmillan, 2018).

83. Schmelzer, "How Colorado Law Enforcement Quietly Expanded its Use
of Facial Recognition."

84. Adele Peters, "Algorithms Are Creating a 'Digital Poorhouse' That Makes
Inequality Worse," *Fast Company*, March 1, 2018, https://www.fastcompany.com
/40534131/algorithms-are-creating-a-digital-poorhouse-that-makes-inequality
-worse.

85. Especially in the United States, marginalized communities have been
made test subjects for medical experiments and invasive technological security
tools. For instance, in the 1930s the U.S. Public Health Service made Black men
subjects of syphilis experiments in the Tuskegee Study. Today, that type of biological racism has expanded to technological racism. Adam McVean, "40 Years
of Human Experimentation in America: The Tuskegee Study," McGill Office of
Science and Society, https://www.mcgill.ca/oss/article/history/40-years-human
-experimentation-america-tuskegee-study (accessed November 15, 2021).

86. Mutale Nkonde, "Automated Anti-Blackness: Facial Recognition in
Brooklyn, New York," *Harvard Kennedy School Journal of African American Policy*
(2019–2020): 30–36.

87. Sam Biddle, "LexisNexis to Provide Giant Database of Personal Information to ICE," *The Intercept*, April 2, 2021, https://theintercept.com/2021/04/
02/ice-database-surveillance-lexisnexis/. ICE calls the data companies' products
"mission critical." Funk, "How ICE Picks Its Targets in the Surveillance Age."

88. "The Deadly Digital Border Wall," Mijente, Just Futures Law, & No
Border Wall Coalition, 2021, https://notechforice.com/wp-content/uploads/2021
/10/Deadly.Digital.Border.Wall_.pdf.

89. "Immigration Cyber Prisons: Ending the Use of Electronic Ankle Shack-
les," Benjamin N. Cardozo School of Law, Kathryn O. Greenberg Immigration
Justice Clinic, Freedom for Immigrants, Immigrant Defense Project, July 2021,
https://static1.squarespace.com/static/5a33042eb078691c386e7bce/t/60ec661ec578
326ec3032d52/1626105377079/Immigration+Cyber+Prisons+report.pdf.

90. Funk, "How ICE Picks Its Targets in the Surveillance Age."

91. Drew Harwell, "ICE Investigators Used a Private Utility Database Covering Millions to Pursue Immigration Violations," *Washington Post*, February
26, 2021, https://www.washingtonpost.com/technology/2021/02/26/ice-private
-utility-data/.

92. Funk, "How ICE Picks Its Targets in the Surveillance Age."

93. "Silicon Valley and Police Create COINTELPRO for the Tech Age," *tele-*

SUR, October 12, 2016, https://www.telesurenglish.net/news/Silicon-Valley-and
-Police-Create-Cointelpro-for-the-Tech-Age-20161012-0005.html.

94. Caroline Haskins and Ryan Mac, "Here Are the Minneapolis Police's Tools to Identify Protesters," *Buzzfeed News*, May 29, 2020, https://www.buzzfeednews.com/article/carolinehaskins1/george-floyd-protests-surveillance-technology.

95. Cristl, "Corporate Surveillance in Everyday Life."

96. Dan Hurley, "Can an Algorithm Tell When Kids Are in Danger?" *New York Times*, January 2, 2018, https://www.nytimes.com/2018/01/02/magazine/can -an-algorithm-tell-when-kids-are-in-danger.html.

97. Elizabeth Brico and Marta Monteiro, "When Data Discriminates," *Weapons of Reason*, April 17, 2019, https://medium.com/the-ai-issue-weapons-of -reason/when-data-discriminates-4791f14c5906.

98. Brico and Monteiro, "When Data Discriminates."

99. Sarah Mancini et al., "Mismatched and Mistaken: How the Use of an Inaccurate Private Database Results in SSI Recipients Unjustly Losing Benefits," National Consumer Law Center, April 2021, https://justiceinaging.org/wp -content/uploads/2021/04/SSADataReport.pdf.

100. Holbrook, "When LexisNexis Makes a Mistake, You Pay For It."

101. Holbrook, "When LexisNexis Makes a Mistake, You Pay For It."

102. Kimble, Megan. "The Blacklist: Screened Out by Automated Background Checks, Tenants Who Face Eviction Can Be Denied Housing for Years to Come, *Texas Observer*, December 9, 2020, https://www.texasobserver.org/ evictions-texas-housing/.

103. "Supplementary Detailed Staff Reports on Intelligence Activities and the Rights of Americans," Final Report of the Select Committee to Study Governmental Operations with Respect to Intelligence Activities, 94th Cong., 2d sess., 1976, S. Rep. 94-755, p. 778.

104. Jesse Marx, "The Mission Creep of Smart Streetlights," *Voice of San Diego*, February 3, 2020, https://www.voiceofsandiego.org/topics/public-safety/ the-mission-creep-of-smart-streetlights/.

105. Claire Lampen, "Yes, LinkNYC Kiosks Are Giant Data-Harvesting Surveillance Cameras, Obviously," *Gothamist*, April 30, 2019, https://gothamist .com/news/yes-linknyc-kiosks-are-giant-data-harvesting-surveillance-cameras -obviously.

106. Annie McDonough, "How New York City Is Watching You," City & State New York, April 30, 2019, https://www.cityandstateny.com/articles/policy/ technology/how-new-york-city-is-watching-you.html.

107. Hoofnagle, "Big Brother's Little Helpers."

108. Hoofnagle, "Big Brother's Little Helpers."

109. Sadie Gurman, "Across US, Police Officers Abuse Confidential Databases," *Associated Press*, September 28, 2016, https://apnews.com/article/699236 946e3140659fff8a2362e16f43.

110. Hoofnagle, "Big Brother's Little Helpers."

111. FBI Office of the General Counsel routing slip, September 16, 2001, p. 5

(obtained from the FBI via FOIA request, https://epic.org/wp-content/uploads/privacy/choicepoint/cpfbic.pdf.

112. Gurman, "Across US, Police Officers Abuse Confidential Databases."

113. "FTC Recommends Congress Require the Data Broker Industry to Be More Transparent and Give Consumers Greater Control Over Their Personal Information," Federal Trade Commission, press release, May 27, 2014, https://www.ftc.gov/news-events/press-releases/2014/05/ftc-recommends-congress-require-data-broker-industry-be-more?utm_source=govdelivery.

114. *Data Broker Accountability and Transparency Act*, S. 2025, 113th Cong., introduced February 12, 2014.

115. Some examples of privacy and data laws beyond the United States include the Brazilian General Personal Data Protection Act (LGPD), Law No. 13.709 (August 14, 2018); Canada's Personal Information Protection and Electronic Data Act (PIPEDA), (S.C. 2000), c. 5; the European Union's General Data Protection Regulation (GDPR), Regulation (EU) (2016/679); New Zealand's Privacy Act 2020 (2020 No 31), and Thailand's Personal Data Protection Act 2019 (PDPA), B.E. 2562.

116. *The Family Educational Rights and Privacy Act of 1974*, 20 U.S.C. § 1232g; *Health Insurance Portability and Accountability Act of 1996*, Pub. L. No. 104-191, § 264, 110 Stat. 1936; and the *Children's Online Privacy Protection Act of 1998*, 15 U.S.C. §§ 6501–6506, Pub. L. No. 105-277, § 112, Stat. 2681; *1978 Right to Financial Privacy Act*, Pub. L. No. 95-630, 92 Stat. 3641; *Gramm-Leach-Bliley Act of 1999*, Pub. L. No. 106-102; and *Fair Credit Reporting Act of 1970*, Pub. L. No. 91-508, 84 Stat. 1127.

117. *The Freedom of Information Act*, 5 U.S.C. § 552.

118. Sarah Mancini et al., "Mismatched and Mistaken: How the Use of an Inaccurate Private Database Results in SSI Recipients Unjustly Losing Benefits," National Consumer Law Center, April 2021, https://justiceinaging.org/wp-content/uploads/2021/04/SSADataReport.pdf.

119. *The Privacy Act of 1974*, 5 U.S.C. § 552a.

120. *The Privacy Act of 1974*, 5 U.S.C. § 552a; Hoofnagle, "Big Brother's Little Helpers."

121. Hoofnagle, "Big Brother's Little Helpers."

122. 18 U.S.C. §§ 2510–2523. The Stored Communications Act, a law that addresses voluntary and compelled disclosure of stored wire and electronic communications and transactional records held by third-party internet service providers, was enacted as Title II of the Electronic Communications Privacy Act of 1986; §§ 2701–2712; Pub. L. 99-508; 100 Stat. 1848, 1860.

123. Chris Hoofnagle, "Facebook and Google Are the New Data Brokers," *Critical Reflections*, Digital Life Initiative at Cornell Tech, January 5, 2021, https://www.dli.tech.cornell.edu/post/facebook-and-google-are-the-new-data-brokers; Cora Currier, "Lawyers and Scholars to LexisNexis, Thomson Reuters: Stop Helping ICE Deport People," *The Intercept*, November 14, 2019, https://theintercept.com/2019/11/14/ice-lexisnexis-thomson-reuters-database/.

124. California's CCPA AB-375, Illinois's PIPA 815 ILCS 530/1, Vermont's protection of personal information law 9 V.S.A. § 2430.

125. "Testimony on Choicepoint and Commercial Data Brokers," Electronic Privacy Information Center, March 17, 2005, https://epic.org/privacy/choicepoint /majorasltr3.17.05.pdf.

126. Samuel D. Warren and Louis D. Brandeis, "Right to Privacy," *Harvard Law Review* 4, no. 5 (1890–1891): 193–220.

127. Dorothy J. Glancy, "The Invention of the Right to Privacy," *Arizona Law Review* 21, no. 1 (1979): 1–40, 37. The famous law review article also warned that anticipating how to apply the law would be "a difficult task." Warren and Brandeis, "Right to Privacy," 214.

128. Fred H. Cate and Beth E. Cate, "The Supreme Court and Information Privacy," *International Data Privacy Law* 2, no. 4 (November 2012): 255–267, https://doi.org/10.1093/idpl/ips024.

129. *Griswold v. Connecticut*, 381 U.S. 479, 484 (1965). A Fourth Amendment right to privacy was established in *Katz v. United States*, 89 U.S. 347 (1967).

130. Martha Minow, "Alternatives to the State Action Doctrine in the Era of Privatization, Mandatory Arbitration, and the Internet: Directing Law to Service Human Needs," *Harvard Civil Rights-Civil Liberties Law Review* 52, no. 1 (Winter 2017): 145–168, 152.

131. *Brentwood Acad. v. Tennessee Secondary Sch. Athletic Ass'n*, 531 U.S. 288, 296 (2000).

132. *Wolotsky v. Huhn*, 960 F.2d 1331, 1335 (6th Cir. 1992).

133. *Burton v. Wilmington Parking Authority*, 365 U.S. 715 (1961).

134. Joshuah Lisk, "Is Batman a State Actor: The Dark Knight's Relationship with the Gotham City Police Department and the Fourth Amendment Implications," *Case Western Reserve Law Review* 64, no. 3 (Spring 2014): 1419–1440.

135. The Supreme Court held that a private nonprofit corporation that operated public access cable channels was not a state actor. *Manhattan Community Access Corp. v. Halleck*, 139 S. Ct. 1921 (2019). A federal court in Texas held that Facebook is not a state actor. *Nyabwa v. Facebook*, 2:17-CV-24 (S.D. Tex. Jan. 26, 2018).

136. *Knight First Amendment Institute at Columbia University v. Trump*, 1:17-cv-05205 (S.D.N.Y.), filed July 11, 2017.

137. *The Fourth Amendment Is Not For Sale Act*, S. 1265, 117th Cong., introduced April 21, 2021.

138. David Segal, "A Matter of Opinion?" *New York Times*, July 18, 2009, https://www.nytimes.com/2009/07/19/business/19floyd.html; *United States v. McGraw Hill Companies, Inc.*, No. 13-00779 (C.D. Cal), Settlement, February 2, 2015, https://www.justice.gov/file/338701/download.

139. *Langdon v. Google, Inc.*, 474 F. Supp. 2d 622 (2007); Brief of Amicus Curiae Electronic Frontier Foundation Supporting Defendants-Appellees at 9; *Prager University v. Google, LLC*, 951 F.3d 991 (2020) (arguing that the First Amendment protects YouTube's right to curate its website); *Jian Zhang v. Baidu*,

10 F. Supp. 3d 433 (2014) (allowing Plaintiffs to sue Baidu for what are in essence editorial judgments about which political ideas to promote would run afoul of the First Amendment).

140. Margot E. Kaminski and Scott Skinner-Thompson, "Free Speech Isn't a Free Pass for Privacy Violations," *Slate*, March 9, 2020, https://slate.com/technology/2020/03/free-speech-privacy-clearview-ai-maine-isps.html.

141. Paulina Firozi, "The Health 202: The Supreme Court Banned Patenting Genes. But Congress Might Change That." *Washington Post*, June 3, 2019, https://www.washingtonpost.com/news/powerpost/paloma/the-health-202/2019/06/03/the-health-202-the-supreme-court-banned-patenting-genes-but-congress-might-change-that/5cf1987f1ad2e52231e8e91b/.

142. Danielle Bernstein, "Why the 'Right to Be Forgotten' Won't Make It to the United States," *Michigan Technology Law Review*, February 14, 2020, http://mttlr.org/2020/02/why-the-right-to-be-forgotten-wont-make-it-to-the-united-states/.

143. *Garcia v. Google, Inc.*, 786 F.3d 733, 743 (9th Cir. 2015).

144. "What Is 'Alt Data', Who Is Using It and Why?" *Radar by Behavox*, June 26, 2019, https://radar.behavox.com/what-is-alt-data-who-is-using-it-and-why/.

145. Zoe Greenberg, "What Is the Blood of a Poor Person Worth?" *New York Times*, February 1, 2019, https://www.nytimes.com/2019/02/01/sunday-review/blood-plasma-industry.html.

146. Cameron F. Kerry and John B. Morris Jr., "Why Data Ownership Is the Wrong Approach to Protecting Privacy," Brookings, June 26, 2019, https://www.brookings.edu/blog/techtank/2019/06/26/why-data-ownership-is-the-wrong-approach-to-protecting-privacy/.

147. *Own Your Own Data Act*, S. 806, 116th Cong., introduced by Senator John Kennedy, March 14, 2019.

148. Hoofnagle, "Big Brother's Little Helpers."

Chapter 3

1. "National Science Foundation (NSF)," grants.gov (accessed November 2, 2021).

2. In 2019, the U.S. government spent $78.7 billion to support research in the higher education sector. "U.S. Research and Development Funding and Performance: Fact Sheet," Congressional Research Service, October 4, 2021, p. 4, https://sgp.fas.org/crs/misc/R44307.pdf.

3. Librarian Micah Vandergrift provides an overview of research impact studies. Micah Vandergrift, "Defining Social Impact," *Accelerating the Social Impact of Research*, Association of Research Libraries, August 18, 2021, https://medium.com/accelerating-the-social-impact-of-research/defining-social-impact-1a68a18f5314.

4. According to the United Nation's Universal Declaration of Human Rights, Article 27, everyone has a right to share in scientific advancement and its benefits.

5. The "academic research oligopoly" includes (1) Reed Elsevier (of the RELX

Group), (2) Wiley-Blackwell, (3) Springer, and (4) Taylor & Francis. Vincent Laviere et al., "The Oligopoly of Academic Publishing in the Digital Era," *PLOS One* 10, no. 6 (June 2015): 11, 10.1371/journal.pone.0127502.

6. "Elsevier," https://www.elsevier.com/ (accessed November 17, 2021).

7. James Ashton, "Stop the Press: How Data Displaced Trade Publishing," RELX, https://stories.relx.com/stop-the-press/index.html; Laura Peek, "A Sense of Purpose at Elsevier," RELX, https://stories.relx.com/elsevier-purpose/index.html.

8. John J. Regazzi, *Scholarly Communications: A History from Content as King to Content as Kingmaker* (Lanham, MD: Rowman & Littlefield, 2015), 52–53.

9. "History," Elsevier, https://www.elsevier.com/about/history (accessed November 17, 2021).

10. As researchers explain, "The ability to rebrand as data analytics and the success of many of these services is a direct result of the disproportionate ownership of academic content that these publishers have historically acquired." Alejandro Posada and George Chen, "Publishers Are Increasingly in Control of Scholarly Infrastructure and Why We Should Care: A Case Study of Elsevier," *The Knowledge G.A.P.: The Geopolitics of Academic Production*, September 20, 2017, http://knowledgegap.org/index.php/sub-projects/rent-seeking-and-financialization-of-the-academic-publishing-industry/preliminary-findings/.

11. Thomson Science launched in 2006, and it became part of Thomson Reuters in the 2008 merger of the Thomson Corporation with the Reuters Group. Bob Grant, "Web of Science Sold for More Than $3 Billion," *The Scientist*, July 15, 2016, https://www.the-scientist.com/the-nutshell/web-of-science-sold-for-more-than-3-billion-33184.

12. "Research Metrics Quick Reference," Elsevier, https://www.elsevier.com/librarians/providing-library-services/research-metrics-quick-reference (accessed November 17, 2021).

13. "About PlumX Metrics," Elsevier, https://plumanalytics.com/learn/about-metrics/ (accessed November 17, 2021).

14. "Welcome to Scopus Preview," Elsevier, https://www.scopus.com/home.uri?zone=header&origin= (accessed November 17, 2021).

15. "Welcome to SciVal," https://www.scival.com/landing (accessed November 17, 2021).

16. Posada and Chen, "Publishers Are Increasingly in Control of Scholarly Infrastructure."

17. Posada and Chen, "Publishers Are Increasingly in Control of Scholarly Infrastructure."

18. These acquisitions and takeovers aren't friendly. An ex-Mendeley employee described how Elsevier bullied Mendeley into selling, forcing Mendeley to remove Elsevier papers from the platform and "ma[king] scary lawyerly noises loud enough to give Mendeley pause." Elsevier suffocated their business until a sale was the only way out. David Dobbs, "When the Rebel Alliance Sells Out," *The New Yorker*, April 12, 2013, https://www.newyorker.com/tech/annals-of-technology/when-the-rebel-alliance-sells-out.

19. Bart G. J.Knols, "Costing Lives," *Index on Censorship* 41, no. 3 (September 2012): 119, https://doi.org/10.1177/0306422012456482.

20. Christophe Boudry et al., "Worldwide Inequality in Access to Full Text Scientific Articles: The Example of Ophthalmology," *PeerJ*, October 30, 2019, https://www.ncbi.nlm.nih.gov/pmc/articles/PMC6825414/.

21. Boudry, "Worldwide Inequality."

22. Justin Peters, "Why Is It So Expensive to Read Academic Research?" *Slate*, April 5, 2016, https://slate.com/technology/2016/04/the-lawsuit-against-sci-hub-begs-the-question-why-are-academic-journals-so-expensive-anyway.html. This article discussed Peter Suber's book *Open Access* (Cambridge, MA: MIT Press, 2012).

23. Jason Schmitt, "Paywalls Block Scientific Progress. Research Should Be Open to Everyone," *The Guardian*, March 28, 2019, https://www.theguardian.com/education/2019/mar/28/paywalls-block-scientific-progress-research-should-be-open-to-everyone.

24. *Paywall: The Business of Scholarship* (movie), 2018, https://paywallthemovie.com/.

25. Alexander Grossmann and Björn Brembs, "Current Market Rates for Scholarly Publishing Services," 2021, https://f1000research.com/articles/10-20.

26. Brian Resnick and Julia Belluz, "The War to Free Science," *Vox*, July 10, 2019, https://www.vox.com/the-highlight/2019/6/3/18271538/open-access-elsevier-california-sci-hub-academic-paywalls.

27. Laviere et al., "The Oligopoly of Academic Publishing in the Digital Era."

28. Gabrielle Emanuel, "Inside the E-Book 'War' Waging Between Libraries and Publishers," *GBH News*, January 6, 2020, https://www.wgbh.org/news/local-news/2020/01/06/inside-the-e-book-war-waging-between-libraries-and-publishers.

29. "Competition in Digital Markets," American Library Association, *Before the U.S. House of Representatives Committee on the Judiciary Investigation of Competition in Digital Markets*, October 15, 2019, http://www.ala.org/news/sites/ala.org.news/files/content/mediapresscenter/CompetitionDigitalMarkets.pdf.

30. Aaron Perzanowski and Jason Schultz. *The End of Ownership: Personal Property in the Digital Economy*. (Cambridge, MA: MIT Press, 2016).

31. "Controlled Digital Lending: Unlocking the Library's Full Potential," Library Futures (2021), https://www.libraryfutures.net/policy-document-2021.

32. *Hachette Book Group, Inc. v. Internet Archive*, No. 20-04160 (S.D.N.Y., October 8, 2020).

33. Swartz was charged with wire fraud and eleven counts of violating the Computer Fraud and Abuse Act.

34. Swartz returned the content to JSTOR. *U.S. v. Swartz*, 11-10260 (D. Mass. 2011).

35. *Elsevier, Inc. v. Sci-Hub*, 15-04282 (S.D.N.Y. 2015).

36. *Elsevier, Inc. v. Sci-Hub*, 15-04282 (S.D.N.Y. 2015). Elbakyan has an upper hand: she lives overseas and can avoid the order. Elbakyan says she's willing to participate in Elsevier's litigation, but only if Elsevier's lawyers "are interested

in the case for the sake of idea, not money." Tragically, Aaron Swartz could not similarly avoid harsh legal actions. He died by suicide before the case concluded. David Kravets, "A Spiritual Successor to Aaron Swartz Is Angering Publishers All Over Again," *Ars Technica*, April 3, 2016, https://arstechnica.com/tech-policy /2016/04/a-spiritual-successor-to-aaron-swartz-is-angering-publishers-all-over -again/.

37. Wolfie Cristl, "Does RELX, the scientific publisher, use personal/be-havioral data on academic scholars who access publications via Elsevier for its data brokerage and risk management services? I don't know. In any case, Sci-enceDirect (RELX/Elsevier) embeds ThreatMetrix (RELX/LexisNexis Risk)," Twitter, August 18, 2020, https://twitter.com/wolfiechristl/status/12956550 4074 1445632?lang=en.

38. They're licensing content, so technically, they aren't buying anything outright.

39. Danielle Cooper and Oya Y. Rieger, "What's the Big Deal? How Re-searchers Are Navigating Changes to Journal Access," Ithaka S+R, June 22, 2021, https://doi.org/10.18665/sr.315570. Cornell's big deal is around $6 million. "Cor-nell University Library and the Big Deals 2019," Cornell University Library, https: //www.library.cornell.edu/about/collections/licensing-electronics-resources/big -deal-faq (accessed November 18, 2021). The University of California's Elsevier contract was valued at $10.5 million dollars a year, increasing annually. Matisse Senkfor, "UC in Negotiations with Publisher Elsevier for Open Access to Journal Articles," *Daily Bruin*, January 8, 2019, https://dailybruin.com/2019/01/08/uc-in -negotiations-with-publisher-elsevier-for-open-access-to-journal-articles. Collec-tively, universities in the United Kingdom paid academic journal platforms over one billion pounds, which equals about $1.3 billion, from 2010 to 2020. Elsevier was paid 394 million pounds, specifically. Jack Grove, "UK Universities 'Paid Big Publishers £1 Billion' in Past Decade," *Times Higher Education World Univer-sity Rankings*, March 12, 2020, https://www.timeshighereducation.com/news/uk -universities-paid-big-publishers-ps1billion-past-decade.

40. "As unplanned and unweeded collections grow . . . works of needed infor-mation are lost in the clutter of outdated and inappropriate materials crowding the shelves." Linda S. Katz, *Weeding and Maintenance of Reference Collections* (New York: Routledge, Taylor & Francis Group, 1990), 1.

41. Resnick and Belluz, "The War to Free Science."

42. Kenneth Frazier, "What's the Big Deal?" *The Serials Librarian* 48, no. 1–2 (2005; 2008): 49–59, https://doi.org/10.1300/J123v48n01_06; Richard Poynder, "The Big Deal: Not Price but Cost," *Information Today* 28, no. 8 (September 2011), https: //www.infotoday.com/it/sep11/The-Big-Deal-Not-Price-But-Cost.shtml.

43. Poynder, "The Big Deal: Not Price but Cost."

44. Poynder, "The Big Deal: Not Price but Cost."

45. *United States v. Loew's Inc.*, 371 U.S. 38 (1962).

46. Aaron S. Edlin and Daniel L. Rubinfeld, "Exclusion or Efficient Pricing— The Big Deal Bundling of Academic Journals," *Antitrust Law Journal* 72, no. 1 (2004): 119–158.

47. Jonathan Tennant and Björn Brembs, "RELX Referral to EU Competition Authority," formal complaint made on October 26, 2018, https://zenodo.org/record/1472045#.YZb-YiNOnBJ.

48. Resnick and Belluz, "The War to Free Science."

49. Martin Paul Eve, "Gov and RCUK Responses to Open Access Inquiry, Eradicating Non-Disclosure Clauses," Open Access Blog, November 26, 2013, https://eve.gd/2013/11/26/gov-and-rcuk-responses-to-open-access-inquiry-eradicating-non-disclosure-clauses/.

50. Theodore C. Bergstrom et al., "Evaluating Big Deal Journal Bundles," *Proceedings of the National Academy of Sciences* 111, no. 26 (July 1, 2014): 9425–9430, https://doi.org/10.1073/pnas.1403006111.

51. "Elsevier's David Tempest Explains Subscription-Contract Confidentiality Clauses," Sauropod Vertebra Picture of the Week, December 20, 2013, https://svpow.com/2013/12/20/elseviers-david-tempest-explains-subscription-contract-confidentiality-clauses/.

52. Bergstrom et al., "Evaluating Big Deal Journal Bundles."

53. Chris Woolston, "Secret Publishing Deals Exposed," *Nature*, June 25, 2014, https://www.nature.com/articles/510447f.

54. "Nondisclosure Clauses," Cornell University Library, https://www.library.cornell.edu/about/policies/nondisclosure (accessed November 19, 2021).

55. Resnick and Belluz, "The War to Free Science."

56. Academics can often maintain control over their preprints (versions of their work that haven't been finalized and reviewed).

57. Taylor Swift, "For years I asked, pleaded for a chance to own my work . . ." Tumblr, June 30, 2019, https://taylorswift.tumblr.com/post/185958366550/for-years-i-asked-pleaded-for-a-chance-to-own-my.

58. Balazs Aczel et al., "A Billion Dollar Donation: The Cost, and Inefficiency of, Researchers' Time Spent on Peer Review," *MetaArXiv Preprints*, March 18, 2021, https://osf.io/preprints/metaarxiv/5h9z4.

59. *Paywall: The Business of Scholarship.*

60. Richard Van Noorden, "Open Access: The True Cost of Science Publishing," *Nature* 495 (2013): 426–429, https://www.nature.com/articles/495426a.

61. Lisa Hoover, "Paywall: The Business of Scholarship—A Review & Discussion with Director Jason Schmitt," *ALA Office of Intellectual Freedom Blog*, May 14, 2019, https://www.oif.ala.org/oif/?p=17751.

62. Grossmann and Brembs, "Current Market Rates for Scholarly Publishing Services."

63. Björn Brembs, "For clues, one may look at Elsevier's tweet from yesterday: https://twitter.com/ElsevierConnect/status/1440632982990049297 'knowledge and analytics' is what they do today—*publishing* is only mentioned as their 'roots' in the past, not something that is relevant today or, let alone, in the future," 5/12, Twitter, September 23, 2021, https://twitter.com/brembs/status/1440942540207820804.

64. Ari B. Friedman, "Prevalence of Medical Journal Websites That Deny Access to Users Who Block Browser Cookies," *JAMA Network Open* 4, no. 3

(March 26, 2021), https://jamanetwork.com/journals/jamanetworkopen/fullarti
cle/2777868.

65. Samuel Moore, "Individuation Through Infrastructure: Get Full Text Research, Data Extraction and the Academic Publishing Oligopoly," *Journal of Documentation* 77, no. 1 (July 28, 2020): 129–141. https://doi.org/10.1108/JD-06 -2020-0090.

66. Ben Williamson et al., "The Datafication of Teaching in Higher Education: Critical Issues and Perspectives," *Teaching in Higher Education* 25 no. 4 (April 29, 2020): 351–365, https://doi.org/10.1080/13562517.2020.1748811; Jun Yu and Nick Couldry, "Education as a Domain of Natural Data Extraction: Analysing Corporate Discourse About Educational Tracking," *Information, Communication & Society*, April 29, 2020, https://doi.org/10.1080/1369118X.2020.1764604.

67. "Data Tracking in Research: Aggregation and Use or Sale of Usage Data by Academic Publishers," DFG, German Research Foundation, October 28, 2021, p. 6, https://www.dfg.de/download/pdf/foerderung/programme/lis/daten tracking_papier_en.pdf.

68. "Data Tracking in Research."

69. Leigh Patel, *Decolonializing Educational Research: From Ownership to Answerability* (Abingdon, UK: Routledge, 2016).

70. Ivan Oransky, "Major Indexing Service Sounds Alarm on Self-Citations by Nearly 50 Journals," *Retraction Watch*, June 29, 2020, https://retractionwatch .com/2020/06/29/major-indexing-service-sounds-alarm-on-self-citations-by -nearly-50-journals/.

71. Finlo Rohrer, "The Perils of Five-Star Reviews," *BBC News Magazine*, June 25, 2009, http://news.bbc.co.uk/2/hi/uk_news/magazine/8118577.stm.

72. Peter A. Lawrence, "Lost in Publication: How Measurement Harms Science," *Ethics in Science and Environmental Publishing* 8, no. 1 (2008): 9–11, https: //doi.org/10.3354/esep00079.

73. Lawrence, "Lost in Publication."

74. Nathan J. Robinson, "The Truth Is Paywalled but the Lies Are Free," *Current Affairs*, August 2, 2020, https://www.currentaffairs.org/2020/08/the -truth-is-paywalled-but-the-lies-are-free/. Here is an example of the paywalled research that could refute YouTube misinformation: Pamela Herd, Melinda C. Mills, and Jennifer Beam Dowd, "Reconstructing Sociogenomic Research: Dismantling Biological and Race and Genetic Essentialism Narratives," *Journal of Health and Social Behavior*, June 8, 2021, https://journals.sagepub.com/doi/abs/ 10.1177/00221465211018682.

75. Roger C. Schonfeld, "Big Deal: Should Universities Outsource More Core Research Infrastructure?" Issue Brief, Ithaka S+R, January 4, 2018, https:// doi.org/10.18665/sr.306032.

76. Posada and Chen, "Publishers Are Increasingly in Control of Scholarly Infrastructure."

77. LexisNexis University Solutions promises to help colleges and universities do everything from providing student and faculty research resources, due

diligence and risk management, and alumni and prospect research. LexisNexis, "LexisNexis University Solutions," https://perma.cc/HBA5-PB6M.

78. Schonfeld, "Big Deal."

79. "Introducing Discrete Analysis, an arXiv Overlay Journal," *Scholastica*, September 29, 2015, https://blog.scholasticahq.com/post/introducing-discrete-analysis-an-arxiv-overlay-journal/.

80. Plan S is an international alliance that advocates for making all publicly funded research open access. In the United States, universities have formed similar coalitions to consider alternatives to the oligopoly, such as Texas Library Coalition for United Action. Marc Schiltz, "Open Access Is Foundational to the Scientific Enterprise," *Plan S*, September 4, 2018, https://www.coalition-s.org/why-plan-s/; "Texas Universities Join Forces to Negotiate Their Future," Texas A&M University Libraries, August 5, 2020, https://library.tamu.edu/news/2020/08/Texas%20Library%20Coalition%20for%20United%20Action.html.

81. Alexander Grossmann and Björn Brembs, "Assessing the Size of the Affordability Problem in Scholarly Publishing," *PeerJ Preprints*, June 18, 2019, https://doi.org/10.7287/peerj.preprints.27809v1.

82. "Business Model," arXiv, https://arxiv.org/about/reports-financials (accessed November 21, 2021).

83. arXiv.org has institutions pay $1,000 to $4,400 a year for membership.

84. Peter Suber, "Open Access Overview," accessed November 21, 2021, http://legacy.earlham.edu/~peters/fos/overview.htm#repositories.

85. Aaron Perzanowski and Jason Schultz. *The End of Ownership: Personal Property in the Digital Economy* (Cambridge, MA: MIT Press, 2016), 22.

86. Limitations on Exclusive Rights: Fair Use, 17 U.S.C. § 107. There's also a copyright exception for libraries and archives. Limitations on Exclusive Rights: Reproduction by Libraries and Archives, 17 U.S.C. § 108.

87. The first-sale doctrine is codified in Section 109 of the *Copyright Act*, 17 U.S.C. § 109.

88. U.S. courts are still sorting out the balance of purchasers' ownership rights and copyright holders' rights in digital media. Cases like *Hachette Book Group, Inc. v. Internet Archive*, U.S. District Court for the Southern District of New York, 1:20-cv-04160, could determine how digital copyrights work in the context of online libraries. In the meantime, libraries are at the whim of publishers' lending decisions. Matthew Chiarizio, "An American Tragedy: E-Books, Licenses, and the End of Public Lending Libraries," *Vanderbilt Law Review* 66, no. 2 (March 2013): 615–644.

89. Courts decide the "fairness" of these four factors on a case-by-case basis. 17 U.S.C. § 107; Kyle Courtney, "COVID-19, Copyright, & Library Superpowers (Part I)," Kyle Courtney Blog, March 11, 2020, discussing *Campbell v. Acuff-Rose Music, Inc.*, 510 U.S. 569 (1994), https://kylecourtney.com/2020/03/11/covid-19-copyright-library-superpowers-part-i/.

90. Fair use for educational purposes has become so limited that legal scholar Ann Bartow calls educational fair use "the incredible shrinking affirmative de-

fense." Ann Bartow, "Educational Fair Use in Copyright: Reclaiming the Right to Photocopy Freely," *University of Pittsburgh Law Review* 60, no. 1 (Fall 1998): 151.

91. Bartow, "Educational Fair Use in Copyright"; Jay Dratler Jr., "Distilling the Witches' Brew of Fair Use in Copyright Law," *University of Miami Law Review* 43, no. 2 (November 1988): 241–245.

92. Justin Hughes, "Fair Use Across Time," *UCLA Law Review* 50 (2003): 775, https://www.uclalawreview.org/wp-content/uploads/2019/09/40_ 50UCLALRev7752002-2003.pdf. Aside from the first-sale and fair use limits on copyright, there's one other part of the Copyright Act that could help libraries get more control over the materials they license from companies like Elsevier. Section 108 of the Act allows libraries and archives to reproduce copyrighted materials for noncommercial research purposes. This special fair-use-like exception codifies the idea that libraries should be able to print and share information for the public good. But librarians, and the rest of the world, rarely invoke these copyright-limiting superpowers. Kyle Courtney points out that Section 108 is rarely discussed or litigated about copyright. He also says that it's written poorly, with passive voice, multiple definitions, and vague terms, so it's hard for librarians, courts, and legal scholars to interpret. In short, nobody's sure how Section 108 works and what its limits are. Kyle Courtney, "COVID-19, Copyright, & Library Superpowers (Part II)," Kyle Courtney Blog, March 16, 2020, https:// kylecourtney.com/2020/03/16/covid-19-copyright-and-library-superpowers-part -ii/.

93. Brian L. Frye, "OK, Landlord: Copyright Profits Are Just Rent," JURIST—Academic Commentary, April 8, 2020, https://www.jurist.org/com mentary/2020/04/brian-frye-copyright-profits/.

94. Karl Kowallis, "Treating Fair Use as an Easement on Intellectual Property," *Brigham Young University Law Review* 2018, no. 5 (2018): 1073–1118.

95. Bartow, "Educational Fair Use in Copyright: Reclaiming the Right to Photocopy Freely," 157.

96. Copyright easements could be built into new laws codifying the presumption of disclosure for government-funded research and data in its final form. "National Task Force on Rule of Law & Democracy: Proposals for Reform, Volume II," Brennan Center for Justice at New York University School of Law, 2019, p. 13, https://www.brennancenter.org/sites/default/files/2019-09/2019_10_ TaskForce%20II_0.pdf.

97. Kowallis, "Treating Fair Use as an Easement on Intellectual Property," 1077.

98. *Aaron's Law Act of 2013*, H.R. 2454, 113th Cong. (2013–2014).

99. Andy Greenberg, " 'Aaron's Law' Suggests Reforms to Computer Fraud Act (But Not Enough to Have Protected Aaron Swartz)," *Forbes*, January 16, 2013, https://www.forbes.com/sites/andygreenberg/2013/01/16/aarons-law-suggests -reforms-to-hacking-acts-but-not-enough-to-have-protected-aaron-swartz/?sh= 198201a6649s.

100. Samuel Moore, "When the market is failing this badly I do think there's a very strong case for the ethics of piracy, especially during an unprecedented crisis in which students are being messed about left, right and centre," Twitter, September 26, 2020, https://twitter.com/samoore_/status/1309795724075429890. As Brandon Butler, head of information policy at the University of Virginia Library puts it, academic piracy is the natural result of information markets in which "people aren't getting what they need at a price that makes sense for them." Resnick and Belluz, "The War to Free Science."

101. Kravets, "A Spiritual Successor to Aaron Swartz Is Angering Publishers All Over Again."

102. "Business Models and Market Structure Within the Scholarly Communications Sector," *ISC Occasional Paper*, International Science Council, September, 2020, https://council.science/wp-content/uploads/2020/06/ISC-Occasional -Paper-Business-Models-and-Market-Structure-within-the-Scholarly-Communi cations-Sector_Rupert-Gatti-3.pdf; Ana Enriquez, "Keeping Up with . . . Antitrust and Competition Law," *Association of College and Research Libraries*, http:/ /www.ala.org/acrl/publications/keeping_up_with/antitrust (accessed November 2, 2021); Gary Price, "Full Text: Complaint Filed with EU Competition Authority Regarding 'Anti-Competitive Practices' of RELX/Elsevier and the Wider Scholarly Publishing Market," *Library Journal Info. Docket*, October 30, 2018, https:/ /www.infodocket.com/2018/10/30/full-text-complaint-filed-with-eu-competition -authority-regarding-relx-and-the-wider-scholarly-publishing-market/.

103. John P. Holdren, Director of the Office of Science and Technology Policy, "Memorandum for the Heads of Executive Departments and Agencies: Increasing Access to the Results of Federally Funded Scientific Research," February 22, 2013, https://obamawhitehouse.archives.gov/sites/default/files/microsites/ ostp/ostp_public_access_memo_2013.pdf.

104. S. 1260, *United States Innovation and Competition Act of 2021*. Section 2527 of the Act would codify the 2013 memorandum.

105. J .C. Correa et al., "The Sci-Hub Effect: Sci-Hub Downloads Lead to More Article Citations," *arXiv*, last modified June 29, 2020, https://arxiv.org/abs /2006.14979.

106. *Paywall: The Business of Scholarship* (movie) 2018, https://paywallthemovie .com/.

Chapter 4

1. Alex West, "Legal Information Vendor Market Survey: Some Surprising Early Results," Feit Consulting, 2020, https://www.feitconsulting.com/feits-20 20-legal-information-vendor-market-survey-some-surprising-early-results/. The survey was described in Public.Resource.Org Submission to the FTC, October 29, 2021, p. 15, https://law.resource.org/pub/us/case/ftc/Public%20Resource%20 FTC%20Submission.pdf.

2. Gail Sullivan, "Steve Wozniak Refutes Apple's Creation Story: 'The Garage Is a Bit of a Myth'," *Washington Post*, December 5, 2014, https://www

.washingtonpost.com/news/morning-mix/wp/2014/12/05/steve-wozniak-refutes
-apples-creation-story-the-garage-is-a-bit-of-a-myth/.

3. Robert M. Jarvis, "John B. West: Founder of the West Publishing Company," *The American Journal of Legal History* L, no. 1 (2008–2010): 1–22.

4. Thomas A. Woxland, "Forever Associated with the Practice of Law: The Early Years of the West Publishing Company," *Legal Reference Services Quarterly* 5, no. 1, October 23, 2008: 116, https://doi.org/10.1300/J113v05n01_07.

5. Ross E. Davies, "West's Words, Ho! Law Books by the Million, Plus a Few," *Green Bag* 2d 14, no. 3, Appendix A (2010–2011): 303.

6. Woxland, "Forever Associated with the Practice of Law," 120.

7. "O.J. Simpson Murder Trial—Shepard's clip," July 16, 2009, https://youtu.be/QFOYoGlgogU.

8. Olufunmilayo B. Arewa, "Open Access in a Closed Universe: Lexis, Westlaw, Law Schools, and the Legal Information Market," *Lewis & Clark Law Review* 10, no. 4 (Winter 2006): 797–840.

9. Josh Chafetz (@joshchafetz), "westlaw is down There Is No Law EVERYTHING IS PERMITTED," Twitter, July 22, 2020, https://twitter.com/joshchafetz/status/1286013823154102273?s=20.

10. Susan Nevelow Mart has done extensive research on the effects of legal research platform algorithms. Susan Nevelow Mart, "The Algorithm as a Human Artifact: Implications for Legal [Re]Search," *Law Library Journal* 109, no. 3 (Summer 2017): 387–422; and Susan Nevelow Mart, "Every Algorithm Has a POV," *AALL Spectrum* 22, no. 1 (September/October 2017): 40–44.

11. Most law librarians have looked for a particular cited law for hours on end, only to discover that it is not real: it's a typo that was written into a case or statute years ago, and that has since spread throughout Westlaw and Lexis, re-cited by law clerks and lawyers.

12. Merritt E. McAlister, "Missing Decisions," *University of Pennsylvania Law Review* 169, no. 4 (March 2021): 1101–1180.

13. "Westlaw Edge," Thomson Reuters, https://legal.thomsonreuters.com/en/c/legal-research-westlaw-edge (accessed November 22, 2021).

14. "Context," LexisNexis, https://www.lexisnexis.com/en-us/products/context.page (accessed November 22, 2021).

15. "Innovative Tools and Features: Pushing the Boundaries of Legal Intelligence," https://www.lexisnexis.com/en-us/products/lexis/innovations.page (accessed October 27, 2021).

16. Laura Peek, "A Sense of Purpose at Elsevier," RELX, https://stories.relx.com/elsevier-purpose/index.html (accessed March 13, 2022).

17. Eduardo R. C. Capulong, "Christopher Columbus Langdell, Black Lives Matter and Legal Education," ed. Brianna Bell, *JURIST*, July 8, 2020, https://www.jurist.org/commentary/2020/07/eduardo-capulong-legal-education/. John B. West's Key Number and Digest system was the first to organize court opinions by legal topic, and the system flows through Westlaw's products and publications. Lexis has a similar system for tagging and organizing legal materials by topic. John B. West, "Multiplicity of Reports," *Law Library Journal* 2 (1909): 1, 4.

18. "Susan Nevelow Mart: The Algorithm as a Human Artifact," *The Future Is Now: Legal Services 2.018*, produced by 2Civility, Illinois Supreme Court Commission on Professionalism, video, May 2, 2018, https://vimeo.com/279257074.

19. Paravathi A. Subbiah, "Representation and Bias: Pushing the Boundaries of Social Data Science," *towards data science*, December 4, 2020, https://towardsdatascience.com/representation-big-data-and-algorithmic-bias-in-social-data-science-c285350ccc2c.

20. Richard Delgado and Jean Stefancic, "Rodrigo's Reappraisal," *Boston University Law Review* 101, Online Symposium: "Critical Legal Research: The Next Wave," 54 (2021), https://www.bu.edu/bulawreview/files/2021/04/DELGADO-STEFANCIC.pdf.

21. Delgado and Stefancic, "Rodrigo's Reappraisal."

22. Susan Nevelow Mart, "The Relevance of Results Generated by Human Indexing and Computer Algorithms: A Study of West's Headnotes and Key Numbers and LexisNexis's Headnotes and Topics," *Law Library Journal* 102, no. 2 (Spring 2010): 241.

23. For instance, both Westlaw and Lexis automatically link headnotes to other cases with the same legal topics.

24. Susan Nevelow Mart, "The Relevance of Results"; 249.

25. Patti Ogden, "Mastering the Lawless Science of Our Law: A Story of Legal Citation Indexes," *Law Library Journal* 85, no. 1 (Winter 1993): 38, fn 169.

26. Kelly Hannah-Moffat, "Algorithmic Adaptability and Ethics Washing—Appropriating the Critique," Ethics of AI in Context Podcast, University of Toronto Ethics of AI Lab, February 3, 2022, Lexis discussion starts at twenty-eight minutes, https://www.listennotes.com/podcasts/ethics-of-ai-in-context-ethics-of-ai-lab-mUlgnk7bPdy/.

27. "Lexis Versus Westlaw Revisited: Comparison of Top Legal Research Platforms," LAC Group, February 22, 2018, https://lac-group.com/blog/lexisnexis-versus-westlaw-revisited/.

28. "The UCLA School of Law paid about $340,000 to Westlaw and $250,000 to LexisNexis for access to the companies' online legal research services for the academic years between 2015 and 2020, according to Westlaw and LexisNexis invoices since 2015." Justin Jung, "UCLA School of Law Holds Contracts with Companies Selling Personal Data to ICE," *Daily Bruin*, July 17, 2020, https://dailybruin.com/2020/07/17/ucla-school-of-law-holds-contracts-with-companies-selling-personal-data-to-ice.

29. Natasha Singer, "No Mug? Drug Makers Cut Out Goodies for Doctors," *New York Times*, December 30, 2008, https://www.nytimes.com/2008/12/31/business/31drug.html.

30. *Shevlin-Carpenter Co. v. Minnesota*, 218 U.S. 57, 68 (1910).

31. *Papachristou v. City of Jacksonville*, 405 U.S. 156, 162 (1972) (quoting *Lanzetta v. New Jersey*, 306 U.S. 451, 453 (1939)).

32. Thomas Jefferson to William Duane, 1810, ME 12:417, https://founders.archives.gov/documents/Jefferson/03-03-02-0001-0002.

33. *Wheaton v. Peters*, 33 U.S. 591 (1834).

34. *Building Officials & Code Adm. v. Code Technology, Inc.*, 628 F.2d 730 (1st Cir. 1980), citing *Banks v. West*, 27 F. 50, 57 (C.C.D. Minn. 1886).

35. Woxland, "Forever Associated with the Practice of Law," 119.

36. "Bluebook Guide: United States Supreme Court," Georgetown Law Library, last modified October 19, 2021, https://guides.ll.georgetown.edu/c.php?g=261289&p=2339383.

37. Some court cases are never published on purpose, because they don't say anything new about the law and aren't of precedential value. Often the same issues are adjudicated time and time again in courts of first entry.

38. Greg Beato, "Tear Down This Paywall," *Reason*, June, 2012, https://reason.com/2012/05/30/tear-down-this-paywall/.

39. "Pricing Frequently Asked Questions," PACER, https://pacer.uscourts.gov/help/faqs/pricing (accessed October 29, 2021); "PACER Pricing: How Fees Work," PACER, https://pacer.uscourts.gov/pacer-pricing-how-fees-work (accessed October 26, 2021).

40. It's no surprise that there are volunteers trying to "free" court records from PACER's paywall by digitizing case law themselves and posting it online. It's also not surprising that people have sued PACER for making millions of dollars on legal information that belongs to the public. "About Free Law Project," Free Law Project, https://free.law/about/ (accessed October 26, 2021); "PACER Fees Class Action," https://www.pacerfeesclassaction.com/Home.aspx (accessed October 26, 2021).

41. Victoria Macchi, "Archives Jackpot: Citizen Archivist Contributions Top One Million," *National Archives News*, National Archives and Records Administration, September 17, 2020, https://www.archives.gov/news/articles/citizen-archivist-one-million.

42. Mary Sauers, "End-of-Term (EOT) Government Website Harvest Enlists Librarians, Educators, Students," NCompass Blog, Nebraska Library Commission, December 29, 2016, http://nlcblogs.nebraska.gov/nlcblog/2016/12/29/end-term-eot-government-website-harvest-enlists-librarians-educators-students/.

43. Sarah Lamdan, "Lessons from DataRescue: The Limits of Grassroots Climate Change Data Preservation and the Need for Federal Records Law Reform," *University of Pennsylvania Law Review Online* 166 (2018): 231–248.

44. *Federal Records Act*, 44 U.S.C. Ch. 21, 29, 31, and 33; *Freedom of Information Act*, 5 U.S.C. § 552.

45. Leslie Street and David R. Hansen, "Who Owns the Law? Why We Must Restore Public Ownership of Legal Publishing," *Journal of Intellectual Property Law* 26, no. 2 (2020): 206, 10.31228/osf.io/xnbcp.

46. Ed Walters, "Copyright of the Annotated Fastcase CEO Discusses Georgia v PublicResource.Org," *Fastcase*, July 8, 2020, https://www.youtube.com/watch?v=ARiFY939tMI&feature=youtu.be.

47. Law librarians have worked for decades to urge states to provide official versions of their laws online with some success, but not with complete adoption in every jurisdiction. "UELMA," American Association of Law Libraries, ac-

cessed October 1, 2021, https://www.aallnet.org/advocacy/government-relations /state-issues/uelma-resources/.

48. Ed Walters, "Tear Down This (Pay)Wall: The End of Private Copyright in Public Statutes," *Vox Populii* (blog), Cornell LII, July 15, 2011, https://blog.law .cornell.edu/voxpop/2011/07/15/tear-down-this-paywall/.

49. For instance, the State of Oregon told Tim Stanley, founder of open access legal websites Justia, to remove Oregon's Revised Statutes from his website. Tim Stanley, "Cease, Desist & Resist—Oregon's Copyright Claim on the Oregon Revised Statutes," *Justia Law Blog*, April 19, 2008, https://lawblog.justia .com/2008/04/19/cease-desist-resist-oregons-copyright-claim-on-the-oregon -revised-statutes/.

50. *Georgia v. Public.Resource.Org*, No. 18-1150, 590 U.S. ___ (2020).

51. *West Publishing Co. v. Mead Data Central, Inc.*, 799 F.2d 1219 (8th Cir. 1986).

52. To amend title 17, United States Code, to exclude copyright protection for certain legal compilations, HR 4426, 102nd Congress (1992).

53. *Georgia v. Public.Resource.Org*, No. 18-1150, 590 U.S. ___ (2020).

54. Ronald Mann, "Opinion Analysis: Sharply Divided Bench Rejects Georgia's Copyright in Annotations of Georgia Statutes," *SCOTUSblog*, April 27, 2020, https://www.scotusblog.com/2020/04/opinion-analysis-sharply-divided-bench -rejects-georgias-copyright-in-annotations-of-georgia-statutes/; Leslie Street and David R. Hansen, "Appendix A: Fifty State Survey of Law Online," in Leslie Street, "Electronic Publication of the Law: Copyright and Contract (Terms of Use)," University of Georgia School of Law, February 21, 2019, https://digitalcommons .law.uga.edu/cgi/viewcontent.cgi?article=1068&context=cle (accessed October 29, 2021).

55. *Georgia v. Public.Resource.Org*, No. 18-1150, 590 U.S. ___ (2020).

56. Ga. Code § 16-6-2 (2012) (declared unconstitutional in *Powell v. State*, 270 Ga. 327 (1998)).

57. *Georgia v. Public.Resource.Org*, No. 18-1150, 590 U.S. ___ (2020).

58. Thomas C. O'Bryant, "The Great Unobtainable Writ: Indigent Pro Se Litigation After the Antiterrorism and Effective Death Penalty Act of 1996," *Harvard Civil Rights-Civil Liberties Law Review* 41, no. 2 (Summer 2006): 299–338.

59. "LexisNexis Sells Its Database to Prisons," *NBC News*, https://www .nbcnews.com/id/wbna4540333 (accessed October 28, 2021). Westlaw has a similar product called Westlaw Correctional. "Westlaw Correctional," *Westlaw*, https: //legal.thomsonreuters.com/en/c/westlaw-corrections (accessed October 28, 2021).

60. LexisNexis, "Inmate Law Library Solutions," perma.cc/VN6E-4JE9 (accessed April 25, 2022).

61. "Westlaw Correctional."

62. "Inmate Law Library Solutions," LexisNexis, https://www.lexisnexis.com /en-us/corrections/default.page (accessed March 13, 2022).

63. State of Missouri, Offender Legal Library Contract, 13, 89, https://doc services.mo.gov/Documents/Contracts/Professional/Awarded/OF13708389.pdf

(accessed March 13, 2022). These records describe inmate tracking on the correctional legal information platform and contain an "Attempted Misuse Incident Report" showing every click an inmate made in the system.

64. Myles McNutt, "*OITNB* Explores the (Slim) Possibility and (False) Promise of Hope in a Broken System," AVClub, July 27, 2019, https://www.avclub.com/oitnb-explores-the-slim-possibility-and-false-promi-1836747849.

65. LexisNexis, "Spoiler Alert! LexisNexis Featured on Netflix's "Orange Is the New Black," *LexTalk* (blog), July 31, 2019, https://perma.cc/8AQ2-NUUA.

66. Carolina Paiz, "Opinion: We Put ICE Detention Centers into 'Orange Is The New Black.' Now I'm Heading Back to One." *Buzzfeed News*, July 29, 2019, https://www.buzzfeednews.com/article/carolinapaiz/ice-detention-centers-orange-is-the-new-black.

67. Sam Biddle, "LexisNexis to Provide Giant Database of Personal Information to ICE," *The Intercept*, April 2, 2021, https://theintercept.com/2021/04/02/ice-database-surveillance-lexisnexis/.

68. Woxland, "Forever Associated with the Practice of Law." 123.

69. Jean O'Grady, "The Law Librarians Revolt: AALL Accuses LexisNexis of Engaging in Unfair Business Practices—Possible Antitrust Violations," *Dewey B Strategic Blog*, June 7, 2018, https://www.deweybstrategic.com/2018/06/law-librarians-revolt-aall-accuses-lexisnexis-engaging-unfair-business-practices.html.

70. *US v. The Thomson Corp.*, 949 F. Supp. 907 (D.C. Cir. 1996).

71. Sam Glover and Aaron Street, "How Westlaw Lost Its Copyright, with Alan Sugarman," *Lawyerist Podcast*, Episode 151, Legal Talk Network, December 20, 2017, https://legaltalknetwork.com/podcasts/lawyerist-podcast/2017/12/151-how-westlaw-lost-its-copyright-with-alan-sugarman/.

72. *Matthew Bender & Co., Inc. v. West Pub. Co.*, 2001 U.S. Dist. LEXIS 8936 (D.D.C. 2001).

73. *Matthew Bender & Co., Inc. v. West Pub. Co.*, 158 F.3d 674 (2nd Cir. 1998).

74. *Thomson Reuters Co. v. Ross Intelligence, Inc.*, No. 20-00613 (D. Del., filed May 6, 2020).

75. Andrew Arruda et al., "Announcement by the Founders," *Ross News*, December 11, 2020, https://blog.rossintelligence.com/post/announcement.

76. Peter Elkind, "The Trouble at Bloomberg," *Fortune*, December 5, 2013, https://fortune.com/2013/12/05/the-trouble-at-bloomberg/.

77. H.R. 1164, 116th Cong. (2019); "Clients Lobbying on H.R.1164: Electronic Court Records Reform Act of 2019," Open Secrets, https://www.opensecrets.org/federal-lobbying/bills/summary?id=hr1164-116 (accessed October 28, 2021).

78. "Thomson Reuters: Annual Lobbying Totals: 1998–2020," Open Secrets, https://www.opensecrets.org/orgs/thomson-reuters/lobbying?id=D000030403 (accessed October 28, 2021).

79. "Clients Lobbying on H.R.1164: Electronic Court Records Reform Act of 2019."

80. "Clients Lobbying on H.R.8235: Open Courts Act of 2020," Open Secrets,

https://www.opensecrets.org/federal-lobbying/bills/summary?id=hr8235-116 (accessed October 28, 2021).

81. Hannah Doenges, "Non-Disclosure Clauses: The Making, Breaking, and Remaking of Relationships" (master's thesis, University of Washington, 2017), https://depts.washington.edu/uwlawlib/wordpress/wp-content/uploads/2018/01/Doenges2017.pdf.

82. Mark Gediman, "After the Love Is Gone," *3 Geeks and a Law Blog*, December 15, 2010, https://www.geeklawblog.com/2010/12/after-love-is-gone.html.

83. Jacob Sayward, "CRIV/Lexis May 2016 Call," *CRIV Blog*, AALL, June 6, 2016, https://crivblog.com/tag/vendor-calls/.

84. Doenges, "Non-Disclosure Clauses," 20.

85. Jung, "UCLA School of Law Holds Contracts."

86. Eric E. Johnson, "The Misadventure of Copyrighting State Law," *Kentucky Law Journal* 107, no. 4 (2018–2019): 593–628.

87. Doenges, "Non-Disclosure Clauses," 9.

88. Jung, "UCLA School of Law Holds Contracts"; West, "Legal Information Vendor Market Survey."

89. "Members of the Free Access to Law Movement (FALM)," FALM, http://falm.info/members/current/ (accessed October 27, 2021). In the United States, the best-known FALM organization is the Cornell Legal Information Institute ("LII").

90. *Federal Records Act*, 44 U.S.C. Ch. 21, 29, 31, and 33.

91. *Presidential Records Act*, 44 U.S.C. Ch. 22.

92. *Freedom of Information Act*, 5 U.S.C. § 552.

93. Shout out to CanLII, AfricanLII, GlobalLex, Free Law Project, and all of the organizations doing this work!

94. Patrice McDermott of Open the Government.Org and I have urged the federal government to provide more funding and resources for digitization and digital access programs for National Archives records. I would suggest similar actions for primary legal authorities. For instance, here is our "Letter to the National Archives and Records Administration Regarding Records Appraisal," December 13, 2019, https://www.ala.org/advocacy/sites/ala.org.advocacy/files/content/govinfo/Sign-ons/NARA%20Records%20Appraisal.pdf and our "Comment on Digitizing Permanent Records and Reviewing Records Schedules," written with Yael Schacher, Senior U.S. Advocate, Refugees International, February 15, 2021, https://govinfowatch.net/wp-content/uploads/2021/02/Comment-on-Digitizing-Permanent-Records-and-Reviewing-Records-Schedules-15-Feb-2021.pdf.

95. *Federal Records Act*, 44 U.S.C. Ch. 21, 29, 31, and 33.

96. 44 U.S.C. § 3301. FRA defines federal records, limiting their scope to only "all recorded information, regardless of form or characteristics, made or received by a Federal agency." This definition includes many kinds of records, but only from agencies. The laws don't preserve court or legislative records, nor do they require any sort of transparency from courts or Congress. Not that we're funding agencies' information infrastructure, either. At the height of the coro-

navirus pandemic, a Health Department official lamented the government's neglected data infrastructure, saying, "We've begged for money over the years to build a solid information highway so that we can collect data rapidly and share it with the people that need it in a timely way . . . but we've never gotten what we needed." Amy Maxmen, "Why the United States Is Having a Coronavirus Data Crisis," *Nature*, News in Focus, August 25, 2020, https://media.nature.com/original/magazine-assets/d41586-020-02478-z/d41586-020-02478-z.pdf.

97. *Federal Register Printing Savings Act of 2017*, Pub. L. No. 115-120 (2018), 44 U.S.C. § 101.

98. *Electronic Freedom of Information Act Amendments of 1996*, Pub. L. No. 104-231 (1996), 5 U.S.C. §552.

99. American Association of Law Libraries, https://www.aallnet.org/advocacy/government-relations/state-issues/uelma-resources/ (accessed October 1, 2021).

100. Graham Greenleaf, "Jon Bing and the History of Computerised Legal Research—Some Missing Links," in *Et Tilbakeblikk på Fremtiden* (Looking Back at the Future), ed. Olav Torvund and Lee Bygrave (Oslo: Institutt for rettsinformatikk, 2004).

101. Courtney Minick, "Universal Citations for State Codes," *Vox Populii* (blog), Cornell LII, September 1, 2011, https://blog.law.cornell.edu/voxpop/2011/09/01/universal-citation-for-state-codes/.

Chapter 5

1. The former type of data is more like what we just read about in Chapter 2, because for data brokers, data about your personal finances is just another type of personal data to sell to advertisers, surveillance programs, and other personal data analytics products, although financial data products have their own personal data analytics products, such as Refinitiv's "Know Your Customer" feature. Alfred Ng and Maddy Varner, "The Little-Known Data Broker Industry Is Spending Big Bucks Lobbying Congress," *The Markup*, April 1, 2021, https://themarkup.org/privacy/2021/04/01/the-little-known-data-broker-industry-is-spending-big-bucks-lobbying-congress.

2. Bloomberg, https://www.bloomberg.com/company/ (accessed December 3, 2021).

3. "Reduce Fraud Risk at Account Opening," LexisNexis, https://risk.lexisnexis.com/products/lexisnexis-fraud-intelligence (accessed November 10, 2021).

4. George H. Pike, "Bloomberg Outage Could Open Doors to Alternatives," *Information Today, Inc.*, May 26, 2015, http://newsbreaks.infotoday.com/NewsBreaks/Bloomberg-Outage-Could-Open-Doors-to-Alternatives-104168.asp.

5. Peter Lynch, *Beating the Street*, rev. ed. (New York: Simon & Schuster, 1994), 307.

6. George H. Pike, "Bloomberg Outage Could Open Doors to Alternatives."

7. Anzhelika Gerasymenko and Viktoriia Svystlnyk, "Evolution of the Information Asymmetry Concepts," chapter 1 in *Knowledge Economy Society: Contem-*

porary Trends and Transformations of Economies and Enterprises, ed. Andrzej Jaki and Tomasz Rojek). (Torún: Cracow University of Economics, 2009).

8. Julie E. Cohen, *Between Truth and Power: The Legal Constructions of Informational Capitalism* (Oxford, UK: Oxford University Press, 2019), 25.

9. Cohen, *Between Truth and Power,* 25.

10. Robert E. Wright, *The Wealth of Nations Rediscovered: Integration and Expansion in American Financial Markets, 1780–1850* (Cambridge. UK: Cambridge University Press, 2002); Tom C. W. Lin, "Reasonable Investor(s)," *Boston University Law Review* 95, no. 2 (March 2015): 484.

11. In 1989, the SEC contracted with BDM International, a subsidiary of Ford Aerospace, to develop EDGAR, and with LEXIS to maintain the system and make it searchable like it did with legal documents. Federal Information Dissemination Policies and Practices, Hearings Before the Government Information, Justice, and Agriculture Subcommittee of the Committee on Government Operations, House of Representatives, 101st Cong., April 18, May 23, and July 11, 1989, pp. 58, 62–63, https://files.eric.ed.gov/fulltext/ED336085.pdf.

12. These companies include SecuritiesMosaic, which parses companies' SEC filings and other public records, and Accuity, a banking data company. Thomson Reuters has similarly acquired companies such as stock data analytics company Vhayu Technologies and Hugin Group, a company that distributes press releases and investor news. Thomson Reuters uses the products it acquires to provide corporate clients with analytics it bills as "effective decisionmaking tools." "Thomson Reuters to Buy Hugin," *Reuters,* September 21, 2021, https://www.reuters.com/article/uk-thomsonreuters-hugin/thomson-reuters-to-buy-hugin-idUKTRE58K0TT20090921.

13. "The Disruption of Bloomberg L.P.," CBI Insights Research Report, September 19, 2018, https://www.cbinsights.com/research/report/bloomberg-terminal-disruption/.

14. Kevin Roose, "Can a Snooping Scandal Break Wall Street's Bloomberg Addiction?" *New York Magazine,* May 13, 2013, https://nymag.com/intelligencer/2013/05/will-wall-streets-terminal-addiction-break.html.

15. James Grimmelmann, "Big Data's Other Privacy Problem," in *Big Data, Big Challenges in Evidence-Based Policy Making,* ed. Kumar Jayasuriya and Kathryn Ritcheske (St. Paul, MN: West Academic, 2015), 212.

16. Today, a Bloomberg Terminal or a Refinitive Eikon subscription cost around $20,000 per year. New York Institute of Technology Library, last updated September 29, 2021, https://libguides.nyit.edu/BloombergTerminal; Jessica Martel and Marisa Figat, "Best Bloomberg Terminal Alternatives," updated May 25, 2021, https://www.wallstreetprep.com/knowledge/bloomberg-vs-capital-iq-vs-factset-vs-thomson-reuters-eikon/#Price_Comparison_at_a_Glance.

17. Grimmelmann, "Big Data's Other Privacy Problem."

18. "Global Spend on Financial Market Data Totals a Record $33.2 Billion in 2020, Rising 5.9% on Demand for Pricing, Reference and Portfolio Management Data—New Burton-Taylor Report," *PR Newswire,* April 8, 2021, https://www

.prnewswire.com/news-releases/global-spend-on-financial-market-data-totals-a
-record-33-2-billion-in-2020--rising-5-9-on-demand-for-pricing-reference-and
-portfolio-management-data---new-burton-taylor-report-301264995.html.

19. Jonathan R. Macey and Geoffrey P. Miller, "Origin of the Blue Sky Laws," *Texas Law Review* 70, no. 2 (December 1991): 347–398, 354.

20. The term "blue sky" floated around bankers' speeches and stuck in 1917 when Supreme Court Justice Joseph McKenna called investments in invisible oil wells, distant gold mines, and other unproven enterprises "speculative schemes which have no more basis than so many feet of blue sky." *Hall v. Geiger Jones Co.*, 242 U.S. 539 (1917).

21. Kansas passed the first Blue Sky law in 1911 and most other states passed similar laws by the mid-1930s. Macey and Miller, "Origin of the Blue Sky Laws," 347–398, 354, 360.

22. "Banking Panics of the Gilded Age: 1863–1913," Federal Reserve History, December 4, 2015, https://www.federalreservehistory.org/essays/banking-panics -of-the-gilded-age.

23. James L. Huston, "Western Grains and the Panic of 1857," *Agricultural History* 57, no. 1 (1983): 14–32.

24. Larry Schweikart and Lynne Pierson Doti, "From Hard Money to Branch Banking: California Banking in the Gold Rush Economy," *California History* 93, no. 1 (Spring 2016): 26–44, 36, https://www.jstor.org/stable/26412652. Originally published in *California History* 77, no. 4 (Winter 1998/1999).

25. Frederic S. Mishkin, "Asymmetric Information and Financial Crises: A Historical Perspective," in *Financial Markets and Financial Crises,* ed. R. Glenn Hubbard (Chicago: University of Chicago Press, 1991), 93, https://www.nber.org /system/files/chapters/c11483/c11483.pdf.

26. Marco Sorrentino, "The 'Production' of Accounting Information Between Regulatory and Free Market Approach: An (Eternally) Open Issue," *Journal of Modern Accounting and Auditing* 11, no. 1 (January 2015): 1–9, doi: 10.17265/1548–6583/2015.01.001.

27. Pub. L. 73-22, 48 Stat. 74, 15 U.S.C. § 77a et seq.

28. Pub. L. 73-22, 48 Stat. 74, 15 U.S.C. § 77a et seq.

29. Pub. L. 73-291, 48 Stat. 881, 15 U.S.C. § 78a et seq.

30. Lin, "Reasonable Investor(s)," 470; Young Han Kim and Felix Meschke, "CEO Interviews on CNBC," Fifth Singapore International Conference on Finance 2011, https://papers.ssrn.com/sol3/papers.cfm?abstract_id=1745085.

31. Unlike Redditors giving advice, hedge funds are regulated to ensure that their investors have plenty of money to spend: accredited hedge funders must have over a million dollars to spend and over $200,000 annual income. Kat Tretina and John Schmidt, "How Do You Invest in Hedge Funds," *Forbes*, June 25, 2021, https://www.forbes.com/advisor/investing/how-to-invest-in-hedge-funds/.

32. Abram Brown, "Reddit Traders Have Lost Millions Over GameStop. But Many Are Refusing to Quit." *Forbes*, February 4, 2001, https://www.forbes.com /sites/abrambrown/2021/02/04/reddit-traders-have-lost-millions-over-gamestop -but-many-are-refusing-to-quit/.

33. Carlos D. Ramirez, "Bank Fragility, 'Money Under the Mattress,' and Long-Run Growth: US Evidence from the 'Perfect' Panic of 1893," *Journal of Banking & Finance* 33, no. 12 (December 2009): 2186, https://doi.org/10.1016/j.jbankfin .2009.05.020; "G-20 Leaders Lay Out Plan to Restore Growth," CNN, March 15, 2009, http://www.cnn.com/2009/BUSINESS/03/14/g20.meeting/index.html?eref =rss_world.

34. Ramirez, "Bank Fragility," 2185–2198.

35. "Asymmetric Information and Financial Crises," 74.

36. The Sarbanes-Oxley Act requires company executives to tell their auditors about weaknesses in their financial controls and to certify the veracity of their financial reports. The *Sarbanes-Oxley Act of 2002*, Pub. L. 107-204, 116 Stat. 745.

37. *Dodd-Frank Wall Street Reform and Consumer Protection Act*, Pub. L. 111-203, 124 Stat. 1376-2223.

38. John C. Doerfer, "The Federal Securities Act of 1933," *Marquette Law Review* 18, no. 3 (April 1934): 147–172, 147.

39. Pub. L. 93-495, 8 Stat. 1521, 15 U.S.C. § 1691 et seq.

40. Colleen Casey, "Low-Wealth Minority Enterprises and Access to Financial Resources for Start-Up Activities: Do Connections Matter?" *Economic Development Quarterly* 26, no. 3 (2012), https://doi.org/10.1177/0891242412452446.

41. Katharina Pistor describes how companies use laws to build wealth and create more capital in *The Code of Capital: How the Law Creates Wealth and Inequality* (Princeton, NJ: Princeton University Press, 2019).

42. Lin, "Reasonable Investor(s)," 480.

43. Form 10-K, Ford Motor Company, for the fiscal year ended December 31, 2019.

44. Richard C. Sauer, "The Erosion of the Materiality Standard in the Enforcement of the Federal Securities Laws," *The Business Lawyer* 62, no. 2 (February 2007): 317–357, https://www.jstor.org/stable/40688521.

45. Enron and Worldcom, for example. John C. Coates, "The Goals and Promise of the Sarbanes-Oxley Act," *The Journal of Economic Perspectives* 21, no. 1 (2007): 91–116, http://www.jstor.org/stable/30033703.

46. Henry T. C. Hu, "Too Complex to Depict—Innovation, Pure Information, and the SEC Disclosure Paradigm," *Texas Law Review* 90, no. 7 (June 2012): 1601–1716.

47. Lin, "Reasonable Investor(s)," 467.

48. Jeffrey N. Gordon and Kathryn Judge, "The Origins of a Capital Market Union in the United States." European Corporate Governance Institute: Law Working Paper N. 395/2018, April 2018, 12–14 (arguing that the lack of a centralized federal bank and loan structure led to a system of market-based debt finance in which railroad companies and other industrial enterprises took advantage of consumers, issuing risky "junk bonds" that led to bank runs, etc.).

49. TLin, "Reasonable Investor(s)," 487.

50. "The End of the Affair," *The Economist* 389, no. 8607 (November 22, 2008): 53, https://www.economist.com/united-states/2008/11/20/the-end-of-the -affair.

51. "The End of the Affair."

52. In 2020, Bloomberg L.P. and Reuters were called the "the fastest and most credible digital information sources in the financial industry." Mark Kolakowski, "Bloomberg vs. Reuters: What's the Difference?" *Investopedia*, June 17, 2021, https://www.investopedia.com/articles/investing/052815/financial-news-comparison-bloomberg-vs-reuters.asp.

53. Scott Patterson, *Dark Pools: High-Speed Traders, A.I. Bandits, and the Threat to the Global Financial System* (New York: Crown, 2012), 230.

54. Lin, "Reasonable Investor(s)," 489. The *Wall Street Journal* reported that people with access to fast SEC filing access through special, subscription-based feeds were able to act on new financial information before anyone else had the chance to see the new data. Ryan Tracy and Scott Patterson, "Fast Traders Are Getting Data from SEC Seconds Early," *Wall Street Journal*, October 29, 2014.

55. Cohen, *Between Truth and Power*, 26.

56. "Audit of the SEC's Progress in Enhancing and Redesigning the Electronic Data Gathering, Analysis, and Retrieval System," U.S. Securities and Exchange Commission Office of Inspector General, September 28, 2017, 1, https://www.sec.gov/files/Audit-of-SECs-Progress-in-Enhancing-and-Redesigning-the-EDGAR-System.pdf.

57. In 2015, SEC Commissioner Kara Stein lamented that EDGAR hasn't kept up with technological advances, and called for an overhaul of the system. Kara M. Stein, "Remarks at the 'SEC Speaks' Conference," February 20, 2015, https://www.sec.gov/news/speech/022015-spchckms.html; Joe Mont, "How Do You Solve a Problem Like EDGAR?" *Compliance Week*, June 9, 2015, https://www.complianceweek.com/how-do-you-solve-a-problem-like-edgar/3296.article.

58. Michael S. Drake et al., "Who Uses Financial Statements? A Demographic Analysis of Financial Statement Downloads from EDGAR," *Accounting Horizons* 31, no. 3 (2017): 55–68, 56, citing https://doi.org/10.2308/acch-51736.

59. Ryan H. Giarusso, "Realizing EDGAR: Eliminating Information Asymmetries Through Artificial Intelligence Analysis of SEC Filings" Open Access Honors Program Thesis, University of Northern Iowa, 2017, p. 1, https://scholarworks.uni.edu/hpt/272/.

60. Grimmelmann, "Big Data's Other Privacy Problem," 214.

61. Hu, "Too Complex to Depict."

62. "Study Regarding Financial Literacy Among Investors, as Required by Section 917 of the Dodd-Frank Wall Street Reform and Consumer Protection Act," U.S. Securities and Exchange Commission, iii, August 2012, https://www.sec.gov/news/studies/2012/917-financial-literacy-study-part1.pdf. The digitization of financial services hasn't made it any easier to understand our finances. We've traded human guides, like bank tellers, for electronic ATMs, and invisible Venmo accounts have replaced visible, countable dollars. New digital banking systems are more complicated than their analog predecessors, and people who can't manage them or afford them have to use analog financial systems: check cashers, pawn shops, payday lenders, and other forms of "fringe finance" that

take advantage of consumers. Rob Aitken, "Capital at Its Fringes," *New Political Economy* 11, no. 4 (December 2006), https://doi.org/10.1080/13563460600990491.

63. Lin, "Reasonable Investor(s)," 484.

64. Grimmelmann, "Big Data's Other Privacy Problem," 212.

65. The Private Securities Regulation Litigation Reform Act of 1995 requires that corporations, and their leaders, limit, and advise consumers to not rely on, forward-looking statements. Companies are especially careful to not make forward-looking statements on air. Application of Safe Harbor for Forward-Looking Statements, 15 U.S.C. 77z-2(c)(1)(A)(i); Kim and Meschke, "CEO Interviews on CNBC."

66. Kim and Meschke, "CEO Interviews on CNBC."

67. Safal Niveshak, "Why I Don't Watch CNBC, and Why Even You Shouldn't," Safal Niveshak Blog, November 13, 2013, https://www.safalniveshak.com/why-i-don%E2%80%99t-watch-cnbc-and-why-even-you-shouldnt/.

68. Kenneth Rapoza, "Can 'Fake News' Impact the Stock Market?" *Forbes*, February 26, 2017, https://www.forbes.com/sites/kenrapoza/2017/02/26/can-fake-news-impact-the-stock-market/?sh=3ec994bd2fac.

69. James Cramer, "To the Moon," *Time*, January 1, 2000, http://content.time.com/time/subscriber/article/0,33009,995808,00.html.

70. Tom Brennan, "Mad Mail: Is Bear Stearns in Trouble?" *CNBC*, March 11 2008, https://www.cnbc.com/id/23575614.

71. The 2010s-era satire show *30 Rock* mocked television stations' product placement. They jokingly sold everything from General Electric microwaves to Verizon phone service in various episodes. In one episode, the show's protagonist, Liz Lemon, says in mock disbelief, "I'm sorry, you're saying you want us to use [our television show] to SELL stuff?" seconds before she and her castmates start talking about how great Snapple is. "*30 Rock* Snapple Product Placement," YouTube, December 10, 2012, https://www.youtube.com/watch?v=b9hepxidZyo.

72. Y. Han (Andy) Kim, "Self Attribution Bias of the CEO: Evidence from CEO Interviews on CNBC," *Journal of Banking & Finance* 37, no. 7 (July 2013): 2472–2489, https://doi.org/10.1016/j.jbankfin.2013.02.008.

73. "Taboola Helps The Motley Fool Australia Achieve 440% Increase In Customer Acquisitions," *B&T Magazine*, https://www.bandt.com.au/taboola-helps-the-motley-fool-australia-achieve-440-increase-in-customer-acquisitions/.

74. Hyunjin Seo et al., "Vulnerable Populations and Misinformation: A Mixed-Methods Approach to Underserved Older Adults' Online Information Assessment," *New Media & Society* 32 no. 7 (2021), https://doi.org/10.1177/1461444820925041.

75. This is especially true for data companies that couple their data services with day-trading services for their subscribers.

76. William Fung and David A. Hsieh, "A Primer on Hedge Funds," *Journal of Empirical Finance* 6, no. 3 (August 1999): 309–331, https://doi.org/10.1016/S0927-5398(99)00006-7.

77. H.R. Rep. No. 1383, 73d Cong., 2d sess., 11 (1934), cited in *Basic Inc. v. Levinson*, 485 U.S. 224 (1988).

78. Harvey R. Miller, "Chapter 11 in Transition—From Boom to Bust and into the Future," *American Bankruptcy Law Journal* 81, no. 4 (Fall 2007): 375–404.

79. Thomas J. Campanella, "Robert Moses and His Racist Parkway, Explained," *Bloomberg CityLab*, July 9, 2017, https://www.bloomberg.com/news /articles/2017-07-09/robert-moses-and-his-racist-parkway-explained;   Merrill Fabry, "Why Is Tennis Scored So Weirdly?" *Time*, August 21, 2019, https://time .com/5040182/tennis-scoring-system-history/.

80. Wright, *The Wealth of Nations Rediscovered*, 4.

81. Bess Levin, "Report: Sen. Kelly Loeffler Downplayed the Coronavirus, Simultaneously Invested in Maker of Protective Gear," *Vanity Fair*, April 1, 2020, https: //www.vanityfair.com/news/2020/04/kelly-loeffler-protective-gear-investment.

82. Annamaria Lusardi et al., "Optimal Financial Knowledge and Wealth Inequality," *Journal of Political Economy* 125, no. 2 (April 2017): 431, https://doi .org/10.1086/690950.

83. Kim Parker and Richard Fry, "More Than Half of U.S. Households Have Some Investment in the Stock Market," Pew Research Center, March 25, 2020, https://www.pewresearch.org/fact-tank/2020/03/25/more-than-half-of-u-s -households-have-some-investment-in-the-stock-market/.

84. Nathan Bomey, "'It's Really Over': Corporate Pensions Head for Extinction as Nature of Retirement Plans Changes," *USA Today*, December 10, 2019, https://www.usatoday.com/story/money/2019/12/10/corporate-pensions-defined -benefit-mercer-report/2618501001/; Lusardi et al., "Optimal Financial Knowledge and Wealth Inequality," 423.

85. Lusardi et al., "Optimal Financial Knowledge and Wealth Inequality," 423.

86. Gary Mottola, "A Snapshot of Investor Households in America," *FINRA Investor Education Foundation Insights: Financial Capability*, September, 2015, https://www.sec.gov/spotlight/fixed-income-advisory-committee/finra-investor -education-foundation-investor-households-fimsa-040918.pdf.

87. Edward N. Wolff, "Household Wealth Trends in the United States, 1962 to 2016: Has Middle Class Wealth Recovered?" National Bureau of Economic Research Working Paper 24085, November 2017, https://www.nber.org/papers/ w24085; discussed in Matt Egan, "The Simple Thing Trump Doesn't Get About the Stock Market," *CNN Business*, September 16, 2020, https://www.cnn.com /2020/09/16/investing/stock-market-trump-economy/index.html. See also Jonnelle Marte, "Trump Touts Stock Market's Record Run, but Who Benefits?" *Reuters*, February 5, 2020, https://www.reuters.com/article/us-usa-trump-speech -stocks-analysis/trump-touts-stock-markets-record-run-but-who-benefits-idUS KBN1ZZ19A.

88. "The top 1% own a lot of stock, the rest of us own a little," said Steven Rosenthal, senior fellow, Urban-Brookings Tax Policy Center. Robert Frank, "The Wealthiest 10% of Americans Own a Record 89% of All U.S. Stocks,"

CNBC, October 18, 2021, https://www.cnbc.com/2021/10/18/the-wealthiest-10per
cent-of-americans-own-a-record-89percent-of-all-us-stocks.html.

89. Disclosure Requirements, 17 C.F.R. § 240.17g-7.

90. Regulation Fair Disclosure, 17 C.F.R. Part 243. The SEC's Regulation
FD prohibits companies from selectively disclosing market-moving information
before it goes public, but it only applies to the publicly traded companies themselves, and their officers, directors, employees, and agents.

91. "Thomson Reuters Suspends Early Release of Consumer Data," *Reuters*,
July 8, 2013, https://www.reuters.com/article/us-thomsonreuters-consumerdata/
thomson-reuters-suspends-early-release-of-consumer-data-idUSBRE9670WE2013
0708.

92. Amy Chozick, "Bloomberg Admits Terminal Snooping," *New York Times*,
May 13, 2013, https://www.nytimes.com/2013/05/13/business/media/bloomberg
-admits-terminal-snooping.html.

93. Michael S. Drake, "Who Uses Financial Statements? A Demographic
Analysis of Financial Statement Downloads from EDGAR," *Accounting Horizons* 31 no. 3 (2017): 56, https://doi.org/10.2308/acch-51736.

94. Milan Babic et al., "Who Is More Powerful—States or Corporations?"
The Conversation, July 10, 2018, https://theconversation.com/who-is-more
-powerful-states-or-corporations-99616.

95. Dilan P. Cook, "Are we sure the United States isn't just Raytheon, Boeing
and Chevron in a trenchcoat?" Twitter, February 17, 2021, https://twitter.com/
dilanpcook/status/1361983354544017411.

96. Troy A. Paredes, "Blinded by the Light: Information Overload and Its
Consequences for Securities Regulation," *Washington University Law Quarterly*
81, no. 2 (Summer 2003): 417–418.

97. Lin, "Reasonable Investor(s)," 461–518.

98. Lin, "Reasonable Investor(s)," 485.

99. Lin, "Reasonable Investor(s)," 485.

100. Hu, "Too Complex to Depict."

101. Wright, *The Wealth of Nations Rediscovered*, 24.

Chapter 6

1. Terhi Rantanen, *When News Was New* (Malden, MA: Wiley-Blackwell,
2009).

2. Mitchell Stephens, *A History of News* (New York: New York University
Press, 1988).

3. Fiona McHardy, "Gossip Was a Powerful Tool for the Powerless in Ancient
Greece," *Aeon*, February 1, 2019, edited by Sam Dresser, https://aeon.co/ideas/
gossip-was-a-powerful-tool-for-the-powerless-in-ancient-greece.

4. Katerina Eva Matsa, "Across Western Europe, Public News Media Are
Widely Used and Trusted Sources of News," Pew Research Center, June 8, 2018,
https://www.pewresearch.org/fact-tank/2018/06/08/western-europe-public-news
-media-widely-used-and-trusted/ .

5. Some nations' "public news" offerings are nothing more than spigots for nationalist propaganda.

6. Amy Mitchell et al., "Americans Who Mainly Get Their News on Social Media Are Less Engaged, Less Knowledgeable," Pew Research Center, July 30, 2020, https://www.journalism.org/2020/07/30/americans-who-mainly-get-their-news-on -social-media-are-less-engaged-less-knowledgeable/.

7. Mitchell et al., "Americans Who Mainly Get Their News on Social Media."

8. "Who Trusts—and Pays for—the News? Here's What 8,728 People Told Us," Donald W. Reynolds Journalism Institute, University of Missouri, Trusting News project, July 27, 2017, https://www.rjionline.org/stories/who-trusts-and -pays-for-the-news-heres-what-8728-people-told-us.

9. Daniel Hallin, "Whatever Happened to the News?" Center for Media Literacy, *Media & Values* 50 (Spring, 1990), https://www.medialit.org/reading-room /whatever-happened-news.

10. Simon Lavington, "Automation: The Machines and the Applications," in *Moving Targets:Elliott-Automation and the Dawn of the Computer Age in Britain, 1947–67* (London: Springer, 2011), https://doi.org/10.1007/978-1-84882-933-6_7.

11. In 1865, Reuters was the first to break the news of Abraham Lincoln's assassination. "Thomson Reuters," *Encyclopedia Brittanica*, https://www.britannica .com/topic/Thomson-Reuters (accessed November 8, 2021); "Company History," Thomson Reuters, https://www.thomsonreuters.com/en/about-us/company-his tory.html (accessed December 6, 2021).

12. "LexisNexis and ALM Extend Strategic Alliance Under New Licensing Agreement," LexisNexis, January 1, 2021, https://www.lexisnexis.com/commun ity/pressroom/b/news/posts/lexisnexis-and-alm-extend-strategic-alliance-under -new-licensing-agreement.

13. "The LexisNexis Timeline," LexisNexis, https://www.lexisnexis.com/an niversary/30th_timeline_fulltxt.pdf; "Start Searching with Nexis," LexisNexis, https://www.lexisnexis.com/en-us/professional/nexis/nexis-features.page (accessed on December 5, 2021).

14. "Nexis® Data as a Service," LexisNexis, https://bis.lexisnexis.co.uk/nexis -daas (accessed November 10, 2021); "Access an Unrivaled Collection of Aggregated Content with Nexis Data as a Service (DaaS)," LexisNexis, https://bis.lexis nexis.co.uk/nexis-daas/content (accessed November 10, 2021).

15. Alfred Snider, *The Code of the Debater: Introduction to Policy Debating*, International Debate Education Association (2018), 141.

16. "Digital Transition: The Future Has Already Happened!" International Press Institute, September 17, 2020, https://ipi.media/digital-transition-the-fu ture-has-already-happened/.

17. Victor Pickard, "American Journalism Is Dying. Its Survival Requires Public Funds," *The Guardian*, February 19, 2020, https://www.theguardian.com /commentisfree/2020/feb/19/american-journalism-press-publishing-mcclatchy.

18. Pickard, "American Journalism Is Dying."

19. Ben Bagdikian, *The New Media Monopoly* (Boston: Beacon Press, 2004), 4–5.

20. *Postal Service Act of 1792.* Washington explained that the federal government would subsidize the transmission of newspapers to distant parts of the country because of the "importance of facilitating the circulation of political intelligence and information." *Fourth Annual Address to Congress,* November 6, 1792.

21. *Postal Reorganization Act of 1970,* Pub. L. 91-375, 84 Stat. 719. The U.S. Postal Service describes this transition in detail on its website. "Postage Rates for Periodicals: A Narrative History," United States Postal Service, https://about .usps.com/who-we-are/postal-history/periodicals-postage-history.htm (accessed December 9, 2021); Richard Pérez-Peña, "A Reminder of Precedents in Subsidizing Newspapers," *New York Times,* January 27, 2010, https://www.nytimes.com/ 2010/01/28/business/media/28subsidy.html.

22. *Public Broadcasting Act of 1967,* Pub. L. 90-129, 81 Stat. 365, codified at 47 U.S.C. Ch. 5 §§ 390–397, 609.

23. John P. Witherspoon, Richard D. Estell, Bernard D. Mayes, and Ralph W. Nicholson, *NPR Articles of Incorporation,* February 26, 1970, https://current .org/1970/02/npr-articles-of-incorporation-1970/.

24. Ethan Zuckerman, "The Case for Digital Public Infrastructure," The Tech Giants, Monopoly Power, and Public Discourse series, Knight First Amendment Institute at Columbia University, January 17, 2020, https://knightcolumbia.org/ content/the-case-for-digital-public-infrastructure.

25. *Communications Act,* 47 U.S.C. § 303(s), *All-Channel Receiver Act,* Pub. L. 87-529, 76 Stat 150, by H.R. 8031 (87th Cong.): An Act to Amend the Communications Act of 1934 in Order to Give the Federal Communications Commission Certain Regulatory Authority Over Television Receiving Apparatus.

26. In 1941, the Federal Communications Commission limited the number of stations a that single entity could own to three. See the history in the Synopsis section of Federal Communications Commission Proposed National Television Multiple Ownership Rule, 83 Federal Register 3661, January 26, 2018, https:/ /www.federalregister.gov/documents/2018/01/26/2018-01404/national-television -multiple-ownership-rule.

27. "President Johnson's Remarks," upon signing S. 1160, Pub. L. 90-129, 81 Stat. 365, November 7, 1967, https://www.cpb.org/aboutpb/act/remarks.

28. "Hear NPR's First On-Air Original Broadcast from 1971," NPR, accessed December 9, 2021, https://www.npr.org/2021/04/28/990230586/hear-nprs-first -on-air-original-broadcast-from-1971.

29. The Telecommunications Act of 1996 reversed rules separating various telecommunications markets, allowing phone companies to provide cable television service and other similar telecommunication crossovers. The law also eliminated rules that stopped national companies from overtaking local news providers. *Telecommunications Act of 1996,* Pub. L. 104-104, 110 Stat. 56; Removal of Barriers to Entry, 47 U.S.C. § 253; 47 U.S.C. §§ 571–573.

30. Some examples of the kinds of opportunities that spurred the Telecommunications Act of 1996 were digital radio and DirecTV, which started the first digital satellite television service in 1994. When Satellite CD Radio (which

would eventually become Sirius XM) proposed satellite radio to the FCC in 1990, the Clinton administration wanted to clear the way for that venture to succeed. Edmund L. Andrews, "F.C.C. Plan For Radio by Satellite," *New York Times*, October 8, 1992, https://www.nytimes.com/1992/10/08/business/fcc-plan -for-radio-by-satellite.html.

31. Geoffrey Cowan and David Westphal, "Public Policy and Funding the News," USC Annenberg School for Communication & Journalism Center on Communication & Leadership Policy, January 2010, https://www.niemanlab.org /pdfs/USC%20Report.pdf.

32. *United States v. AT&T*, 310 F. Supp. 3d 161 (D.D.C. 2018).

33. Jack Shafer, "The Media Monotony", *Slate*, August 4, 2004, https://slate .com/news-and-politics/2004/08/the-media-monotony.html.

34. Bagdikian, *The New Media Monopoly*.

35. Paul Farhi, "NPR May Be 'Public' Radio, But It's Feeling the Economic Pain of the Pandemic. More Trouble Lies Ahead." *Washington Post*, July 21, 2020, https://www.washingtonpost.com/lifestyle/media/npr-may-be-public-radio-but -its-feeling-the-economic-pain-of-the-pandemic-more-trouble-lies-ahead/2020/ 07/21/8f08958a-c6a4-11ea-a99f-3bbdffb1af38_story.html.

36. Richard L. Hasen, "Cheap Speech and What It Has Done (to American Democracy)," *First Amendment Law Review* 16, Symposium (2017): 200, 203.

37. Reuters plans to put all of its news content behind a paywall as soon as it gets legal clearance to do so. Kenneth Li, "Reuters Postpones Website Paywall Amid Refinitiv Dispute," *Reuters*, May 27, 2021, https://www.reuters.com /business/media-telecom/reuters-postpones-website-paywall-amid-refinitiv -dispute-2021-05-27/.

38. Anna Heward, "The Story Behind the Unjust Shutdown of Gothamist and DNAinfo," *The New Yorker*, November 14, 2017, https://www.newyorker .com/culture/culture-desk/the-story-behind-the-unjust-shutdown-of-gothamist -and-dnainfo.

39. Meredith Broussard, "The Irony of Writing Online About Digital Preservation," *The Atlantic*, November 20, 2015, https://www.theatlantic.com/tech nology/archive/2015/11/the-irony-of-writing-about-digital-preservation/416184/.

40. Nathan J. Robinson, "The Truth Is Paywalled but the Lies Are Free," *Current Affairs*, August 2, 2020, https://www.currentaffairs.org/2020/08/the-truth-is -paywalled-but-the-lies-are-free/.

41. Today, public news organizations are usually set up as nonprofit corporations, underwritten by taxes, government funding, and corporate underwriting. They are often supplemented with donation drives, the source, for example, of New York City's ubiquitous WNYC public radio station totebags.

42. Jennifer 8. Lee, "On Minot, N.D., Radio, a Single Corporate Voice," *New York Times*, March 31, 2003, https://www.nytimes.com/2003/03/31/business /media-on-minot-nd-radio-a-single-corporate-voice.html.

43. Jack Shafer, "What Really Happened in Minot, N.D.?" *Slate*, January 10, 2007, https://slate.com/news-and-politics/2007/01/the-whole-story-about-that -toxic-spill-and-the-clear-channel-monopoly.html.

44. In 2020, 18 percent of adults in the United States said they primarily get their news information from platforms like Facebook, YouTube, and Twitter. Mitchell et al., "Americans Who Mainly Get Their News on Social Media Are Less Engaged, Less Knowledgeable."

45. 47 U.S.C. § 230.

46. Section 230 was passed after conflicting court cases left the issue of liability for online content providers uncertain. In *Cubby, Inc. v. CompuServe Inc.*, 776 F. Supp. 135 (S.D.N.Y. 1991), a federal court found that CompuServ could not be held liable for content that appeared on its forums. In contrast, in *Stratton Oakmont, Inc. v. Prodigy Services Co.*, 1995 WL 323710 (N.Y. Sup. Ct. 1995), a Long Island stockbroker tried to sue the company for libel after an anonymous poster on one of Prodigy's finance-themed bulletin boards said that the stockbroker had committed criminal acts. In *Stratton Oakmont*, a New York Court held that the online serivce provider could be held liable for the speech of its users.

47. Alina Selyukh, "Section 230: A Key Legal Shield for Facebook, Google Is About to Change," *NPR*, March 21, 2018, https://www.npr.org/sections/all techconsidered/2018/03/21/591622450/section-230-a-key-legal-shield-for-facebook -google-is-about-to-change, discussing SESTA-FOSTA legislation, *Stop Enabling Sex Traffickers Act*, H.R. 1865, and *Fight Online Sex Trafficking Act*, H.R. 115-572, Pub. L. 115-164 (2018).

48. Tom Foremski, "Media Company or Tech Platform? The Hugely Important Battle to Redefine Facebook," *ZDNet*, November 18, 2016, https://www.zd net.com/article/media-company-or-tech-platform-facebook-definition-has-huge -fallout/.

49. Giulia Segreti, "Facebook CEO Says Group Will not Become a Media Company," Reuters, August 29, 2016, https://www.reuters.com/article/us-face book-zuckerberg-idUSKCN1141WN.

50. Foremski, "Media Company or Tech Platform?"

51. Deepa Seetharaman and Emily Glazer, "How Mark Zuckerberg Learned Politics," *Wall Street Journal*, October 16, 2020, https://www.wsj.com/articles/ how-mark-zuckerberg-learned-politics-11602853200.

52. "Here's the Latest Official Saying Facebook Should Be Treated as a Media Company," *Fortune*, November 23, 2016, http://search.ebscohost.com.law.ezproxy .cuny.edu/login.aspx?direct=true&db=bth&AN=119658070&site=ehost-live.

53. Rebecca Tushnet, "Power Without Responsibility: Intermediaries and the First Amendment," *George Washington Law Review* 76, no. 4 (June 2008): 986–1016.

54. Brandy Zadrozny, "In a Pennsylvania Town, a Facebook Group Fills the Local News Void," *NBC News*, April 5, 2021, https://www.nbcnews.com/tech/ social-media/pennsylvania-town-facebook-group-fills-local-news-void-rcna577.

55. Zadrozny, "In a Pennsylvania Town, a Facebook Group Fills the Local News Void."

56. For example, the Society of Professional Journalists Code of Ethics focuses first on accuracy and fact-checking. "SPJ Code of Ethics," accessed December 7, 2021, https://www.spj.org/ethicscode.asp.

57. Laura Edelson et al., "Far-Right News Sources on Facebook More Engaging," Cybersecurity for Democracy, March 3, 2021, https://medium.com/cybersecurity-for-democracy/far-right-news-sources-on-facebook-more-engaging-e04a01efae90.

58. Gregory J. Martin and Josh McCrain, "Local News and National Politics," *American Political Science Review* 113, no. 2 (May 2019): 372–384.

59. Jacey Fortin and Jonah Engel Bromwich, "Sinclair Made Dozens of Local News Anchors Recite the Same Script," *New York Times*, April 2, 2018, https://www.nytimes.com/2018/04/02/business/media/sinclair-news-anchors-script.html.

60. Tina Nguyen and Mark Scott, "How 'SharpieGate' Went from Online Chatter to Trumpworld Strategy in Arizona", *Politico*, November 5, 2020, https://www.politico.com/news/2020/11/05/sharpie-ballots-trump-strategy-arizona-434372.

61. Davey Alba and Jack Nicas, "As Local News Dies, a Pay-for-Play Network Rises in Its Place," *New York Times*, October 18, 2020, https://www.nytimes.com/2020/10/18/technology/timpone-local-news-metric-media.html.

62. Alba and Nicas, "As Local News Dies."

63. Priyanjana Bengani, "As Election Looms, a Network of Mysterious 'Pink Slime' Local News Outlets Nearly Triples in Size," *Columbia Journalism Review*, August 4, 2020, https://www.cjr.org/analysis/as-election-looms-a-network-of-mysterious-pink-slime-local-news-outlets-nearly-triples-in-size.php.

64. Alba and Nicas, "As Local News Dies."

65. Eric Hananoki, "A Supplement Company Is Using Conservative Radio to Market Itself as a Coronavirus Defense and Treatment," Media Matters for America, April 1, 2020, https://www.mediamatters.org/coronavirus-covid-19/supplement-company-balance-nature-using-conservative-radio-market-itself.

66. Joshua Goodman, "Voting Company Sues Fox, Giuliani Over Election Fraud Claims," *AP News*, February 4, 2021, https://apnews.com/article/smartmatic-sues-fox-news-giuliani-2a8d83df2e6d73b750dd85f92f4fd7ef.

67. Timothy Libert, "This Article Is Spying on You," *New York Times*, September 18, 2019, https://www.nytimes.com/2019/09/18/opinion/data-privacy-tracking.html.

68. Michael Beckel, "Media Outlets Capitalize on Political Committees' Use of Subscriber Lists," Open Secrets News & Analysis, April 6, 2011, https://www.opensecrets.org/news/2011/04/subscriber-lists-valuable-assets/.

69. "Data Broker Registration for Taboola, Inc.," State of California Department of Justice, https://oag.ca.gov/data-broker/registration/186589 (accessed November 9, 2021). Companies like Taboola and Outbrain post ads designed to resemble news stories on digital news sites, personalizing what appears on the basis of the particular user's browser history. Outbrain and Taboola are paid by the companies whose ads they share, and by second- and third-party data brokers that purchase their data products.

70. Perhaps this is because the fall of public access news has been so visible and well-reported.

71. Victor Pickard and Timothy Neff, "Strengthen Our Democracy by Funding Public Media," *Columbia Journalism Review*, June 2, 2021, https://www.cjr.org/opinion/public-funding-media-democracy.php.

72. Mike Rispoli, "Why the Civic Info Consortium Is Such a Huge Deal," Free Press, September 30, 2020, https://www.freepress.net/our-response/expert-analysis/insights-opinions/why-civic-info-consortium-such-huge-deal.

73. New York State Senate Bill S. 6784 (2019–2020); New York State Assembly Bill A. 8662 (2019–2020).

74. *Saving Local News Act of 2019*, H.R. 3126, 116th Cong., introduced June 5, 2019.

75. David Ardia, Evan Ringel, Victoria Smith Ekstrand, and Ashley Fox, "Addressing the Decline of Local News, Rise of Platforms, and Spread of Mis- and Disinformation Online," UNC Center for Media Law and Policy, https://citap.unc.edu/local-news-platforms-mis-disinformation/ (accessed December 10, 2021).

76. Ethan Zuckerman, "The Case for Digital Public Infrastructure," The Tech Giants, Monopoly Power, and Public Discourse series, Knight First Amendment Institute at Columbia University, January 17, 2020, https://knightcolumbia.org/content/the-case-for-digital-public-infrastructure.

77. Timothy Karr and Craig Aaron, "Beyond Fixing Facebook," Free Press, February 2019, https://www.freepress.net/sites/default/files/2019-02/Beyond-Fixing-Facebook-Final_0.pdf; Paul Romer, "A Tax That Could Fix Big Tech," *New York Times*, May 6, 2019, https://www.nytimes.com/2019/05/06/opinion/tax-facebook-google.html; Zuckerman, "The Case for Digital Public Infrastructure."

78. Mark Zuckerberg, "Facebook Can Help the News Business," *New York Times*, October 25, 2019, https://www.nytimes.com/2019/10/25/opinion/sunday/mark-zuckerberg-facebook-news.html.

79. Jasmine Enberg, "Global Digital Ad Spending 2019," *Insider Intelligence*, March 28, 2019, https://www.emarketer.com/content/global-digital-ad-spending-2019.

80. Zuckerman, "The Case for Digital Public Infrastructure."

81. Robinson, "The Truth Is Paywalled but the Lies Are Free."

82. "About Us," Associated Press, https://www.ap.org/about/ (accessed November 9, 2021).

83. Pickard and Neff, "Strengthen Our Democracy by Funding Public Media."

84. For example, the Federal Radio Commission that regulated radio stations like public utilities. *The Radio Act of 1927*, Pub. L. 69-632, H.R. 9971, 69th Cong.

85. Victor Pickard, "The Answer to the Media Industry's Woes? Publicly Owned Newspapers," *Washington Post*, May 18, 2020, https://www.washingtonpost.com/outlook/2020/05/18/answer-media-industrys-woes-publicly-owned-newspapers/.

86. Adam Ragusea, "Topple the Towers: Why Public Radio and Television Stations Should Radically Reorient Toward Digital-First Local News, and How

They Could Do It," Knight Foundation, 2017, https://knightfoundation.org/public-media-white-paper-2017-ragusea/.

87. Robinson, "The Truth Is Paywalled but the Lies Are Free."

Conclusion

1. Nantina Vgontzas and Meredith Whittaker, "These Machines Won't Kill Fascism: Toward a Militant Progressive Vision for Tech," *The Nation*, January 29, 2021, https://www.thenation.com/article/society/tech-labor-progressive/.

2. Ari Notis, "No One Can Fully Explain This Baffling *Roblox* Ad Scam," *Kotaku*, August 5, 2021, https://kotaku.com/no-one-can-fully-explain-this-baffling-roblox-ad-scam-1847431110.

3. Ethan Zuckerman, "The Case for Digital Public Infrastructure," The Tech Giants, Monopoly Power, and Public Discourse series, Knight First Amendment Institute at Columbia University, January 17, 2020, https://knightcolumbia.org/content/the-case-for-digital-public-infrastructure.

4. Ethan Zuckerman, "Digital Public Infrastructural Possibilities," Reclaiming Digital Infrastructure for the Public Interest series, Session #1, October 20, 2020, https://pacscenter.stanford.edu/event/digital-public-infrastructural-possibilities/.

5. Tim Wu, *The Curse of Bigness: Antitrust in the New Gilded Age* (New York: Columbia Global Reports, 2018).

6. Heather Timmons, "Washington Failed to Regulate Big Tech—and Now It's About to Discover That It Can't," *Quartz*, October 3, 2017, https://qz.com/1089907/why-washington-dc-is-incapable-of-regulating-the-worlds-tech-giants/.

7. Meg Leta Jones, "Does Technology Drive Law? The Dilemma of Technological Exceptionalism in the Law," *Journal of Law, Technology, and Policy* 2018, no. 2 (2018): 250–284.

8. Jones, "Does Technology Drive Law?," 278.

9. Alexis C. Madrigal, "What Facebook Did to American Democracy," *The Atlantic*, October 12, 2017, https://www.theatlantic.com/technology/archive/2017/10/what-facebook-did/542502/.

10. Dan Milmo, "Facebook Failing to Protect Users from Covid Misinformation, Says Monitor," *The Guardian*, November 1, 2021, https://www.theguardian.com/technology/2021/nov/02/facebook-failing-to-protect-users-from-covid-misinformation-says-monitor.

11. Paul Mozer, "A Genocide Incited on Facebook, with Posts from Myanmar's Military," October 15, 2018, *New York Times*, https://www.nytimes.com/2018/10/15/technology/myanmar-facebook-genocide.html.

12. Tiffany C. Li, "FaceApp Makes Today's Privacy Laws Look Antiquated," *The Atlantic*, July 20, 2019, https://www.theatlantic.com/ideas/archive/2019/07/faceapp-reveals-huge-holes-todays-privacy-laws/594358/.

13. Amanda Lenhart and Kellie Owens, "Good Intentions, Bad Inventions: The Four Myths of Healthy Tech," Data & Society, 2020, p. 3, https://datasociety.net/wp-content/uploads/2020/10/Healthy-Tech-Myths-DataSociety-20201007.pdf.

14. For example, practices such as product tying, pricing informational

products far above market value, and forcing purchasers to sign nondisclosure agreements.

15. Robin Berjon, "Competition & Privacy: It's Both or Nothing," Robin Berjon Blog, December 13, 2021, https://berjon.com/competition-privacy/.

16. Samantha Cole, "Archivists Are Preserving Capitol Hill Riot Livestreams Before They're Deleted," January 7, 2021, Motherboard, Vice, https://www.vice.com/en/article/3an5e3/archivists-are-preserving-capitol-hill-riot-livestreams-before-theyre-deleted.

17. Jathan Sadowski, Salomé Viljoen, and Meredith Whittaker, "Everyone Should Decide How Their Digital Data Are Used—Not Just Tech Companies," *Nature*, July 1, 2021, https://www.nature.com/articles/d41586-021-01812-3?proof=t%253B.

18. Chris Gilliard and Hugh Culik, "Digital Redlining, Access, and Privacy," Common Sense Education Blog, May 24, 2016, https://www.commonsense.org/education/articles/digital-redlining-access-and-privacy.

19. Gilliard and Culik, "Digital Redlining, Access, and Privacy."

20. Camille Marcos Noûs, "Message from the Grassroots: Scholarly Communication, Crisis, and Contradictions," *Canadian Journal of Academic Librarianship* 7 (2021), https://cjal.ca/index.php/capal/article/view/36448/28824.

21. April Hathcock, "Racing to the Crossroads of Scholarly Communication and Democracy: But Who Are We Leaving Behind?" *In the Library with the Lead Pipe*, August 22, 2018, https://www.inthelibrarywiththeleadpipe.org/2018/racing-to-the-crossroads-of-scholarly-communication-and-democracy-but-who-are-we-leaving-behind/.

22. Chris Edwards, "Who Owns U.S. Infrastructure?" *Cato Institute Tax and Budget Bulletin*, no. 78 (June 1, 2017), https://www.cato.org/tax-budget-bulletin/who-owns-us-infrastructure.

23. The company responsible for a major Brooklyn ferry hub stranded passengers on the shore when it sold its investment to a new company without including continued ferry service in the deal. Edward Ongweso Jr., "NYC Ferry Limits Service Because New Pier Owner Won't Let It Dock," Motherboard, Vice, October 19, 2020, https://www.vice.com/en/article/akdw4g/nyc-ferry-limits-service-because-new-pier-owner-wont-let-it-dock; Elizabeth Adams, "Greenpoint @ NYCferry stop out of commission 'indefinitely' bc the developer sold the property. This isn't how public transit functions. And here's how commuters are being notified this morning: from a boat operater calling out to people as the ferry goes by. Seriously @NYCEDC," Twitter, October 19, 2020, https://twitter.com/ElizabAdams/status/1318171382803501057.

24. Gabriel Sandoval, "NYC Ferry Gets New $64 Million Boost from de Blasio-Controlled Board," *The City*, December 15, 2021, https://www.thecity.nyc/transportation/2021/2/4/22267583/nyc-ferry-de-blasio-financial-boost.

25. *Highway Trust Fund*, 26 U.S.C. § 9503.

26. "The Federal Net Neutrality Debate: Access to Broadband Networks," Congressional Research Service, updated February 24, 2021, https://sgp.fas.org/crs/misc/R40616.pdf.

27. Zuckerman, "The Case for Digital Public Infrastructure."

28. Zuckerman, "The Case for Digital Public Infrastructure."

29. Zuckerman, "The Case for Digital Public Infrastructure"; *Radio Act of 1927*, Pub. L. 69-632, codified at 47 U.S.C. Ch. 4, repealed by *Telecommunications Act of 1934*.

30. Licenses, 47 U.S.C. § 307(a).

31. *Radio Act of 1927*, Pub. L. 69-632, codified at 47 U.S.C. Ch. 4, repealed by *Telecommunications Act of 1934*.

32. Federal Communication Commission, "The Public and Broadcasting," updated September 2021, https://www.fcc.gov/media/radio/public-and-broadcasting.

33. Zuckerman, "The Case for Digital Public Infrastructure"; Paul Romer, "A Tax That Could Fix Big Tech," *New York Times*, May 6, 2019, https://www.nytimes.com/2019/05/06/opinion/tax-facebook-google.html.

34. John Gastil and Todd Davies, "Digital Democracy: Episode IV—A New Hope*: How a Corporation for Public Software Could Transform Digital Engagement for Government and Civil Society," *Digital Government: Research and Practice* 1, no. 1, Article 6, January 2020, https://dl.acm.org/doi/pdf/10.1145/3342194.

35. Jefferson Pooley, "Collective Funding to Reclaim Scholarly Publishing," Common Place, Series 1.2: The Business of Knowing, 2021, https://doi.org/10.21428/6ffd8432.250139da.

36. Tech companies avoid taxes by using tax havens, overreporting taxes, and using their digital services to work around tax requirements that apply to traditional brick-and-mortar businesses. Jim Tankersley, "Tech Giants Shift Profits to Avoid Taxes. There's a Plan to Stop Them." *New York Times*, October 10, 2019, https://www.nytimes.com/2019/10/09/us/politics/tech-giants-taxes-oecd.html.

37. "Common Public Library Funding Myths," OCLC, June 25, 2015, https://www.webjunction.org/documents/webjunction/advocacy-in-action/common-public-library-funding-myths.html. While public library systems are established on state and local levels, Congress has designated federal funds for libraries, as well. *Library Services and Technology Act*, Pub. L. 104-208, 110 Stat. 3009-925 (1996). Funding was reauthorized in 2018 in the *Museum and Library Services Act of 2018*, 20 U.S.C., Pub. L. 115-410. The law is codified at 20 U.S.C. 9101 et seq.

38. Eli Pariser, "To Mend a Broken Internet, Create Online Parks," *Wired*, October 13, 2020, https://www.wired.com/story/to-mend-a-broken-internet-create-online-parks/.

39. "PubMed User Guide," Pub.Med.gov, National Library of Medicine, last updated November 2, 2021, https://pubmed.ncbi.nlm.nih.gov/help/.

40. India's government has proposed nationalizing access to subscription databases by buying bulk subscriptions to research services and providing free access to all. Amitabh Sinha, "Govt Proposes to Buy Bulk Subscriptions of All Scientific Journals, Provide Free Access to All," *The Indian Express*, January 1, 2021, https://indianexpress.com/article/india/pune/one-nation-one-subscription-govt-draft-policy-7128799/.

41. Aaron Perzanowski and Jason Schultz. *The End of Ownership: Personal Property in the Digital Economy.* (Cambridge, MA: MIT Press, 2016).

42. Internet Archive and HathiTrust have been sued for attempting to implement controlled digital lending programs that allow internet users to look at materials one at a time (like people checking out a book in a physical library would) and for attempting to host "orphan works," copyright-protected materials whose owners are impossible to contact or find. See *Authors Guild v. HathiTrust,* 755 F.3d 87 (2d Cir. 2014) and *Hachette v. Internet Archive,* 20-04160 (S.D.N.Y. 2020).

43. Siva Vaidhyanathan, "Making Sense of the Facebook Menace," *The New Republic,* January 5, 2021, https://newrepublic.com/article/160661/facebook-menace-making-platform-safe-democracy.

44. Chris Hoofnagle, "Big Brother's Little Helpers: How ChoicePoint and Other Commercial Data Brokers Collect and Package Your Data for Law Enforcement," *North Carolina Journal of International Law and Commercial Regulation* 29, no. 4 (2004): 624. Courts have used different tests to decide whether an enterprise is a state actor, assessing whether companies are performing a public function traditionally and exclusively performed by the government, whether the government compelled a private entity's actions, or whether a private actor was "pervasively entwined with public institutions." Government data brokers could be described as state actors under any of these inquiries. *Manhattan Cmty. Access Corp. v. Halleck,* 139 S. Ct. 1921, 1933 (2019); *Am. Mfrs. Mut. Ins. Co. v. Sullivan,* 526 U.S. 40, 52–58 (1999); *Brentwood Acad. v. Tenn. Secondary Sch. Athletic Ass'n,* 531 U.S. 288, 298–302 (2001).

45. Jack M. Balkin, "The Fiduciary Model of Privacy," *Harvard Law Review Forum* 134, no. 1 (2020): 11–33.

46. Balkin, "The Fiduciary Model of Privacy," 14.

47. Balkin, "The Fiduciary Model of Privacy," 20.

48. Sherrod Brown, " Privacy Isn't a Right You Can Click Away," *Wired,* June 29, 2020, https://www.wired.com/story/privacy-isnt-a-right-you-can-click-away/.

49. Salomé Viljoen, "A Relational Theory of Data Governance" *Yale Law Journal* 131, no. 2 (November 2021): 573–654, https://www.yalelawjournal.org/feature/a-relational-theory-of-data-governance.

50. Siva Vaidhyanathan, "Making Sense of the Facebook Menace," *The New Republic,* January 5, 2021, https://newrepublic.com/article/160661/facebook-menace-making-platform-safe-democracy.

51. Carl Malamud, "Who May Swim in the Ocean of Knowledge?" *The Wire,* March 2, 2018, https://thewire.in/education/who-may-swim-in-the-ocean-of-knowledge.

INDEX

academic metrics, xi, xii, 51, 52; inequality compounded by, 63–64; manipulation of, 65

academic research, xii, xiii, 3, 5, 7, 14, 16, 19, 25, 50–71

Accurint, 18, 28, 43

All-Channel Receiver Act (1962), 116

Amazon, 4–5, 10, 11, 15, 20, 35, 128, 129

AMC Theaters, 100

American Association of Law Libraries (AALL), xi, 89, 92

American Lawyer Media, 113

Anduril, 32

Apple Computer, 110

article processing charges (APCs), 67

artificial intelligence (AI), 76–77

arXiv, 67

Asher, Hank, 28–29

Associated Press, 125

AT&T (American Telephone & Telegraph), 9–10, 32

authenticating, of law, 82

Automating Inequality (Eubanks), 39

AutoTrack, 29

background checks, 18, 42

Bagdikian, Ben, 9

BBC (British Broadcasting Corporation), 113

Bear Stearns, 106

Benjamin, Ruha, 32

BePress, xiii, 53, 64

Bertelsmann, 116

Biden, Joe, 123

biometrics, 19

Black Panther Party, 32

Bloomberg, Michael, 98

Bloomberg L.P., 3, 88, 94–95, 98, 103, 104, 109–11

blue sky laws, 99

body cameras, 42

Boolean searching, 76, 80

Bork, Robert, 10

Bradford, Marion, 61

Brandeis, Louis, 45

Breitbart News Network, 123

Brown, Sherrod, 142

bundling, 58–59, 71, 89, 90

California, 45
cartels, 8–9
Chafetz, Josh, 75
cheese, 8
Chicago school of economics, 10, 22
Chicago Tribune, 116
Children's Online Privacy Protection
    Act (COPPA, 1998), 44
child welfare agencies, 22, 28, 31, 32,
    33, 41
ChoicePoint, 28, 30, 43, 49
citizen authorship, 79
Citrix, 108
civil rights movement, 32
Clarivate (Thomson Science), 52–53,
    64
Clark, Marcia, 74
Clean Air Act (1963), 142
Clean Water Act (1972), 142
Clear Channel, 118
Clearview AI, 27
Clinton, Bill, 20–21, 115
CNBC, 105, 106
CNN, 3, 118
Cohen, Julie, 97
COINTELPRO, 32, 41
collusion, 8
Communications Act (1934), 115
Communications Decency Act (1996),
    119
Computer Fraud and Abuse Act
    (1986), 70
confidentiality, xi, xiv
confidentiality clauses, 59
Consolidated Lead Evaluation and
    Reporting (CLEAR), 30
Consumer Financial Protection
    Bureau (CFPB), 100
consumer protection, 11, 23
copyright, 48, 57, 67–70, 92, 139–40
Cornell University, 67, 90
Corporation for Public Broadcasting,
    114, 125–26
Covid pandemic, 5, 16, 108, 116, 123

Cramer, Jim, 106
credit rating, credit reporting, 18, 44,
    109
cryptocurrency, 108
The Curse of Bigness (Wu), 129
Customs and Border Patrol (CBP), 40

Data Broker Accountability and
    Transparency Act, 43
data brokering, 27–49
Data Corporation, 74
dating apps, 2, 34
Department of Homeland Security
    (DHS), 40
deregulation, 21
digital lending, 56
Dinkins, James, 22
disclosure, of financial information,
    99, 101, 108–9, 110–11
Discrete Analysis (mathematics jour-
    nal), 67
Disney Company, 115
DNA identification, 36, 40
dossier effect, 35–36, 40–41
Dropbox, 80
DuPont, 108

EBSCO, 117
EDGAR (Electronic Data Gathering,
    Analysis and Retrieval), 98, 103,
    110, 111, 139
Eisen, Michael, 61–62
Ekeland, Tor, 70
Elbakyan, Alexandra, 57, 70, 71
Electronic Communications Privacy
    Act (ECPA, 1986), 44–45
Electronic Court Records Reform Act
    (2019), 88–89
Elsevier, xii, xiii, 5, 7, 17, 22, 97;
    copyright abused by, 68; cost of
    abandoning, 66, 67; as oligopolist,
    51–71
Elzevier, Louis, 51
employers, xi, 2, 15, 28, 38, 41, 44

Enron Corporation, 100
entwinement test, for state action, 46
environmental protection, 23
Environmental Protection Agency
    (EPA), 142
Erasmus, Desiderius, 51
Experian, 44
Equal Credit Opportunity Act (1974),
    101
Equifax, 3, 44
errors, in data files, 38, 132
Eubanks, Virginia, 39

Facebook, 11, 15, 18, 20, 128, 129–30;
    as data broker, 27; local reporting
    funded by, 125; as news source,
    118–21
facial recognition, 18, 19, 39, 40, 41
Fair Credit Reporting Act (FCRA,
    1970), 44
fair use doctrine, 68, 69
Family Educational Rights and Pri-
    vacy Act (FERPA, 1974), 44
Federal Bureau of Investigation (FBI),
    32, 43, 141
Federal Communications Commis-
    sion (FCC), 115
Federal Records Act (FRA, 1950), 81,
    90, 92
Federal Register, 91
Federal Trade Commission (FTC),
    xiii, 29–30, 43, 71
fiduciaries, 137, 141
Fifth Amendment, 45
financial data, xii, 22, 24, 25, 94–111;
    disclosure of, 99, 101, 108–9, 110–11
Fios1 (local news channel), 124
First Amendment, 46, 47
first-sale doctrine, 68–69
Florida, 45
Floyd, George, 41
food stamps, 33
Ford Motor Company, 101
forum shopping, 14

Fourth Amendment, 36, 45, 46, 141
Fox News, 118, 122, 123
Free Access to Legal Movement
    (FALM), 90–91, 92
freedom of association, 46
Freedom of Information Act (FOIA,
    1974), 44, 81, 90, 92
freedom of speech, 47
free riding, 138
Friedman, Milton, 10
Frye, Brian, 69

Galileo Galilei, 51
GameStop, 100
Gannett Company, 123
Georgia v. Public.Resource.Org (2020),
    83, 89–90
Get Full Text Research, 62–63
geospatial data, 12, 19
Glossa (online journal), 66–67
Google, 10–12, 18, 35, 47, 119, 125, 128,
    130
Google Drive, 80
Gothamist (online news site), 117
government edicts doctrine, 79, 82,
    90, 92
Gowers, Timothy, 67
GPS (global positioning system), 12,
    36
Gramm-Leach-Bliley Act (1999), 44
Great Depression, 99
Grygiel, Jennifer, 121

Hathcock, April, 144
HathiTrust, 139, 140
HBO (Home Box Office), 117
healthcare, xi, 18, 24, 27, 41
Health Insurance Portability and
    Accountability Act (HIPAA, 1996),
    44
Hearst Publication, 116
Hoofnagle, Chris, 49
housing, xi, 2, 15, 18–19, 39–40, 42
Hu, Henry, 111

HyperLaw, 88

Icahn, Carl, 111
Illinois, 45
Immigration and Customs Enforce-
    ment (ICE), ix–xii, xiii, 19, 23, 31,
    34, 40, 85, 141
India, 16
information asymmetries, 96, 97, 109,
    110
information cascades, 99–100, 122
InfoWars, 122
insider trading, 109
Inskeep, Steve, 126
insurers, xi, 2, 14, 18, 27, 33, 41
Internet Archive, 56, 139, 140
Ito, Lance, 74

Jobs, Steve, 73
Johnson, Lyndon, 115
journal publishing, 15; as academic
    lifeblood, 50; digitization of, 51–52;
    fees charged in, 4, 6–7; global
    inequality compounded by, 54;
    market concentration in, 3; privacy
    concerns surrounding, xiii, 57;
    sharp practices in, 56–60
JPMorgan Chase, 110
JSTOR, 56

Kansas, 99
KeyCite, xiv
King, Martin Luther, Jr., 32
Kodak Company, 45

legal information, 72–93
Legal Information Institute (LII),
    90–91
Lehrer, Jim, 115
Lexis, ix–xi, xiii, 19, 22, 42, 66, 73,
    74, 97, 109, 111; bundling by, 90;
    "correctional" product line of, 64–
    65; financial data compiled by, 94,
    97–98; law privatized by, 79–80;

law shaped by, 75–78; one-sided
    contracts of, 89; state law compiled
    by, 81–82; in television series, 85–
    86; user-friendliness of, 80
LexisNexis Special Services, Inc.
    (LNSSI), 30
libel, 119, 123, 124
lightbulbs, 8
Lin, Tom C. W., 111
Linda Hall Library, 56
Lingua (journal), 66
Loeffler, Kelly, 108
Lofgren, Zoe, 70
Los Angeles Municipal News, 126
Los Angeles Times, 116
Lumen (facial recognition tool), 39, 41
Lynch, Peter, 96

Maas, Heiko, 120
machine learning, 76–77
MacNeil, Robert, 115
malaria, 16
Malcolm X, 32
maple syrup, 8
Markey, Ed, 43
Mart, Susan Nevelow, 77
Mead Corporation, 73
Mendeley, 53
Microsoft, 10, 20
mistaken identity, 18, 42
Moore, Samuel, 63–64
Moses, Robert, 107
Mother Jones, 120, 123
Motley Fool, 107
MSNBC, 118
Murdoch, Rupert, 116

National Archives, 81
National Crime and Information
    Center, 43
National Public Radio (NPR), 113–16,
    119, 126
National Security Agency (NSA), 31
Nestlé, 3–4

Netflix, 54, 55
net neutrality, 138
news, xii, 2, 3, 112–26; data compa-
    nies' retreat from, 15; deregulation
    and, 20–21; digitization of, 114–15
News Corporation, 116
New York City, 42
New York Times, 116, 123
NextDoor, 120
nondisclosure agreements, 5, 57, 59–
    60, 71, 89
Norway, 124

Obama, Barack, 22
O'Grady, Jean, 87
O'Neil, Cathy, 28
OPEC (Organization of Petroleum
    Exporting Countries), 8, 9
open access, 24, 66–67, 71, 92–93,
    133–36
Oracle, 3, 123
Orange Is the New Black (television
    series), 85
Own Your Own Data Act, 48

Palantir Technologies, 19, 32
Patterson, Scott, 103
Paywall (documentary film), 61
pharmaceuticals, 8
Pickard, Victor, 126
"pink slime" news, 123
piracy, 70
plasma donation, 48
policing, 2, 14, 27, 29–30; of immi-
    grants, 19; racist underpinnings of,
    xii, 18, 26, 32–33; rules limiting, 42–
    43; after September 11 attacks, 31
Presidential Records Act (1978), 90
Preston, James, 73, 74
price discrimination, 59, 89
price fixing, 8
privatization, xii, 2, 6–7, 80
prisoners, xii, 16, 84
Privacy Act (1974), 44, 141

profiling, 32
Prohibition, 32
property rights, for personal data,
    47–48
ProQuest, 117
Public Access to Court Electronic
    Records (PACER), 80–81, 89, 139
Public Broadcasting Act (1967), 114
Public Broadcasting Service (PBS),
    113, 116
public goods, 23, 25
public transportation, 135–36, 142
public utilities, 8, 23, 126, 135, 136–40

radio, 20, 115, 119, 137
Radio Act (1927), 137
Reddit (social media platform), 100,
    122
redlining, 33, 101
Reed Elsevier LexisNexis (RELX), ix,
    x–xi, xiii, 2, 8–9, 49, 66, 117, 141;
    sanalytics software developed by,
    13–14; copyright exploited by, 68;
    during Covid pandemic, 5; as data
    broker, 27–29, 31; duty to correct
    disclaimed by, 44; early history
    of, 113; fees charged by, 4, 7, 23,
    53; financial data compiled by, 95,
    97–98; governments dependent on,
    22, 40, 41; informational commons
    privatized by, 15–16; informational
    reach of, 14–15, 18, 19, 35–36, 51–52;
    legal information controlled by,
    72; Lexis acquired by, 74; lobbying
    and campaign contributions by, 23,
    88–89; low profile of, 11–12; market
    power of, 3–4, 6, 7, 10, 11–12, 29–
    30; publishing deemphasized by, 15;
    quality control problems at, 16–17,
    86–87; surveillance linked to, 19,
    37–38, 85; warrant requirements
    circumvented by, 37
Refinitiv Eikon, 94, 95, 103, 104, 109,
    111

rent seeking, 54
Reuters, xii, 15, 113, 117
Rich, Steven, 33
Right to Financial Privacy Act
    (RFPA, 1978), 44
risk, xi, xii, 2, 15, 27–30, 34, 35, 49;
    false assessments of, 18–19, 42; fi-
    nancial, 94–95, 96, 101, 104; varied
    understandings of, 104–5
Roberts, John, 83
Rockefeller, John D., IV, 43
Romigh, Deanna, 120
ROSS (information company), 88

Sage Publications, 62, 66
San Diego, 42
San Francisco Chronicle, 116
satellite radio, 20
Schafer, Sarah, 1
Schumer, Charles, 71
ScienceDirect, 57, 71
Sci-Hub, 57, 71
Scopus, 52, 64
search warrants, 36, 42–43, 46, 141
Securities Act (1933), 99
Securities and Exchange Act (1934), 99
Securities and Exchange Commission
    (SEC), 22, 97, 99, 101, 110, 111s
self-incrimination, 46
September 11 attacks, 31
Sesame Street, 117
Shepard's citations, xiv, 74
Simpson, O. J., 74
Sinclair Broadcast Group, 122, 123
Smith, Adam, 8, 96
Sotomayor, Sonia, 37
Souter, David, 25
Springer, 58, 62
SSRN (Social Science Research Net-
    work), 53, 64
Standard & Poor's, 47
Standard Oil Company, 9–10
Starbucks, 110

state actor test, 46–47
state law, 81
subprime mortgage crisis, 102
sufficient nexus test, for state action,
    46
Sugarman, Alan, 88
Supplemental Nutrition Assistance
    Program (SNAP), 34
surveillance, ix–xi, 18, 19, 22, 25, 26,
    30–31; by data brokers, 63; on news
    websites, 123
surveillant advertising, 125
Swartz, Aaron, 56–57, 70
Swauger, Shea, 38
Sweden, 124
Swift, Taylor, 61
symbiotic relationship test, for state
    action, 46

Tanzania, 16
Taylor & Francis, 62
Telecommunications Act (1996),
    115–16
Tempest, David, 59
Third Amendment, 46
third-party doctrine, 37, 46
Thomson Reuters, ix–xii, 2, 8–9, 49,
    111, 141; analytics software devel-
    oped by, 13–14; copyright exploited
    by, 68; as data broker, 27–30; duty
    to correct disclaimed by, 38–39, 44;
    early history of, 113; fees charged
    by, 5; financial data compiled by,
    97; governments dependent on, 22,
    40, 41; informational commons
    privatized by, 15–16; informational
    reach of, 14–15, 18, 19, 35–36, 51; in-
    formation prereleased by, 109; legal
    information controlled by, 72; lob-
    bying by, 88–89; market power of,
    3–4, 6, 7, 10, 11–12; quality control
    problems at, 16–17, 86–87; Reuters
    division of, xii, 15, 113, 117; surveil-

lance linked to, 19, 38, 57; warrant requirements circumvented by, 37; Westlaw acquired by, 74, 87
Thomson Reuters Special Services (TRSS), 30, 31
ThreatMetrix, 57
tie-ins, 5, 58, 89, 90
Time Warner, 116
Toyota, 54
TransUnion, 44
Tribune Company, 116
Trump, Donald, 122
Twitter, 18, 46–47, 118, 134

Uniform Electronic Legal Material Act (UELMA), 92
United Kingdom, 124
Universal Declaration of Human Rights, 26, 50
USA PATRIOT Act (2001), 31
U.S. Marshals Service (USMS), 43, 44
utilities, 8, 23, 126, 135, 136–40

Vaidhyanathan, Siva, 142
Verizon, 45, 124
Vermont, 45
Vgontzas, Nantina, 127
Viacom, 116
Vietnam War, 115
vitamins, 8

Walmart, 54, 110
Warren, Samuel, 45
Washington, George, 114
Washington Post, 116
Watergate scandal, 115
Weapons of Math Destruction (O'Neil), 28
West, John B., 73, 76, 79
Westlaw, ix–xiv, 73; bundling by, 90; "correctional" product line of, 64–65; law privatized by, 79–80; law shaped by, 75–78; state law compiled by, 81–82; surveillance linked to, 85; user-friendliness of, 80; "star pagination" system of, 83
West Publishing, 73–74
Whittaker, Meredith, 127
Wikipedia, 138
Wiley, 62
wiretapping, 32, 45
Wiretap Act (1968), 45
WorldCom, 100
Wright, Robert E., 111
Wu, Tim, 129
Wyden, Ron, 47

Yahoo, 47
YouTube, 18, 47, 119, 123, 134

Zuckerberg, Mark, 73, 119, 125, 130
Zuckerman, Ethan, 125

CPSIA information can be obtained
at www.ICGtesting.com
Printed in the USA
JSHW022122100922
30312JS00002B/2